The Security State in Pakistan

The War on Terror, a war which has directly contributed to growing security regimes in its frontline states, has been going on for over a decade, and it shows no signs of winding down in the near future.

This book focuses on the legal dimensions of the War on Terror and security in Pakistan. It highlights the growth of the security state in Pakistan and questions the growing, and now entrenched, legal security regime in the country. The book traces the roots of the present security laws in colonial and postcolonial times. One broader dimension through which the legal security regime of Pakistan is analysed in this book is in highlighting specific issues concerning the legal identity of the subject, such as the rights of aliens (in the background of state power versus liberal constitutionalism) and the rights of terrorism suspects (in the background of deploying a death sentence as a tactical, psychological tool in contrast with the absolute right to life of every individual). By critically reflecting on the increasingly institutionalized form of the security apparatus in Pakistan, the book (indirectly) suggests the legal ways to resist the growing legal security regime and its derogation from human rights.

Offering a theoretically engaged and critically reflective overview of the current state of individual identity, rights, and freedoms in face of a burgeoning legal regime of security in Pakistan, this study makes advances in critical legal studies and critical International Relations. It will be of interest to academics working in the fields of security studies and South Asian Studies (particularly Pakistan), and those with an interest in the War on Terror.

Syed Sami Raza received his PhD from the University of Hawai'i at Mānoa, US. He is Assistant Professor in the Department of Political Science at the University of Peshawar, Pakistan.

Routledge Studies in South Asian Politics

9 **Pakistan's Democratic Transition**
Change and Persistence
Edited by Ishtiaq Ahmad and Adnan Rafiq

10 **Localizing Governance in India**
Bidyut Chakrabarty

11 **Government and Politics in Sri Lanka**
Biopolitics and Security
A. R. Sriskanda Rajah

12 **Politics and Governance in Bangladesh**
Uncertain Landscapes
Edited by Ipshita Basu, Joe Devine and Geoffrey Wood

13 **Constitutional Democracy in India**
Bidyut Chakrabarty

14 **Radical Politics and Governance in India's North East**
The Case of Tripura
Harihar Bhattacharyya

15 **The Security State in Pakistan**
Legal Foundations
Syed Sami Raza

For more information about this series, please visit: https://www.routledge.com

The Security State in Pakistan

Legal Foundations

Syed Sami Raza

Routledge
Taylor & Francis Group
LONDON AND NEW YORK

First published 2019
by Routledge
2 Park Square, Milton Park, Abingdon, Oxon OX14 4RN

and by Routledge
52 Vanderbilt Avenue, New York, NY 10017, USA

First issued in paperback 2020

Routledge is an imprint of the Taylor & Francis Group, an informa business

British Library Cataloguing-in-Publication Data
A catalogue record for this book is available from the British Library

Library of Congress Cataloging-in-Publication Data
A catalog record has been requested for this book

ISBN 13: 978-0-367-58686-7 (pbk)
ISBN 13: 978-1-138-30910-4 (hbk)

Typeset in Times New Roman
by codeMantra

For my parents
Prof. Jawed Hussain & Perveen Jawed

Contents

Preface

The initial idea of this book began to turn over in my mind in the summer of 2011. The impetus came from two incidents of cold-blooded violence at the hands of law enforcement agencies that took place in Pakistan. These incidents, or parts of them, were incidentally captured on camera and soon afterwards became available on both electronic and social media. One incident related to the killing of a group of aliens/foreigners at a check-post outside Quetta and another of a young man near a park in metropolitan Karachi. In both cases, the law enforcement agencies claimed to have operated under the security legal regime, even though they used excessive force. They also tried to cover up the incidents, but in the latter case, failed, as the Supreme Court intervened.

These violent incidents and the diametrically different response that they received from the superior judiciary made me think of the nature of our criminal justice system. I also began to think of the legal regime of security and how it is impervious to judicial intervention as well as how it derogates from substantive and procedural rights. As I began more and more to think about and conduct research on these questions, as well as on the problematic in general, I became gripped with the (entrenched) nature and historical growth of the legal regime of security. My initial response was published the following year (2012) in a section in my PhD dissertation. Later, as I kept working in this direction, my second response was published in a couple of articles, which I mention later. To give the gist of my findings, I would say that the legal regime of security in Pakistan has grown gradually with long-drawn exposures to states of emergency. The distant roots of the regime stretch back to the colonial security corpus, while its recent branches entangle with the current Anglo-American anti-terrorism laws. Since much of the security legal regime is based on procedural laws, it is therefore more susceptible to executives' control, while judiciary's writ has often been truncated through creation of special courts and/or through placing outright constitutional and statute bars.

Given the (apparently) unending project of the War on Terror, it doesn't seem that Pakistan will be able to wind down its expanded and, by now, entrenched legal regime of security. It is also difficult to guess whether the regime has yet reached its peak. Moreover, it needs to be noticed that the War on Terror was just one more stimulus to the recent growth of the security regime, which was in fact already maturing by the time the War on Terror began. Accordingly, since it seems as if it will remain in force for quite some time, and since it will keep encroaching upon our both substantive and procedural rights, the legal regime of security is of urgent and abiding significance. Although much has been written on Pakistan's War on Terror and counter-insurgency programmes, not much has been written on the legal dimension of the war and the security regime. This book is a modest effort to fill part of this academic gap.

I would like to acknowledge that some threads of thought in the first two chapters were published earlier, in the fourth chapter of my dissertation—"Constitutional Order in Pakistan: The Dynamics of Exception, Violence and High Treason"—and in an article entitled "Anti-Terrorism Legal Regime of Pakistan," published in *Review of Human Rights*. Chapter 5 was published earlier in a journal called *Counter Terrorist Trends and Analysis* with a slightly different title ("After the Peshawar School Attack: Law and Politics of the Death Sentence in Pakistan"). Chapter 6 and the epilogue were also published earlier with slightly different titles: "Legal Sovereignty on the Border: Aliens, Identity, and Violence on the Northwestern Frontier of Pakistan" in *Geopolitics* and "Divine Violence after the Kharotabad Killings" in *Review of Human Rights,* respectively.

Acknowledgement

I owe much of my thinking, ideas, and analysis in this book to the camaraderie of scholars, practitioners, and students working at the intersections of law, politics, and theory. In this regard, I extend my first note of gratitude to my teachers. I have learnt a great deal from my teachers at the University of Hawaiʻi at Mānoa, especially Michael J. Shapiro, Sankaran Karishna, Manfred Henningsen, and Nevzat Soguk. I have also learnt a great deal more from my graduate office mates, small writing circles, and class-fellows: Alvin C. Lim, Samson Opondo, Melisa Casumbul, Umi Perkins, Rohan Kalyan, Amir Moheet, Ozge, Rex Troumbly, Guenpei, Brianne Gallagar, Noah Viernes, Jason Adams, David Toohey, Jimmy Weir, and Lorenzo Renilli.

At the University of Peshawar, I learnt the basics of political science at the hands of Nazir Kakakhel and Taj Moharram Khan. I would also like to mention some other colleagues and friends, in Pakistan and elsewhere, who have inspired me in different ways: Qibla Ayaz, Rasul B. Rais, Abdul Rauf, Shahida Amaan, Noreen Naseer, Ayub Jan, M. Zubair, Amir Raza, Hassan Abbas, Jan Peter Hartung, and James Caron.

I am thankful to Dorothea Schaefter, editor of Routledge Studies in South Asian Politics, for her interest in this book project and for encouraging me through all stages of the editorial process. In this regard, I am also indebted to Lily Brown for her quick correspondence and facilitation.

I owe my special gratitude to my parents, who have remained the source of my strength: Jawed Hussain and Perveen Jawed. My brothers Tahir, Ali, and Faisal and my sisters Saima and Anbarin have all been waiting to see this project materialise, for which I am thankful.

Dulcis in fundo I would like to thank my little family—Ghazala Rafi and Aryan Raza. It is their patience, courage, and love to which I owe the finishing of this project. I owe special thanks to my wife for making me excellent cups of coffee, which kept me going.

Abbreviations

AACPR	The Actions (in Aid of Civil Power) Regulations (2011)
AIR	All India Reporter
ARCA	The Anarchical and Revolutionary Crimes Act (1919)
ATA	Anti-Terrorism Act (1997)
ATC	Anti-Terrorism Court
CrPC	The Code of Criminal Procedure (1898)
DIA	Defence of India Act (1915 & 1939)
DIR	Defence of India Rule (1915 & 1939)
DORA	The Defence of the Realm Act (1914)
DPO	The Defence of Pakistan Ordinance (1965 & 1971)
DPR	The Defence of Pakistan Rules (1965 & 1971)
EBDO	The Elective Bodies (Disqualification) Ordinance, 1959
FATA	The Federally Administered Tribal Areas
FC	Frontier Corps
FCR	Federal Court Reporter
FCR	The Frontier Crimes Regulation (1901)
JJSO	The Juvenile Justice System Ordinance (2000)
KPK	Khyber-Pakhtunkhwa province
LEAs	Law Enforcement Agencies
MLD	Monthly Law Reports
MPOO	The Maintenance of Public Order Ordinance (1960)
NAP	The National Action Plan (2014)
NIEPA	The Northern Ireland (Emergency Powers) Act (1973)
PAA	The Pakistan Army Act (1952)
PAFO	The Pakistan Armed Forces (Acting in Aid of Civil Power) Ordinance (1998)
PATA	The Provincially Administered Tribal Areas
PCrLJ	Pakistan Criminal Law Journal
PLD	The All Pakistan Legal Decisions
PLJ	Pakistan Law Journal
PPA	The Pakistan Protection Act (2014)
PPO	The Pakistan Protection Ordinance (2013)

PRODA	The Public and Representative Offices (Disqualification) Act, 1949
SCA	The Special Courts for Speedy Trials Act (1992)
SCMR	Supreme Court Monthly Review
SPA	The Security of Pakistan Act (1952)
STAA	The Suppression of Terrorist Activities (Special Courts) Act (1975)
TAAA	The Terrorist Affected Areas (Special Courts) Act (1992)
TSNM	Tehreek-e-Nafaz-e-Shariat Mohammadi
TTP	Tehreek-e-Taliban
YLR	Yearly Law Reporter

Introduction

What is the security state?

Before I discuss the legal foundations of the security state in Pakistan, it seems to be an imperative to define what I mean by the concept of security state. Broadly speaking, a security state can be defined in a number of ways. It depends on the state's historical context, present challenges, and future orientations, as well as on subject matter such as the policies adopted, laws made, and governmental machinery or law enforcement infrastructure raised at a given time. Moreover, any definition will also have to draw on a certain academic approach or a school of thought. To instantiate this, let us have a look at certain broad and widely used definitions of the security state, after which I will present my own understanding of it, based on my inductive analysis of Pakistan. This understanding, or definition, will remain our point of reference for the analysis I make in the book.

One widely accepted definition of the security state, which comes from the realist school of thought in International Relations (IR), places the state in its international political context where strife and struggle among the community of states is an ever-present condition. On the international stage, states are almost always faced with insecurity, and therefore they have to make security arrangements on their own. From the point of view of this school of thought, the security state can be defined as "a state that accords primacy to the protection of national borders, physical assets, and core values largely through military means."[1] In line with the general approach adopted in the realist school of thought, this definition warns the state about the anarchical nature of international politics. Given the growing presence of warfare in the world, each nation state is expected to develop a certain defence policy—for instance, raising a large army and/or making alliances with other states—to protect its borders, sovereignty, people and national interests.

Another somewhat similar definition, also based on the context of an international system, says: "the national security state is that, in any state, [where] the political institutions [are] responsible for the conduct of foreign security policy."[2] This definition comes from mainstream IR, as it relates security to foreign policy and thinks of security as an external threat. A critical variation of the two previous definitions is the critical IR school of thought, which defines the security state from the ontological vantage ground. Based on the theory of critical IR, this definition holds the view that the security state creates, or else benefits from, the political ontology of "us" versus "them" and "inside" versus "outside." It believes that the modern security state consciously engages in seeking or conjuring up the enemy.[3] Accordingly, it also criticises that the political discourse of the War on Terror is part of the strategy of the security state's war-making policy.

There are other scholars who define the security state from a domestic, institutional context. They believe that a security state is one that has "institutionalized the provisions of security and prioritized it over all other functions of state."[4] One study, for instance, refers to the enactment of the National Security Act in the United States in 1947, under which security apparatus such as the National Security Council (NSC) and the Central Intelligence Agency (CIA) began to develop. This definition points to yet another relevant concept, by Harold D. Lasswell, of the "garrison state."[5] A garrison state is one dominated by the military–industrial complex, which seeks to promote an economy heavily dependent on military and war spending.[6] For Lasswell, the United States grew as a garrison state during the Cold War era, developing a war economy on the one hand and curtailing civil liberties on the other. Lasswell writes,

> ...we are moving toward a world of "garrison states"—a world in which the specialists on violence are the most power group in the society. From this point of view the trend of our time is away from the dominance of the specialist on bargaining, who is the businessman, and toward the supremacy of the soldier.[7]

The concept of garrison state has also been applied to Pakistan and has generated considerable debate.[8]

For the purposes of this book, I present a definition of the security state which is based on the vantage point of law, especially security law and the state of emergency. By security state, I mean a state that is faced with (again) a real or perceived state of emergency. This state of emergency arises from a real or perceived external threat to the state's defence and security or from an internal threat to its public order. The state also feels insecure about its control over the physical means of violence. Due to this real or perceived state of emergency, the security state responds by creating a relatively large corpus of security laws. These laws result in the making of an almost parallel criminal code as well as an abridged criminal procedure. The superior courts receive a large number of writ petition cases for safeguarding individuals' liberties and fundamental rights. The security state also provides for a wide range of powers to law enforcement agencies, including the power to detain and kill. A variety of forces are normally involved in coping with the problem of insecurity, fear, and violence—including the civil and paramilitary forces and intelligence agencies, even though these agencies are not trained for either policing or counterterrorism.

Political context: the state of emergency

One of the crucial factors in the development of the security state in Pakistan is its long-drawn exposure to the state of emergency. By the state of emergency, I mean its three manifestations at the minimum: the state of emergency declared (a) in the wake of a war, (b) after a *coup d'état* and (c) under the power granted in the constitution. No matter what type of emergency was declared in Pakistan, it exhibited the tendency on the part of the government to prolong it. In simple words, states of emergency in Pakistan have tended to extend well beyond the events that produced the need for them in the first place. And interestingly, often one manifestation of emergency has led to another. It is during these prolonged emergencies that the legal regime of security has grown and thrived in Pakistan.

In recent times, an eminent philosopher of law and politics, Giorgio Agamben, has made certain crucial observations about the state of emergency that are quite relevant for the purpose of the present study. First, he has observed that the state of emergency tends to continue even after the emergency event. It is the emergency event that affords the pretext for making the elaborate structure of emergency laws and the government's discretionary powers. Second, he has observed that the modern state uses security and emergency as a tool of governance.[9] In the case of Pakistan, both these observations hold true, and I would, in the course of this study, explain and keep them as our point of reference.

Let me point to another of Agamben's observations here, which regards the historical growth of the paradigm of security in Europe, especially in England. I point to this observation because it is relevant in the context of this study or, rather, the point of my beginning in the present study. He says that the modern paradigm of security in Europe began with World War I.[10] In the wake of the war, a state of emergency was imposed in England, and the Defence of the Realm Act and Rules (1914) were enforced in the country. Towards the end of the war, the emergency continued and a new law—the Emergency Powers Act (1920)—was enforced. With these emergency laws, during and after the war, the government was able to restrict subjects' liberties and rights. In 1915, in India, the colonial administration also declared a state of emergency and enforced a similar law, the Defence of India Act and Rules (1915). Just as Agamben has pointed out that World War I and emergency laws paved the way for the modern security paradigm in England, I suggest similarly that the state of war and emergency laws also prepared the ground for the paradigm of security in colonial India. And just as new emergency laws were enforced in England, in colonial India, the Anarchical and Revolutionary Crimes Act (1919) was enforced, which indirectly continued the emergency.

Elsewhere, Agamben points out that the distant legal roots of the modern state of security in England stretch back to the Mutiny Acts of the 17th and 18th centuries.[11] In Chapter 1 of this book, I similarly demonstrate that the legal roots of the colonial paradigm of security in India are also related, although indirectly and distantly, to these English Mutiny Acts. To explain this, I point to the introduction of Regulation X of 1804 in colonial India, which was one of the foremost criminal and security regulations. The colonial administration designed this regulation on the model of English Mutiny Acts. Just as the English Mutiny Acts envisaged martial law and courts in England, the Regulation X also envisaged martial law and courts in colonial India. Furthermore, in England, in the late 18th and early 19th centuries, the government, in the wake of the war with France, passed laws for suspension of *habeas corpus*. Soon afterwards, in India, in 1818, the British colonial administration introduced Regulation III, which allowed suspension of *habeas corpus* in the form of "safe custody" and preventive detention.

The colonial state of security that began during World War I further expanded throughout the interwar period, and by World War II (when once again the emergency and the Defence of India laws were invoked) it reached its peak. In 1935, colonial India was given a so-called Constitution—the Government of India Act (GIA) (1935). The Constitution came without having entrenched fundamental liberties and rights. It was, rather, burdened with the provisions of preventive detention. Later, after independence, when Pakistan and India drafted their respective constitutions, they adopted this colonial constitution as their model and incorporated the provisions of preventive detention. During World War II, the Federal Court of India, however, ventured to try and wrestle some ground for the fundamental liberties and rights of colonial subjects. It did so by way of exercising its judicial review power in favour of subjects' rights, but unfortunately, the government frustrated the Court through its overbearing powers and tactics. Nevertheless, the Federal Court set a decent precedent for the postcolonial states' higher courts to follow suit.

When the war ended and colonial India achieved independence, the legal foundations of the colonial security state were inherited by the postcolonial states of Pakistan and India, especially due to the adoption of much of the colonial legal corpus. In the initial years after independence, there were several security laws in place, both at the national level and in the provinces in Pakistan. Often, at the expiry of one security law, a new one was enforced. Moreover, the new laws were often given retrospective effect to continue the unbroken chain of security regime. With the passage of time, the state also began to consider consolidation of the security laws and bringing uniformity in them throughout the country. For instance, the different security ordinances and acts were combined in the Security of Pakistan Act (1952) and the various provincial and the central public safety ordinances and acts were consolidated into the Maintenance of Public Order Ordinance (1960). On the north-western border in the tribal areas, the Frontier Crimes Regulation (FCR) (1901) was allowed to continue. Even after the adoption of the constitution (1956) the tribal areas neither were reorganised to make them settled areas nor was the FCR removed from them. Rather, the Supreme Court's decision in the *Dosso* (1958) gave further life to the FCR. Since then, the higher courts have not been able to exercise their jurisdiction there nor provide relief relating to fundamental liberties and rights to the tribal people.

In 1965, when a war broke out between Pakistan and India, President Ayub Khan declared a state of emergency and the colonial defence laws were once again invoked in the forms of the Defence of Pakistan Ordinance and the Defence of Pakistan Rules (1965). Although the war ended in about seventeen days, the emergency and the laws that were enforced in its wake continued for the next two decades. Over time, they were supplemented with more security laws and even with two martial laws. President Ayub Khan also laid the foundation for trial of civilians in martial courts by introducing two ordinances—Ordinance III and IV of 1967—that amended the Army Act (1952). Later, the Supreme Court in *F.B. Ali* (1973) upheld these ordinances as constitutional. However, in 1977, when Zulfikar Ali Bhutto's democratic government enforced martial law and wished to create martial courts in Karachi, Hyderabad, and Lahore, the Supreme Court made a bold decision and struck them down. But to the Court's dismay, only few months afterward, General Zia-ul-Haq took power, once again imposed martial law, and later, set up hundreds of martial courts throughout the country.

In the early 1990s, the Nawaz Sharif government was faced with the menace of local terrorism in the country. Accordingly, it initially enacted two laws for creating special courts, which tried certain heinous offences through speedy trial. These laws also afforded wide-ranging powers to the law enforcement agencies. Later, in 1997, his government replaced these acts with a more comprehensive law, the Anti-Terrorism Act (ATA).

In October 1999, Pakistan faced yet another emergency in the form of a military *coup d'état*. General Pervez Musharraf took over and suspended the Constitution. The jurisdiction of higher courts was restricted, and fundamental liberties and rights were withdrawn. Through this emergency, Musharraf's government continued to work on the ATA (1997). A couple of weeks before the terrorist attacks of September 11, 2001 in New York City, Musharraf's government introduced an amendment to the ATA (1997). This amendment made several changes to the act, including one to its definition of terrorism, redefining terrorism based on the definition in the British Terrorism Act (2000). After the 9/11 attacks, when the United States began its international war against terrorism, Pakistan joined the war and, in fact, became a frontline state. In 2005, Pakistani armed forces began their own operations in South Waziristan. The same year, an amendment was made to the ATA (1997) to increase punishments for various offences of terrorism. After the operations in South Waziristan, more operations began in other tribal agencies. In 2008 and 2009, the armed forces carried out massive operations in the Swat valley and its neighbouring districts and agencies. During these operations, thousands of terrorism suspects were arrested and detained in internment camps specifically set up for this purpose, though without proper legal and constitutional sanction. Accordingly, in 2011, the government exercised its emergency powers under Article 245 to issue the Actions (in Aid of Civil Power) Regulations (AACPRs), which provided legal framework to these prolonged detentions.

The next set of security laws were passed by Nawaz Sharif's third government beginning in 2013. By then, the country was faced with the highest-ever level of incidence of terrorism. The government set up a committee to propose reforms to the ATA (1999). Later, in December 2014, when terrorists attacked a school in Peshawar, the government announced the National Action Plan and resolved to make tougher anti-terrorism laws. The laws that were eventually made included proposed amendments to the ATA (1997), the Protection of Pakistan Ordinance and Act (2013 and 2014), the Army (Amendment) Acts (2015 and 2017) and two constitutional amendments (21st Amendment, 2015 and 28th Amendment, 2017). The most notable of these laws included amendments to the Army Act, which authorised the Armed Forces to set up martial courts and try civilian suspects of terrorism. To protect the martial courts from the judicial review power of the higher courts, the government also passed two constitutional amendments.

Legal foundations

What are the legal foundations of the security state in Pakistan? In other words, how does the security state ground itself in law? To answer these questions, we need to begin by understanding the nature of the security law. The security law in Pakistan is procedural in nature, rather than substantive. The Supreme Court, in a decision in 2001, also acknowledged this fact with the following words: "[...] although this act [the ATA, 1997] to some extent contains the substantive law [...] it is procedural in nature."[12] What we need to know is the difference between the two—procedural versus substantive law—as well as why it is important to know this difference. In 1969, the Supreme Court described the difference between the two by drawing on Sir John Salmond's opinion. The Court said:

> True it is not easy to draw a line between substantive and procedural law, but the task is not impossible if the essential difference is kept in mind. 'The law of procedure may be defined as that branch of the law which governs the process of litigation...All the residue is substantive law, and relates, not to the process of litigation, but to its purposes and subject matter.'[13]

On the question as to what constitutes substantive law, the Supreme Court, in a number of decisions, has relied on Black's Law Dictionary, defining substantive law as "an essential part or constituent or relating to what is essential."[14] In light of these definitions, the security law in Pakistan can be understood as the one describing criminal procedure adopted in the process of litigation. The substantive part in it is little: for example, the definition of terrorism and what it constitutes. But we know that this definition only came in its refined form in 2001 through the amendment made to the ATA (1997). The rest of the ATA, and for that matter, other security laws, detail the procedure adopted in dealing with suspects: the use of force, the mode of arrest and detention, the creation of special courts, the procedure adopted for trial, and the punishable offences and the amount of punishment for them.

Since the security law is more procedural in nature, it is also more prone to government's control. For instance, the government can make any number of special courts, send any number of cases to them and/or from one court to another and include any number of scheduled offences through a simple notification. Similarly, the executive can restrict procedural rights more easily than substantive rights. Since the criminal procedure given in the security laws is often abridged, it becomes difficult to defend procedural rights otherwise guaranteed in the Code of Criminal Procedure (1898) and established through case law. However, it is worth noticing that the higher courts have noted that substantive rights (compared to procedural rights) of subjects or of accused persons remain unaffected in case of the procedural laws of security.[15]

Security laws normally come with the provision of overriding effect. However necessary and logical the provision may appear, the precedence/override of security laws over the ordinary criminal law shows how a security state is different from other states—or even from itself, at a different time when it relies upon its regular criminal justice system. The overriding effect of security laws also enhances the government's discretionary power. The government can enforce or withdraw a security law anywhere in the country with a simple notification and thus override the ordinary criminal justice system. The government can incorporate any offence into the list of scheduled offences through a simple notification and can send cases to special courts as well as remove cases from ordinary courts and send them to special courts. The provision of the overriding effect became crucial when the question of conflict between the ATA (1997) and the Juvenile Justice System Ordinance (JJSO) (2000) arose. Both these laws came with the provision of overriding, and the courts were asked to decide on the question. Although different courts made different decisions, a trend seemed to develop in favour of the ATA. Later, the same conflict arose between the Army (Amendment) Act (2015) and the JJSO (2000). Once again, the higher courts decided in favour of the former, which provided for setting up military courts.

Inasmuch as security laws are special laws, they have necessitated the making of special courts for their adjudication. Although not all security laws provide for special courts, for the government, they have been an imperative, because only with them could the government hope to achieve the objectives of both speedy dispensation of justice and enhancing its own powers. The special courts have normally been given similar powers to a Session Court and those of the First Class Magistrate, as well as the same power to issue contempt of court available to the High Court. Moreover, just as the security laws enjoy precedence over ordinary criminal laws, the special courts also enjoy jurisdictional precedence over ordinary criminal courts. However, they normally take cognizance of cases when the government decides to send them.

It is worth mentioning here that the creation of special courts has remained a bone of contention between the executive branch and the higher courts for a long time. This is because the creation of special courts has consequences for the doctrine of separation of judicial power from the power of the executive branch. Since special courts can be created through both regular legislation and executive's ordinance-making power, the judiciary has always feared executive encroachment in the judicial sphere. This fear has haunted the judiciary since 1943, when the governor-general created special courts through his ordinance-making power, and the Federal Court challenged the governor-general's power. However, whether created by the legislature or the executive, the higher courts have jealously guarded against the creation of special courts, which lead to the creation of a *parallel judiciary*. In other words, the judiciary has almost always insisted upon its appellate, supervisory, and administrative jurisdiction over special courts, while the executive branch has also always tried to bring the special courts under its control. The historical evidence shows that the executive branch has been considerably successful in developing and maintaining its control over special courts. The government has sought to achieve this control through a number of ways. First, it has often provided for a lower level of qualifications for the appointment of special judges. By lower level we mean that just any practicing lawyer could be appointed as a special judge on government's discretion, without meeting the regular requirement of passing competitive examination organized by a public service commission. Second, in the appointment process the executive branch has also often exercised its discretion in picking and choosing from among the existing regular judges and magistrates. Moreover, the executive branch has at times provided in security laws that for appointment of special judges consultation with chief justices of the concerned High Courts was not required.

It was not until the *Mehram Ali* (1998) and *Liaquat Hussain* (1999) that the Supreme Court effectively brought the special courts under the oversight of higher courts. The Supreme Court set guidelines for the appointment and tenure of the judges of special courts. It also struck down the appellate special court and instructed that all appeals should go to the relevant High Courts. Moreover, the Supreme Court advised that, while speedy trials should be carried out in the Anti-Terrorism Courts (ATCs), the regular criminal procedure should be followed as nearly as possible. To these instructions, however, the government responded by making changes to the ATA (1997); but it also later resorted to setting up martial courts that did not follow these instructions.

Historically speaking, military courts have been set up during martial law, as well as during civilian rules. Let me point out quickly that it is the military courts set up during civilian rules that are the matter of our interest in this study. As early as in *Asma Jilani* (1972), the Supreme Court denounced the imposition of the 1969 martial law. However, the next year, in *F.B. Ali* (1973), the Supreme Court, in order to curry favour with Bhutto's government, decided that martial courts set up under the amended Army Act (1952) could validly try civilians who were indirectly involved in offences under that act. The possibility of trying civilians in martial courts was, in fact, created by President Ayub Khan, who had promulgated two ordinances earlier—Ordinance III and IV of 1967. In *F.B. Ali* the Court simply upheld these ordinances and said that they did not contravene with the separation of powers doctrine or with the fundamental rights guaranteed in the Constitution. Later, in 1977, when Bhutto tried to impose martial law in Karachi, Lahore, and Hyderabad, and wished to create martial courts, the Supreme Court struck down both the martial law and its courts.

Recently, in 2015, Nawaz Sharif's government decided to cope with terrorism through military courts. The decision came in the wake of the cold-blooded attack on an Army public school in Peshawar. Accordingly, the Army Act (1952) was amended, and this amendment was further protected by an amendment within the Constitution.[16] Initially, these courts were set up for a period of two years, but towards the end of that period, their life was extended for two more years. What is important to note about the present military courts is that they can try civilians, as well as aliens, but only when cases are sent to them by the government. However, in their functioning, they remain almost outside both the control of the government and the jurisdiction of the civilian higher courts. This aspect has been established by the Supreme Court in a case (2015) challenging military courts.[17] The Court decided, on the same lines as set in *F.B. Ali* (1973), that the higher courts could not exercise jurisdiction over martial courts except on two conditions: *mala fide* and *corum non judice*.

Apart from giving special courts enhanced powers and jurisdiction, the security state also equips them with special criminal procedure. What is special about the criminal procedure is that it is meant to achieve speedy trials, and for that purpose, it can let go of certain features of regular criminal procedure. The special procedure includes the following aspects: the special courts are required to hear a case every day without giving adjournments (the special courts do not give adjournments, except in exceptional circumstances); the maximum period in which they are asked to give a decision varies from one month to seven days; they do not need to hear a witness again or recall evidence; they can also hold trials in absentia and trials in camera; and finally, a limited time is given to appeal against the decisions of special courts.

With the special procedure, the special courts try scheduled offences. Technically speaking, the major security laws of Pakistan do not prescribe any new offences. The offences that are provided in the schedules attached to the security laws are those offences already available in the Penal Code or other laws. For instance, the categories of heinous offences and so-called offences against the state are often provided in security laws, which are borrowed from the Penal Code. Once these offences are provided as scheduled offences in security laws, they are, however, related to different purpose and design. In the ATA (1997), for instance, we find that the offences punishable as terrorism are mostly heinous offences, offences against the state and certain other offences taken from other laws, but they are all linked to the political purpose and design of causing fear, insecurity, and terror in the public.

While security laws in Pakistan often derogate from fundamental liberties and rights, they normally seek their sanction from the Constitution. For instance, the preventive detention laws seek their legality from Article 10 of the Constitution, which provides for safeguards against arbitrary arrest and detention. Similarly, the laws relating to requisitioning the armed forces in aid of civil authorities seek their legality from Article 245. Under this article, the armed forces are called in for emergency purpose, but they are also given the regular powers of law enforcement and policing even when they are not trained for that. As long as they provide aid to a civil authority, the fundamental liberties and rights effectively remain suspended. However, the civilian courts keep functioning, and military tribunals do not replace them.[18] The armed forces have been called in aid of civil authority in Karachi a number of times since the 1990s, and recently, they have been called in for operations in the Federally Administered Tribal Areas (FATA) and Provincially Administered Tribal Areas (PATA).

Apart from Article 245, a more serious form of emergency power is available to the government under Article 232. Under this article, the President can implement emergency in the entire country or in any part of it, and under Article 233 can suspend the fundamental rights guaranteed in the Constitution. Zulfikar Ali Bhutto had declared the first emergency under the present Constitution only few hours after its adoption. Later, this emergency took the form of a martial law under Zia-ul-Haq. In 1999, and again in 2008, General Pervez Musharraf declared emergency in the country and suspended fundamental rights. The second time he declared emergency, he had to face tough resistance at the hands of a movement led by judges and lawyers, which eventually led to his removal.

Even as the security state seeks to base security laws in the Constitution, their constitutionality is mediated by the judicial review power of the higher courts. The history of such exercise of judicial review goes back to the colonial Federal Court, as I mentioned earlier. The Court struck down a number of the executive branch's arrest and detention orders, as well as the legal provisions on which they were based. In the postcolonial state of Pakistan, the Federal Court continued to exercise judicial review power. However, in the 1970s, Zulfikar Ali Bhutto curtailed the power of judicial review and jurisdiction of higher courts through passing constitutional amendments. For the next couple of decades, the higher courts exercised their judicial review power only sparingly. Towards the end of the 1990s, however, the Supreme Court once again began to make some bold decisions, as in *Mehram Ali* (1998) and *Liaquat Hussain* (1999). In 2008, the Supreme Court had a direct confrontation with the executive branch over the declaration of emergency. The judges, led by Chief Justice Iftikhar Chaudhry, refused to accept the emergency declaration and take fresh oaths. Eventually, when President Pervez Musharraf stepped down from power and a new democratic government was elected, the judiciary reclaimed its independence through the constitution's 18th Amendment.

Although the security regime might not survive without constitutional ground or constitutionality, it also has roots in case law and the legal debate both inside and outside the courts. The higher courts have explained, clarified, and at times, fixed the meaning, scope, and applicability of security laws. While it is not possible to present an account here of the long history of legal debate and case law relating to the security regime, I want to point to certain key dimensions that are important for this book. First, the case law shows that the superior judiciary has remained torn between upholding executive powers and individual liberties and rights. Nevertheless, when seen in the long view, the judiciary's approach seems to show an inclination towards the latter. Second, a number of precedents have been set in reviewing the powers and/or orders of the executive under the security laws. The courts have often set these precedents at the risk of losing their own wider jurisdiction and judicial review power. Third, even though case law shows a check on the making of a parallel judiciary in the form of special courts, nowhere has it declared (in line with a liberal criminal justice system) that special courts are unconstitutional or outside the law-making power of the executive branch and the legislature. Lastly, with more and more decisions in constitutional cases, the scope of security laws often become restricted with the passage of time, but then it creates the need for new security laws with even more strong protections.

Overview of the book

For more than a decade now, the War on Terror has gone on with no signs of winding down in the near future. Accordingly, through this book I propose that it is high time that we revisit and critically reflect on the growing legal regime of security in the frontline state of Pakistan. As this regime of security takes a more institutionalised form by grounding and entrenching the security apparatus in the law, there is need to (a) trace its development, (b) highlight its operation, and (c) critique its relationship with the notion of a liberal criminal justice system in the country. And just as we focus on the security laws of Pakistan, we need to discern their normative and discursive linkages with security laws of the allied states (the United States and the United Kingdom), especially to keep the larger global paradigm of security in the backdrop. This book teases out and makes sense of the normative and ethical aspects of the state control regime in Pakistan.

The book approaches the debate on the legal regime of security by taking up some specific and urgent issues: for instance, the rights of aliens (within the background of state power versus liberal constitutionalism), and the rights of terrorism suspects (including the deploying of death sentences as a tactical, psychological tool contrasted with the absolute right to life of every individual). Another urgent issue the book discusses is the relationship between the border and freedom of mobility and state controls. Moreover, the book also indirectly suggests legal ways to resist the growing legal security regime and its derogation from human rights. The methodological scope of the book makes advances in critical legal studies and critical International Relations fields. However, the initial discussions begin with descriptive, genealogical, and/or illustrative approaches. More detail about each chapter is given below.

In the first chapter—"The Colonial State of Security"—I shed light on the genealogy of the anti-terrorism legal regime, from preventive indefinite detention to special courts and speedy trials. Moreover, because this regime is often criticised in the West as Pakistan's failure to defend human rights, I trace the genealogy of this legal regime in Pakistan to highlight its historical linkages with Anglo-American legal regimes. I demonstrate that there is much in common between Anglo-American and Pakistani legal regimes. Furthermore, I point out that the latter bases its legal form and substance on the former.

The second chapter—"The Postcolonial State of Security"—follows the genealogical threads of the colonial security regime into the postcolonial state of Pakistan. I shed light on the development of security and the anti-terrorism legal regime of Pakistan after its independence, with an emphasis on the most recent developments. In this chapter, I use the same genealogical and comparative approaches, and highlight the linkages between Pakistani and Anglo-American security regimes.

In the 1990s, Pakistan saw unprecedented amount of violence, especially sectarian and ethnic bloodshed. This violence reached its peak by the mid-1990s. To cope with the growing menace of violence, the government passed the ATA in 1997, which is the focus of the third chapter. Through this act, terrorism was not only defined for the first time but also became central to the official discourse on security. What practically constituted terrorism was not anything new, but rather, the already existing offences, such as offences against the state or heinous offences. Under the ATA, these offences were now to be coped with through increased police power, special courts, and an abridged criminal procedure. However, the Supreme Court reviewed the constitutionality of the act and struck down certain provisions of it that contravened with higher courts' jurisdiction and/or fundamental rights. But with the beginning of the international War on Terror, the Act became at once more relevant and timely.

In the fourth chapter, "Expansion and Entrenchment of the Legal Regime of Security in Pakistan," I analyse the anti-terrorism laws in the second decade of the War on Terror (2010–2017), especially with the view to see how they lead to further expansion and entrenchment of the legal regime of security. In this decade, a number of important legislations were passed, among these the Actions (in Aid of Civil Power) Regulation (2011); the Protection of Pakistan Ordinance (2013); the Protection of Pakistan Act (2014); the National Action Plan (2014); the Military (Amendment) Act (2015); the Constitution (21st Amendment) Act (2015); the Military (Amendment) Act (2017); and the Constitution (28th Amendment) Act (2017). Apparently, these security legislations came in the wake of the resurgence of terrorism. For instance, according to the Global Terrorism Index in 2013, Pakistan ranked second among the most terrorism-hit countries in the world, with casualties soaring up to three thousand. In this decade, the government has carried out both large- and small-scale military operations in the border tribal territories as well as in certain major cities. To support the armed forces in their operations, the government passed some of these legislations and provided for preventive detention, special courts, military courts, and speedy trials. Within the criminal justice system of the country, the most worrisome of all these laws were the amendments made to the Army Act that allowed for trying civilians in martial courts.

The December 2014 terrorist attack on the Army public school in Peshawar brought the question of death sentences for terrorism convicts back into the public debate. However, this meant not only arriving at a consensus to lift the six-year-long moratorium, but also justifying death sentences as a worthwhile tool in fighting terrorism. In the fifth chapter, entitled "Security and the Absolute Right to Life: Critical Reflections on the Revival of Capital Punishment," I reflect, though relatively briefly, on the politics of legitimising death sentences, in the context of local political scene and its criminal justice system. The chapter discusses the law and politics of capital punishment from four different dimensions: (a) the pathos of national politics, (b) the menace of expanding necro-power, (c) the ethos of Islamic jurisprudence, and (d) the aporia of modern justice dispensation.

In the summer of 2011, two incidents of cold-blooded violence took place at the hands of law enforcement agencies (LEAs) in Pakistan. One incident involved the killing of a group of foreigners/aliens traveling across the Pakistan–Afghanistan border near Kharotabad, and the other involved the killing of a citizen in an area under curfew in the metropolitan city of Karachi. The Supreme Court of Pakistan took a *suo moto* action in the case of the latter incident, while remaining silent on the former. Meanwhile, the Pakistani government, instead of reviewing the powers of LEAs, increased them by passing new security laws in the following years. In the sixth chapter—"Aliens, Identity, and Legal Regime of Security on the Border"—I focus on these two incidents of violence to question how and why aliens are treated differently from citizens in Pakistan's criminal justice system. I trace the legal genealogy of that differential treatment and highlight the different stages of its growth. I also shed light on the way lethal force was used on the victims in order to show the drawbacks of the operational side of law enforcement. Finally, I engage critical theory to understand the nature of this violence, which now resides in the structure of the legal regime of security.

In the epilogue, "Kharotabad Killings: Security and Political Responsibility," I focus again on the incident of violence at Kharotabad. The incident took place on May 17, 2011. The group, consisting of five people (including three women), was stopped at a checkpoint outside the city of Quetta, Baluchistan and were killed by law enforcement on suspicion of being suicide bombers. Interestingly, the incident was recorded on camera, as the media had arrived on the spot before the order to kill them was given. The government tried to defend the actions of law enforcement, but failed because of the video and photographs that were taken by the media and subsequently made public. One of these photographs became iconic. In this photograph, an injured woman is shown lying on the ground near the sandbag-covered checkpoint, stretching her arm upward and pointing to the sky. This photograph became so sensational that it later forced the government to carry out a judicial inquiry into the incident. In this epilogue, I discuss the politics of aesthetics related with the photograph. In other words, I critique the precarity of what Agamben calls "bare life" when it is faced with security *dispositif* (apparatus).

Notes

1 The definition is based on Deudney, "Nuclear Weapons and the Waning of the Real-State"; Ripsman and Paul, *Globalization and the National Security State*, 10.
2 This definition is based on the idea of Ripsman, *Peacemaking by Democracies: The Effect of State Autonomy on the Post-World-War Settlement*; Ripsman and Paul, *Globalization and the National Security State*, 11.
3 Shapiro, *Cinematic Geopolitics*; Shapiro, *Violent Cartographies*; Raza, "Desiring Enemy: An Ontological Reading of the Military Operations and Small Wars on the North West Frontier."
4 This definition is based on the ideas of Yergin, *Shattered Peace*; Raskin, *Essays of a Citizen: From National Security State to Democracy*; Ripsman and Paul, *Globalization and the National Security State*, 11.
5 Lasswell, "The Garrison State."
6 For a recent take on the military–industrial complex economy, see Der Derian, *Virtuous War*.
7 Lasswell, "The Garrison State," 455.
8 See, for instance: Ahmed, *Pakistan: The Garrison State*; Siddiqa, *Military, Inc.: Inside Pakistan's Military Economy*. For a perspective on the colonial garrison state in the Punjab, see Yong, *The Garrison State*.
9 Agamben, "For a Theory of Destituent Power."

10 Agamben, *State of Exception*. Especially, see Chapter 1.
11 Ibid., 18.
12 *Mumtaz Ali Khan Rajban v. Federation of Pakistan*, PLD 2001 SC 169.
13 *Nabi Ahmad v. Home Secretary, Govt. of W. Pak*. PLD 1969 SC 599.
14 See *Hakim Khan and 3 others v. Government of Pakistan through Secretary Interior and Others*, PLD 1992 SC 595; *Mahmood Khan Achakzai and others v. Federation of Pakistan and others*, PLJ 1997 SC 550.
15 *Mehram Ali v. Federation of Pakistan*, MLD 1998 1411.
16 The Military (Amendment) Act 2015, the Constitution (21st Amendment) Act, the Military (Amendment) Act 2017, the Constitution (28th Amendment) Act 2017.
17 *District Bar Association, Rawalpindi*, PLD 2015 SC 401.
18 *Liaquat Hussain and others v. Federation of Pakistan*, PLD 1999 SC 504.

1 The colonial state of security

Introduction

According to Charles Kennedy, an eminent political scientist, Pakistan's security regime is quite unprecedented. Giving a critical account of Pakistan's security regime in an essay, Kennedy concludes with the following note: "The tortured history of Pakistan's anti-terrorism regime should give pause to prospective latecomers to the process (e.g., the United States, Britain, EU, Australia)."[1] Innocuous as it may appear, Kennedy's advice at once begs the question: are the Western states really latecomers in introducing legal security regimes? Apparently, in the short view, the answer might be affirmative. We know that one of the major anti-terrorism laws in Pakistan was passed in 1997 and later amended on August 14, 2001, about a month before the terrorist attacks of 9/11. On the other hand, in the United States and the United Kingdom, some of the major anti-terrorism laws were not passed until after the 9/11 attacks.

However, when we view the security regimes of the West in the long term, or approach them with a genealogical lens, we come to the contrary conclusion: (a) the Western security regimes are much older, and (b) they have constituted the main source of the security regimes of the postcolonial states of Pakistan and India. In fact, these postcolonial states have inherited security laws from the British colonial state of security in India. Similarly, in making their latest anti-terrorism acts (ATAs), Pakistan and India have drawn on more recent Anglo-American security laws. In this chapter, and in the next, in the genealogical account that I give of Pakistan's security regime, I try to make these points. However, let me also clarify at the outset that my aim is not to discover which state has the oldest security regime. Rather, I aim, where possible, to highlight how the Western and Pakistani security regimes have been historically related.

On a broader level, our focus on the security regime of Pakistan takes place within the scope of two juridical derogations that this security regime entails: (a) the suspension of the rule of law and (b) the suspension of civil courts or parts of their jurisdictions. The former derogation results from provisions that allow for preventive detention, and the latter results from provisions for special courts, such as anti-terrorist and martial courts, as well as from providing for speedy and extraordinary trial procedures. I point out that the genealogy of these derogations, along with the juridical categories underpinning them (in Pakistan and, for that matter, in India), can be traced back to early-19th-century colonial laws, especially Regulation X of 1804 and Regulation III of 1818. The legal form and substance of these regulations were both drawn from certain security laws of England, especially the law of high treason. Once introduced within colonial India, these juridical derogations thrived through the colonial era and were kept on in Pakistan and India after independence. After surviving through the post-independence era, they have, only recently, in the wake of the War on Terror, come to converge with the global paradigm of security.

The colonial state of security

The colonial security state in India began with the introduction of certain criminal regulations, as mentioned previously, in the early 19th century. When we trace further the genealogical roots of these regulations, we find that they go back to the English Mutiny Acts of the 17th and 18th centuries. It is also interesting to notice, as one recent genealogical account demonstrates, that the Mutiny Acts have been foundational to the Western, or at least the British, paradigm of security.[2] On the indication of this genealogical account, it can be further conjectured that the first Mutiny Act of 1689 provided the elemental basis for two exceptions to the rule of Common Law: it made martial law courts relevant to peacetime and applicable at home. However, at the time, the exceptions were hardly consequential for the rule of (Common) law—they neither implied the suspension of law nor yielded a new prerogative to the sovereign to proclaim martial law within the realm. While the exceptions would take time to manifest their legal consequences, the object of the act was quite manifest and consequential. It was to provide for the security of the sovereign and the realm, especially in the face of the fledgling institution of a standing army, which, it was feared, could pose a potential threat of rebellion/mutiny. However, even as the object of the act was clear, it can be argued that it did not set out anything new. The security of the sovereign and the realm had long been an enduring political concern, one that was well recognised in Common Law and ensured by a severely punitive law—the law of high treason. Accordingly, should we endeavour to trace the normative origins of the paradigm of security in England, we will have to stretch our genealogy further back to the high treason acts. The mutiny acts, for their part, came as corollaries to the law of high treason, especially at the time when the expediency of disciplining a fledgling standing army on the one hand, and the constraints imposed by the Petition of Rights of 1628 on the sovereign's martial law powers on the other, produced room for them.[3]

The law of high treason had, at a minimum, two key substantive elements that link it to the colonial and modern paradigms of security. One key element was loyalty to the sovereign and hence, the urgency of his security, which, as the object of the law for a long time, was sanctioned as paramount and above the very basic rights of subjects. Another key element, which follows from the first, was the subject of the law: the offences directed against the security of the sovereign and the Realm. These offences primarily included levying war or taking up arms, aiding and abetting the enemy, and rebellion. The normative relationship between the law of high treason and the colonial and modern states of security evolved gradually, I presume; these key elements of the law of high treason, with some adaptation in their form but not much in their substance, were passed on to the colonial and modern states, especially to their security and anti-terrorism laws, over the course of the following two centuries. In this long course, one of the initial, crucial junctures came in the shift in security concern from the person of the sovereign to the political entity of England. It came, or at least began, in the middle of the 19th century, when the Treason Acts of 1842 (and later of 1848) marked "a departure from equating the monarch's personal safety with the essential security of the state," which is obvious in the provisions for the reduction of certain high treason offences to high misdemeanour and felony.[4] In other words, the defining aspect of this departure was how the key elements of the law of high treason created the occasion for *the offences against the state*, or simply put, political offences. Accordingly, we can argue that the early signs of the modern paradigm of security in England emerged during this time, with the unpacking of (or "ambivalence toward"[5]) the law of high treason and the rise of the offences against the state. However, it is important to note that it was not until World War I and the passage of the Defence of the Realm Act (DORA) in 1914 that the paradigm of security in England became manifest and legally consequential. In other words, it is in the DORA that we see the convergence of the two exceptions mentioned earlier: (a) the exception of martial law and martial courts, originally conceived in the Mutiny Acts, and (b) the supremacy of the security of state over the rights of subjects, originally grounded in the law of high treason.

The convergence of the key substantive elements of the laws of high treason and mutiny in the DORA (1914), however, was not the first of its kind. About a century earlier, in the colonial state of Bengal, the British had attempted this convergence in the form of Regulation X of 1804. In other words, the English laws of high treason and mutiny provided the key elements for designing this colonial law of security. The offences that were deemed treasonous under the Treason Act 1351 were provided in Regulation X almost verbatim and were subject to martial law jurisdiction. Three such categories of offences are worth noticing. First, the offence of "levy[ing] war against our lord the King" provided in the High Treason Act was phrased in Regulation X as follows: "to have borne arms in open hostility to the authority." Second, the offence of "be[ing] adherent to the King's enemies in his realm, giving to them aid and comfort in the realm or elsewhere" provided in the High Treason Act was phrased in Regulation X as follows: to have "abetted and aided the enemy." Third, the petty treason in the Common Law was provided in Regulation X as follows: to have "committed acts of violence and outrage against the lives and properties of the subjects."[6] From their experience at home, the British colonial administrators were well aware of the fact that the trial procedure of high treason was considerably cumbersome and often lengthy and hence not suitable to their interests in the colonial state. Therefore, the administration chose to introduce a different law, Regulation X, and empowered the colonial administration to try treasonous offences in martial courts.

Regulation X provided that the Governor-General in Council could (a) establish martial law, (b) suspend or direct any public authority or officer to suspend the ordinary Criminal Courts of Judicature, and (c) direct an immediate trial by courts martial. The regulation not only provided for punishment by death, but also provided for the punishment of forfeiture of property and effects real and personal (as in the case of high treason). Later, Act V of 1841 provided that the government could issue commissions to set up tribunals competent to try offences mentioned in Regulation X.[7] Two decades later, the Indian Councils Act 1861 empowered the Governor-General to issue ordinances to authorise special tribunals, during times of emergency (the existence of which he himself determined), to try offences contained in Regulation X.

In England, by the turn of the 18th century, it had become evident to the government that the law of high treason and the severe punishment it awarded was, at times, not enough to guarantee the security of the sovereign. Meanwhile, the nature and understanding of a threat to the security of the sovereign was undergoing crucial change from a concern for revolts and rebellions to that of commotion, rioting, and public disorder. These latter forms of offences, although directed against the state, could not be dealt with through the law of high treason, due partly to both the difficulty of a lengthy trial procedure and to the question of proportionality of punishment. In order to deal with these offences, the government came up with a different solution. It chose to suspend *habeas corpus* and to place individuals under extended detentions. For instance, in the last decade of the 18th century, during its wars against revolutionary France, the government suspended *habeas corpus* twice—from May 1794 to July 1795 and again from April 1798 to March 1801. Later after end of the war, as a violent proletariat movement for parliamentary reforms began, and especially when the Prince Regent's coach was attacked in January 1817, the parliament enacted the Habeas Corpus Suspension Act 1817.

The following year in Bengal, Regulation III—A Regulation for the Confinement of State Prisoners—was passed, which authorised the colonial administration to suspend *habeas corpus*, even before such a right was constitutionally guaranteed.[8] A year later, a similar regulation was enacted in

Madras. The suspension of *habeas* powers were justified for "the reasons of state"—a phrase that corresponded to the predominant political rationality of the time, the *raison d'état*—which was said to be the maintenance of alliances formed by the British government, preservation of tranquillity in the dominions, and prevention of internal commotion. The Regulation declared:

> Whereas reasons of state...occasionally render it necessary to place under personal restraint individuals against whom there may not be sufficient ground to institute any judicial proceeding, or when such proceeding may not be adapted to the nature of the case, or may for other reasons be unadvisable or improper.[9]

Apart from depriving the detainee of the right to be presented before a magistrate and to a legal counsel for defence, he was also deprived of the right to be informed of the grounds of his detention. These procedural rights were an important part of the rule of law in England. The officer under whose custody the detainee was placed prepared a bi-annual report "on the conduct, the health, and the comfort of such state prisoner, in order that the Governor-General in Council may determine whether the orders for his detention shall continue in force or shall be modified." Hence, on his discretion, the Governor-General in Council could extend detention of "a state prisoner"—a new juridical category that stood between the categories of a regular prisoner and a prisoner of war—every six months and potentially make it indefinite. There was no provision for judicial oversight through an advisory board. Apart from authorising preventive detention, the regulation also gave powers to the colonial government to take away a prisoner's estates and property. This kind of punishment exhibits a link to the high treason laws mentioned earlier. However, according to one opinion, "the subject was protected in that only a very high authority, the Governor-General [... or the Governors] were empowered to order detention, and not a subordinate official or police officer."[10]

Although Regulation III introduced preventive detention in colonial India, it was not well defined. The regulation only envisioned it to be "personal restraint" exercised by the head of colonial administration. A century later, the British higher judiciary in *Rex v Halliday* (1917) tried to explain preventive detention as different from punitive detention, thus laying the ground for its acceptability and reasonability: "It is not punitive, but precautionary measure." The judiciary further argued that in time of emergency "it [was] essential to public safety that there should exist in the executive a power of preventive detention." On the other hand, in his commentaries, Blackstone had already made the task easier for the judges by justifying preventive detention as an emergency measure on the ground that it was Parliament, rather than the Crown, that would determine whether the emergency existed. Thus he wrote that Parliament could "authorise the Crown, by suspending the Habeas Corpus Act for a *short and limited time*, to imprison suspected person without giving any reason for so doing"[11] (emphasis mine). Blackstone would, however, never know that a few years after his death, the power to suspend the Habeas Corpus Act and the right enshrined within it would become a permanent tool of governance in the hands of the Crown. In colonial India, once the power to suspend *habeas corpus* was sanctioned in 1818, its exercise continued for the entire colonial period. Later, the postcolonial states happily adopted it.

In 1850, the Governor-General's territorial jurisdiction under Regulation III (1818) was extended to all conquered territories of the East India Company. Moreover, a proviso was added regarding "the removal of doubts" of courts relating to the question of whether state prisoners could be "lawfully detained" in the territories under their jurisdiction.[12] Eight years later, the regulation was introduced in the provinces of Madras and Bombay with another added proviso: that the Governor-General in Council could order the removal of state prisoners from one place of confinement to another, within the territories controlled by the Company. Moreover, the power to detain was also made available to provincial governors.[13] In 1861, the Indian Council Act promised to bring "peace and good government" to the country, but only after reiterating the Governor-General's power to authorise preventive detention by way of issuing ordinances.[14] Finally, in 1872, Regulation III was extended to the province of the Punjab, and it remained in force until after independence.[15]

In the first half of the 19th century, the colonial administration was engaged in preparing a uniform code of penal laws; in fact, it was a legal imperative of the colonial administration. In 1837, the Law Commissioners of India presented to the Governor-General in Council a brief copy of the penal code. On the top of the enumerated list of crimes was the category of "offences against the state." These offences were almost the same as those already provided in Regulation X of 1804 and Regulation III of 1818: especially the offences of waging of war, aiding and abetting and/or instigation and conspiracy for and during war against the state, and waging war against an ally or committing depredation on the territories of a state that was at peace with colonial India. Apart from the provision of these offences, some new provisions were also proposed, some related to these offences and some that stood alone. First, the copy of the code proposed that the offences against the state should be made subject to the jurisdiction of civil courts with a uniform criminal procedure, which, it was indicated, was underway. This provision, however, was not meant to eliminate the martial law jurisdiction. Second, Section 109 introduced a new offence: that of the "previous abetting" of waging war or rebellion. The offence referred to initial activities involved in the process of waging war or rebellion. Interestingly, it was being introduced in India at the time when courts in England, as well as in the United States, were taking pains to restrict it by restricting the construction of the law of treason.[16] However, in defence of introducing this new offence, the Law Commissioners reasoned:

> As the penal law is impotent against a successful rebel, it is consequently necessary that it should be made strong and sharp against the first beginnings of rebellion, against treasonable designs which have been carried no further than plots and preparations.[17]

With regard to offences against the state, the commissioners apportioned the highest punishment: death. They reasoned that the highest punishment should be apportioned for the highest offences, which they thought were "either murder or the highest offence against the State."[18] Logically and on the scale of punitive proportion, they had placed the security of the state on an equal level with the security of the life of an individual. The balance was, however, further upset in favour of the former by a proviso that added the additional punishment of forfeiture of property, hence likening offences against the state with the offence of high treason. Accordingly, in the punitive respect, offences against the state were considered worse than homicide. Third, the act (or omission) of concealing the existence of any design of waging war was declared punishable by up to a fourteen-year sentence and fine.

Finally, the colonial state wished to address the problem of political resistance in the code. The subject matter was spread over two chapters: Chapter V, containing the offences against the state, and Chapter VII, containing the offences against public tranquillity. In the former chapter, it was provided that any act that affected the government's use of legal powers or that "overawes by means of a riotous assembly," or overawed the government in any other way, would be punished with imprisonment for up to seven years and a fine. Moreover, it was provided that causing "disaffection to the Government" by words, signs, or representation would be punished with banishment for life or imprisonment for three years and a fine. In Chapter VII, the issue of public tranquillity was spread over eleven sections, whereas in Regulation X of 1804 it was covered in only a few words. It was provided in the code that an assembly of twelve or more people with the object to overawe the government would be considered "a riotous assembly." Other offences against the public tranquillity included showing resistance to the execution of law and causing a person "fear or hurt."

The penal code was passed and then enacted in 1860. Once enacted, it remained in force throughout the entire colonial period and is still in force to this day in both Pakistan and India. More details in the form of illustrations, explanations, and notes were added in the Code, especially with the aim to address as many gaps and exceptions as could possibly arise, though "the frame-work and phraseology," the framers stated, remained the same.[19] Just as in the 1837 copy of the code, the Code of 1860 placed the offences against the state on the top of the list. They were further divided, and graded according to the severity of the offence and punishment, into three classes: (a) offences against the Queen and her Government, (b) offences concerning relation of the Indian government with other governments, and (c) offences relating to the custody of prisoners of the state and of war. The second class of offences reflected the provisions of Regulation X of 1804, while the subject matter of the third class went back to Regulation III of 1818. The first class of offences included waging of war, attempting to wage, or abetting the waging of war against the Queen. This class was to be punished with death or transportation for life as well as forfeiture of all property. The offence of "previous abetting" was removed, and in its place to "prepare to wage war" was given as an offense. This offence was made punishable by transportation for life or up to ten years of imprisonment as well as forfeiture of property. Concealing the design of waging war was made punishable by up to ten years and a fine.

In the explanatory note, the framers explained the first class of state offences in the context of the English law of high treason. The framers wrote that while the occasion for an offence against "the person of the Sovereign and the members of the royal family" would "scarcely arise in India," treasonous offences could still be done against the Queen. They could be indirectly done in the form of offences against Her Majesty's Government in India and elsewhere in the Empire. The framers indicated that just as high treason was an offence directed against the allegiance–protection relationship between the Queen and her subjects, the offences against the state were also directed against this relationship between the Queen's Indian government and her subjects. These offences, they said, "threatened to destroy or injure the whole fabric of political society," although they didn't care to explain the exact nature of that political society or how it had come into existence. Because subjects received protection from Her Majesty's Government in India, they were duty-bound to show "true and faithful" obedience. In the absence of a civil law of rights—as stated, the absence was acknowledged by the framers in the 1837 copy of the code—it seemed that the emphasis of the colonial state was centred more on duties than on rights.

The chapter on public tranquillity was expanded in the code. In the 1837 copy of the code, there were only eleven sections. The number increased to twenty, and the chapter in which they were included was provided with illustrations and explanations. In the introductory note to the chapter, the framers stated that the offences against the public tranquillity "hold a middle place between State offences on the one hand, and crimes against person and property on the other." The chapter, they wrote, primarily focused on "unlawful assemblies of persons who, whether they assemble tumultuously or otherwise, have a common unlawful purpose in their minds, the execution of which will disturb public order and excite alarm." One of the important provisions related to the distinction between an unlawful assembly and a riotous assembly. Section 141 provided that an unlawful assembly was one having five or more persons with the common objective to "overawe" the government, resist execution of law, commit mischief or criminal trespass, or overawe a subject. Members of an unlawful assembly were liable to receive imprisonment up to six months, which might include fine. Section 146 provided that if force or violence was used in pursuance of the common object, even by just one member, such unlawful assembly would be considered riotous assembly, and all of its members would be liable to receive up to two years of imprisonment.

As the framers attended to these details, they began to realise how asymmetric the overall legal system had grown. Penal laws were among the first that were codified, even as they acknowledged that penal laws were/are subsidiary and auxiliary to civil law. Because it prescribed rights and duties of subjects as well as delimited the powers of the executive, civil law was/is the principal substantive law. Moreover, the framers argued that at the time of their making, penal laws or a penal code assumed the existence of civil laws or a civil code. But even as they made this honest statement, given their acknowledgement of the asymmetric relationship between different "departments" of law or code(s), the framers were also apparently apologetic, registering a proleptic defence of what they called the "uncertainty and obscurity" of the penal code. Hence, in order to defend the Code, which they and their predecessors had taken pains to author, compile, and edit, they acknowledged its shortcomings—but only by way of putting the blame on the "dark and confused" state of other departments of law. To quote them:

> A Penal Code[...]is then an auxiliary to the other departments of the law. If many important questions concerning rights and duties are undetermined by the Civil law, it must often be doubtful whether the provisions of the Penal law do or do not apply to a particular case [...] A Penal Code therefore necessarily partakes of the vagueness and uncertainty of the rest of the law. It cannot be clear and explicit while the substantive Civil law and the law of procedure are dark and confused.[20]

The framers acknowledged that the laws that ideally should have been auxiliary and supportive had replaced the principal laws and taken centre stage in the legal system. Interestingly, they might (not) have realised that their acknowledgement would expose how the legal system of the colonial security state was being run on subsidiary and auxiliary laws.

Instead of paying attention to introducing constitutional law guaranteeing fundamental rights and prescribing defined duties, the British sought to claim some credit for the framing of a consolidated and uniform penal code for all territories of India. It is true that the legal system of the colonial state moved a step forward, from individual regulations, which often differed on the temporal and territorial scales, to a unified system of penal laws and procedure. But again, the claim to this achievement could not last long as, in the first quarter of the 20th century, especially with the outbreak of World War I, the legal process began to undergo a reversal from a unified system of penal laws back to individual security regulations. And it is worth noticing that this change, or a similar one, first took place in England.

The DORA (1914), its amendment in 1915, and its associated regulations virtually replaced the rule of Common Law. The DORA authorised the trial of British subjects by martial courts, thus materialising the possibility that was only latent in the Mutiny Acts of the 17th century and that was once heatedly debated in the case of the rebellion in Jamaica in 1865. Due to severe public criticism, an amendment was made to the DORA on March 16, 1915 to substitute martial courts with civil courts and trials by jury. The relief was, however, available only to British subjects and not to anyone who fell under the category of aliens. Interestingly, the amendment also provided such relief to British women married to aliens (Section 8). In this way, the amendment was tantamount to clearly drawing a line between subjects and aliens, hence making legally consequential the individual's *divisiones personarum*. Nevertheless, the relief did not diminish the nature of the offence of contravening the DORA, which was to be considered a felony punishable by penal servitude for life and, in cases of assisting the enemy, by death and forfeiture of property. The amendment specifically provided that if any case qualified as a case of high treason it would still be tried as a case of felony. Evidently, this provision was made to avoid the cumbersome and often lengthy trial procedure of the law of high treason. Moreover, the amendment provided for two procedural novelties. First, it said that "for the purpose of speedy trial" a case could be initiated anywhere in the country, not just where the offence actually took place. Hence the notion of speedy trial—in fact, speedy procedure of trial, not speedy justice as such—took its initial roots in this act. Second, it gave courts the authority "to exclude the public," or certain attendees, from the court, purportedly in "the interests of national safety." This provision amounted to a crucial procedural change in the trial of felony cases, or what was earlier considered high treason or, in India, offences against the state.

The DORA authorised preventive detention under Regulation 14(b). Under the regulation, the government could detain civilians of "hostile origin or associations"—a juridical category that has survived and which has become even more significant in present times—and restrict their movement for indefinite amounts of time. Such preventive detentions were challenged, but the British courts decided that government had valid discretion to detain anyone, even on mere suspicion. For instance, in *Rex v Halliday* 1917 (and later in *Liversidge v Anderson*, 1942) the court accepted the principle of "subjective satisfaction," as opposed to that of "objective satisfaction," on the part of government, as sufficient criteria for the reasonableness of suspicion needed to detain individuals.

On March 19, 1915, three days after the passage of the amendment to the DORA in England, the Governor-General gave assent to the Defence of India (Criminal Law Amendment) Act, or DIA. The DIA, taking its legal form and substance from the DORA, authorised the colonial government to make rules or regulations in the name of public safety and in the defence of the country. Just like the DORA, it was preoccupied with political offences, which it classified under the term "certain offences." By now this phrase was more than a century old and still referred to almost the same offences as in Regulation X of 1804: waging war, assisting the enemy, and causing disaffection. These offences were once provided through individual regulations, later made part of the Penal Code and now placed under the DIA. While in Regulation X these offences were subject to courts martial, as well as under the DORA, the DIA provided for special tribunals "for the more speedy trial." The essence of all these courts of different generations was speed. The speedy trials, in practice, entailed circumvention of the regular, lengthy, and cumbersome trial procedure of the Code of Criminal Procedure, 1898. Under the DIA, each special tribunal was to consist of three commissioners, two of whom were required to have legal experience and qualifications. The tribunals were given the power to award capital sentences in cases of waging war or assisting the enemy. Moreover, it was provided that the decision was "final and conclusive." There was no right to appeal against the decision, and no other court had the power to revise the decision or exercise "any jurisdiction of any kind in respect of any proceedings under this Act."

The DIA and its associated rules, which curtailed several freedoms including the freedom of movement, applied both to subjects and aliens. However, the war put aliens at a greater disadvantage. All aliens were suspected enemy aliens. Many European enemy aliens were transferred to India and placed in camps. Towards the end of the war, the Government of India Act 1919 transferred the power of dealing with matters relating to aliens to the central government. The following year, the Passport Act was passed, which placed a new set of regulatory rules on the entry and movement of aliens in India. Because a passport was a new requirement, many countries had not yet developed the system, nor would many aliens even be aware of what it was, and as a result they were left at the mercy of the discretionary powers of colonial officers. In addition, the passport requirement also meant that any British Indian subject wishing to travel abroad would need a passport and, hence, the consent of the government. The act also gave powers to police officers above the rank of sub-inspector to make arrests without warrant of person violating any provision of the act.

In the aftermath of the war, three Imperial Conferences (1918, 1921, and 1923) took place. In these conferences, the power of the state to exclude an alien from entering, traveling, and residing was accepted without reservations by all participants, including Indian members. (In fact, in January 1920, the Government of India decided to completely bar the entry of enemy aliens for a period of five years after the conclusion of peace.) The Conference members ignored the fact that it was the Imperial War that had created and/or exacerbated the category of aliens (which now included enemy aliens, refugees, stateless people, and asylum seekers), and that following the end of the war they were now restricting, oppressing, and humiliating them.

Around the same time, in the United States, a century-old debate on the rights of aliens was coming to an end. The debate that had begun with the Alien and Sedition Acts (1798) revolved around the question of whether aliens should enjoy protections and rights under the constitution. Although the debate mostly affected the rights of white, European aliens, it was, however, significant as a test of the scope of American constitutionalism. The Federalists took the position that aliens were not party to the compact (i.e. the Constitution), and therefore they could not claim rights or protections under it. They emphasised that aliens were subject to the law of nations rather than to the municipal law. The Republicans, on the other hand, took the position that the Constitution was fundamentally a law that subjected everyone to its command and therefore guaranteed equal protection and rights to "persons," not just to citizens.[21]

While this debate went on through the course of the 19th century, many individual states accorded rights to *alien friends* under their constitutions, including the right to political suffrage. The Supreme Court also accepted a degree of formal juridical equality of citizens and aliens in normal times to hear the justiciable claims of aliens. The court observed that aliens were under the government's protection while within the territory and inasmuch as they obeyed the laws (*Carlisle v United States*, 1873). Towards the end of the century, as the demand for immigrant workers plummeted, feelings of ambivalence, and then hostility, began to emerge. Asians and black people were already facing discrimination; European aliens also began to lose their privileged position.

Following World War I, "the rabidly anti-alien decade of the 1920s" began.[22] States that were hitherto vying for immigrant aliens began to develop a mistrust of them. State legislatures introduced legislation placing increased restrictions on them. The Court also yielded to legislative judgment that aliens could not be trusted. Legislatures thus barred aliens from certain occupations, activities, and rights. For instance, they were barred from owning billiard halls, in the name of the public good (*Clarke v Deckebach*, 1927), owning rifles and shotguns, to preserve wildlife (*Patsone v Pennsylvania*) and owning land, to benefit citizens (*Terrace v Thompson*, 1927). The Court accepted the political argument that the alien lacked allegiance to the state, which made him untrustworthy, and therefore the state's discrimination against him was legitimate.

The Supreme Court's response to federal and state legislation in this era, according to one insightful observer, was shaped by concern for balancing the fear of the other with the fear of governmental tyranny.

> Aliens were understood to present a direct threat to the continued existence and security of the nation. Hence when the Court perceived the threat to citizens' liberty posed by aliens to be greater than that posed by government—as it did in the great majority of cases—it would allow the government to regulate. Only when the Court perceived the threat

> to liberty posed by governmental action to be greater than the threat posed by aliens would it intervene and strike down the regulation at issue.[23]

In India, towards the end of World War I, it was expected that the government would end the exercise of emergency powers in six months, as declared in both the DORA and the DIA. However, the expectations were not met and new emergency laws were enacted at the end of the war. On March 21, 1919, in the wake of a stepped-up political resistance to colonial rule, the government enacted the Anarchical and Revolutionary Crimes Act (ARCA). In England, a year and a half later, the Emergency Powers Act was enacted. In the case of the ARCA, the stated purpose was to "supplement" the ordinary criminal law and to make emergency powers "exercisable." However, the act did not define what it generically termed anarchical and revolutionary movements and crimes. Instead, it took out a list of offences from the Penal Code, put them together in the form of a schedule, and attached it to the act. These penal crimes were to be treated as anarchical and revolutionary offences and would also justify the invoking of emergency powers. However, the major offences were, once again, the same: waging war, assaulting or overawing the government, and (abetting) mutiny or sedition. Moreover, several lesser crimes from the Penal Code were included: for instance, rioting, extortion, criminal intimidation, banditry and robbery, murder or culpable homicide, damage to public infrastructure, mischief by fire or explosive substance, and lurking, housebreaking and entering. All of these offences were made subject to the jurisdiction of special courts, to be set up under the direction of a high court, each consisting of three judges of that, or any other, high court. The ARCA provided in detail a special procedure of trial and declared that court decisions were to be final and conclusive. Some notable features of the special procedure included: (a) the discretion of the government to initiate proceedings; to prepare charges and serve the accused; and to determine the place of court sitting, (b) that the court was not bound by rules of adjournment, (c) that the court could order to prohibit or restrict the disclosure or publication of proceedings, (d) other superior courts were excluded from exercising jurisdiction over the trial, and (e) that the recorded evidence of a person who later died, disappeared, or was incapable of giving evidence was made admissible. For two reasons, the ARCA was a prototype of modern security laws. First, it demonstrated well the new technique of borrowing crimes from the Penal Code, listing them in a schedule, and giving them a generic name. Second, it provided a detailed special procedure of trial, barred the regular superior courts from interference, whether judicial or administrative, and restricted the appeal against decisions.

In 1935, the British government adopted a Constitution for India—the Government of India Act, GIA.[24] Although a comprehensive document, the GIA did not guarantee fundamental rights. However, it authorised both federal and provincial governments to make laws and rules for preventive detention. The GIA provided constitutional sanction of preventive detention laws, whether already existing—such as the Bengal Regulation III of 1818—or to be made in future. The federal government was authorised to make preventive detention laws for the state for reasons relating to defence and foreign affairs, and the provincial governments for the maintenance of public order.[25]

In April 1939, just months before the outbreak of World War II, the Registration of Foreigners Act was introduced. There was some debate in the legislative assembly on the act, especially regarding the question of who was to be considered an alien. Some members complained that the government previously used the 1864 Act to exclude native Indians of princely states and autonomous or border territories when they were involved in civil resistance movements. The government, heeding these concerns, explained that people who were domiciled in India, including within the princely states and other territories, as well as those in the United Kingdom, would not be excluded. However, the subjects of other British colonies would be considered foreigners. The punishment for contravening the act was increased from two months to one year's imprisonment. The surveillance of foreigners continued (from the 1864 Act), and foreigners were to report both their arrival and departure, as well as carry their proof of identity at all times.

With the outbreak of World War II, the Defence Acts were once again invoked. This time, the Defence of India Act, 1939, came with more details. The government was authorised to make rules on virtually anything related to defence and public safety—the two subjects that were drawn from the DIA 1915—or to public order, efficient prosecution of war, and maintenance of supplies and services essential to the life of community. Apart from that, under the "generality of the powers" to make rules, a phrase used in the act, it provided for thirty-five specific subjects on which government could make rules. However, in one way or another, much of the government's focus was on a few specific subjects, especially the waging of war, assisting the enemy, and causing disaffection. Accordingly, the act provided for "enhanced penalties" for these offences and by 1943 made them subject to the Enemy Agents Ordinance—an ordinance that was severely derogatory to the British principles of equality before—and equal protection of—the law.

Aliens and foreigners were put under stricter control. Accordingly, they could neither enter nor leave the country without permission, and the government could also place a complete ban on entry and departure of foreigners. The government could order them to submit photographs, thumb impressions, and handwriting samples. A foreigner not only could be detained in safe custody but also removed to prescribed areas and makeshift camps. The term of imprisonment for contravening these orders was increased to five years. The officials were given discretionary powers to reject the object of pursuit or reasons of entering/travelling and, if already present, the reasons to extend his stay. While these rules were set up for a war emergency, at the end of war, the nationalist colonial legislature appropriated them into a permanent peacetime law—the Foreigners Act 1946.

On November 13, Sardar Vallabhbhai Patel introduced the Bill. He argued that the 1939 Act needed a supplemental and more robust act. He proposed the repeal of the 1864 Act on the grounds that it was "used or abused for treating Indians as foreigners in India." However, he had designed the bill on the pattern of the 1864 Act, and had added provisions from certain wartime laws, especially the DIA, 1939, and the Foreigners Act, 1940. The new act provided that a foreigner be required to stay in a prescribed area with "restrictions on his movement." He could be required to submit himself to medical tests, prohibited from associating with any prescribed group of people and/or activities and/or from carrying any items. He could be detained and those wishing to access him could also be turned away. If he was ordered to remove himself from any place or the country, then he was to bear the cost of it. Government could control and even shut down places frequented by foreigners. Regarding the identity of a foreigner, the act added a new provision. In case the identity of a foreigner was unknown or contradictory, the government would decide on his identity/nationality. Finally, the act gave indemnity to actions of the police and other officials (Article 15): "No suit, prosecution or other legal proceeding shall lie against any person for anything which is in good faith done or intended to be done under this Act."

One of the crucial legal aspects of the DIA, 1939, was the provision for creation of special tribunals. The Act provided for special tribunals whose rules of constitution and procedure were modelled on the pattern of the DIA, 1915, and the ARCA, 1919. However, some of the provisions were either notably different or were modified, and they caused further derogation from justice. First, the qualification of members of tribunals came down to the district magistrate or session judge. Only one member was to qualify as a judge of High Court. Second, the tribunals were authorised to award punishments, which included the death sentence, transportation for life and long-term imprisonment. Those who were awarded capital sentences were given the right to appeal their case to a high court, but they had no right of appeal against the awarded sentence. Third, the government could transfer any case to a special tribunal from any other special or ordinary criminal court. Fourth, a special tribunal could take cognizance of an offence even if it was not trying the accused. Fifth, a special tribunal was not required to record evidence at length in writing except in the case of capital sentences, and even in that category, it would "cause a memorandum of the substance of what each witness deposes." Sixth, a special tribunal was not bound to recall and rehear any witness. Rather, it could proceed on with the trial on the basis of already recorded evidence. Lastly, a special tribunal could try the accused in his absence if he had appeared once.

The special tribunals set up under the Enemy Agents Ordinance, 1943, went a step further in the derogation from justice. The ordinance did away with the three-member composition of special tribunals. Under it, a special tribunal consisted of one judge who was appointed by the government and was to be a session judge or an assistant session judge. The government not only determined the time and place of sitting but also could transfer cases from one special judge to another. Appeals against decisions of special courts were to be reviewed by another special judge, who was chosen from the judges of a high court. The decision of the appeals special judge was final. The higher courts were barred from exercising their administrative authority to transfer a case from a special court to an ordinary court. The ordinance further provided that an accused individual had the right to be defended by a legal pleader, but that "such pleader shall be a person whose name is entered in a list prepared in this behalf by the Government or who is otherwise approved by the Government." Similarly, the accused was given the right to receive a copy of the decision and other documents relating to the case, but he was supposed to return them within ten days after the end of proceedings and must not disclose information to anyone regarding the trial. After independence, Pakistan adopted this ordinance, while its special procedure also made its way into the Army Act (1952). Under the Army Act, civilians can be tried in a martial court with a similar special procedure.

Just like its predecessor, the DIA (1939) also provided for preventive detention and other restrictions on the freedom of movement. In connection with this, Rule 26, for instance, provided:

> So long as there is in force in respect of any person such an order as aforesaid directing that he be detained, he shall be liable to be detained in such place, and under such conditions…

On the other hand, Rule 129 provided that any officer, whether of police or administration so authorised could arrest any person without warrant "whom he reasonably suspect[ed] of having acted, of acting, or of being about to act" in such a way "to assist any State at war with His Majesty, or in a manner prejudicial to the public safety or to the efficient prosecution of war," "or to assist the promotion of rebellion." It is worth mentioning here that just as the DIA and DIR (Defence of India Rules) (1939) curtailed civil liberties of Indian subjects, the higher courts stepped in to defend them, at least initially. I explain this crucial point at some length later.

Since *Rex v Halliday* (1917), the colonial higher courts seemed to have accepted the executive branch's power in relation to making orders of arrest and preventive detention. The subjective satisfaction on the part of the executive, rather than the objective one, was deemed enough to keep an Indian subject in preventive detention for almost indefinite time period, especially during emergencies. However, beginning in the summer of 1942, the Federal Court of India made a series of decisions which were based on nuanced interpretation of provisions of civil liberties and their relationship with criminal and emergency laws. First, in *Niharendu Butt Mazumdar* (1942), the Federal

Court redefined sedition in relation to freedom of speech and expression.[26] Mazumdar had spoken in the Bengal Legislative Assembly about the failure of the provincial government of Bengal to handle the Dacca riots. The Court carefully analysed his speech and termed it a political speech rather than a seditious one. The Court said: "...the time is long gone when a mere criticism of government, even abusive language, was sufficient to constitute sedition." The Court was of the opinion that "honest and reasonable criticism" could be justified in politics; indeed, it played a vital role in political opposition.

A nuanced interpretation of the subjective satisfaction criterion in the cases of arrest and detention under the DIA and its rules came in *Keshav Talpade* (1943).[27] The Court pointed out that in Rule 26 of the DIA, the executive had exceeded its rule making authority as envisioned in the Clause X of Section 2(2) of the DIA. Rule 26 had given almost *carte blanche* to the executive in matters relating to arrest and detention. This was evident in the actual practice of arrests and detentions at the hands of police, who were not preparing specific reports in each individual case. Since the Civil Disobedience Movement was going on against the colonial government and mass arrests were taking place, the police prepared reports in which they specified almost verbatim a number of the grounds given in Rules 26 and 129.[28] This clearly showed, as the Court pointed out, that the executive was not applying its mind to individual detention orders. The Federal Court, therefore, stressed that the DIA (1939) required making rules for arrest and detention only on line of *reasonable suspicion* relating to persons of hostile origin or those acting in a manner prejudicial to the safety and interest of the empire. The Court acknowledged the existence of grave emergency, but it also insisted upon its judicial review power. The Court said that it was expected not only to exercise judicial review whenever the executive exceeded in the exercise of power conferred upon it by the legislature but also to safeguard the civil liberties of subjects.

The decision in *Keshav Talpade* alarmed the colonial government because the declaration of Rule 26 as invalid could have led to the release of thousands of detainees. Therefore, the Governor-General, within a few days, promulgated an ordinance making the necessary correction in Clause X of Section 2(2) of the Defence of India Act.[29] The correction made was declared to have retroactive effect, thus validating all arrests and detentions made under Rule 26. With this ordinance, the subjective satisfaction on the part of the executive, which had initially received precedence over objective satisfaction, was then made law. The ordinance had made the matter of preventive detention rest on the touchstone of subjective satisfaction alone. Another consequence, although indirect, of this provision in the ordinance was that the judicial review power of higher courts was curtailed. Thus, commenting on this consequence, the Chief Justice of the Lahore High Court said:

> There seems to be persistent endeavour on the part of the Executive these days not only to ignore and flout the legislature, but even to

> interfere with and curtail the powers of the judiciary as well. The judiciary have, therefore, to be extra vigilant to preserve and maintain their authority and prestige intact.[30]

The decision in *Keshav* encouraged other detainees to appeal for *habeas corpus* in the Federal Court. In these appeals, the Court was also asked to strike down the ordinance on the same basis as it did Rule 26. The Court heard several appeals in *Sibnath Banerjee* (1943). However, the Court declined to put the ordinance to judicial review or strike it down. It instead upheld the principle of subjective satisfaction on the part of the executive. Nevertheless, the Court maintained that a detention based on the recommendation of police was not a satisfactory test of the executive's application of its mind to a case. This line of argument was again stressed in *Emperor v Keshav Gokhale* (1945).

In 1944, another ordinance (Ordinance III) was promulgated to replace the earlier ordinance. The principle of subjective satisfaction in the new ordinance remained the same. However, it required the executive to communicate grounds of detention to detainees, and any other particulars as requested, so as to enable them to make representation, unless such communication was conflicted with the public interest. On the one hand, this procedural right was given to detainees, but on the other, the ordinance took away the power of the High Courts under Section 491 (relating to *habeas corpus*) of the Criminal Procedure Code (1898). Moreover, the ordinance allowed the executive to extend detention for a further period of six months beyond the initial period of six months. Although the higher courts could not review the ordinance, they were not happy about it. For instance, the Chief Justice of the Allahabad High Court protested that the ordinance had paralysed the higher courts to consider even the basic questions of legality and propriety of arrests and detentions made by the executive.[31]

In 1942, the Governor-General promulgated Ordinance II for creating special criminal courts for speedy trials. The ordinance conferred authority upon provincial governments to create special criminal courts in provinces and specify their procedure, jurisdiction, and the sentences they could award. The criminal special courts, thus created, adopted a substantially abridged criminal procedure. The procedural requirements of recalling witnesses and evidence, grant of bail, adjournment, trial by jury, punishments and appeal to higher courts were modified to ensure expedited trials. However, the Federal Court in *Emperor v Benoari Lall Sharma* (1943), struck down the ordinance.[32] The Court argued that the executive could not create special criminal courts through an ordinance. The Court said that special courts could be created only by the legislature. Moreover, the Court criticised the government's indirect curtailing of the judicial review power of higher courts through the ordinance. The government responded by issuing a fresh ordinance, modelled exactly after the previous ordinance, and recreated special criminal courts.[33] However, in the new ordinance, the government allowed the making of appeal to higher courts and conceded to the judicial review power of higher courts. The new ordinance was challenged on the grounds established in the case that struck down the earlier ordinance. The following year (1944), the Federal Court decided with a considerably different opinion from the one given earlier.[34] The Court argued that since civil liberties were not constitutionally protected in India through the Government of India Act, 1935, they could therefore be made subject to the ordinary lawmaking power of both the legislature and the executive.

It is interesting to notice that the challenge to emergency laws began in the summer of 1942 and continued for only a couple of years. This was the time when civil disobedience by the Quit India Movement was going strong. On the other hand, the British Government was facing a tough fight in the war on different fronts. Thus the legal battle between the executive and the higher courts kept the Indian politics engaged, with hope pinned in the courts. For two years, this legal battle made headlines in newspapers and radio newscasts. The media remained gripped, explaining the court debates and their potential consequences for fundamental rights *vis-à-vis* the executive's powers. Interestingly, by the time the decision in *Piare Dusadh* (1944) came along, the war pressure on the British Government had considerably eased. With this we can also see that the legal battle between the executive and the judiciary phased out, with the executive let off the hook.

Conclusion

By the time World War II ended and as British India approached its independence, the security regime of the colonial state had immensely expanded. Let us recall that in the early 19th century, the fledgling colonial state had begun with a legal system that barely constituted few individual security regulations. The legal form and the substance of these regulations were all drawn from the English law of high treason. In particular, the legal form of treason helped create the category of offences against the state. Martial courts and special commissions were introduced in lieu of the jury procedure for treason trials, while in cases where a charge was difficult to establish, the law of preventive detention was given to provide a solution. By the mid-19th century, security regulations were consolidated into a penal code for the purposes of greater uniformity throughout the colonial state. But by the first quarter of the 20th century, especially with the outbreak of WWI, security regulations once again came to centre stage. These security regulations had by now created a powerful colonial security regime, but obviously at the expense of other "departments" of the legal system. Given this reliance on security regulations, it can well be argued that the colonial state began and ended with security regulations and special procedures.

Notes

1 Kennedy, "The Creation and Development of Pakistan's Anti-Terrorism Regime, 1997–2002," 411.
2 Agamben, *State of Exception*, 18.
3 The affinity between the Mutiny Acts and the law of high treason can be seen in the Mutiny Act, 1703, which stipulated that any correspondence with the enemy would be considered an act of high treason.
4 Steffen, *Defining a British State*, 160–161.
5 Fletcher, "Ambivalence about Treason."
6 Assault and violence against the king's subjects were petty treason in Common Law. See Steinhaus 1955, 254.
7 The Act V of 1841 also aimed to achieve "greater uniformity of the process upon trials for State offences." The act was repealed by Act X of 1872, which provided for regulating the procedure of the courts of criminal judicature.
8 The next year the Madras State Prisoners Regulation II was passed and in 1827 the Bombay State Prisoners Regulation XXV was passed.
9 The reader might find it interesting that the reasoning giving in the quoted passage from the Regulation of 1818 has recently been presented by President Barrack Obama to justify detentions at Guantanamo Bay. He might not be aware of this Regulation as he said: "There may be a number of people who could not be prosecuted for past crimes, in some case because the evidence maybe tainted, but who nonetheless poses a threat to the security of the United State." Maddow, "Obama Justifies FEMA Imprisonment of Civilians!"
10 Mahmood, *The Law of Preventive Detention*, 4.
11 Blackstone, *Commentaries on the Laws of England*, 136.
12 An Act for the better Custody of State Prisoners, Act XXXIV of 1850. The act was passed on August 23, 1850.
13 The State Prisoners Act, Act III of 1858.
14 Indian Council Act of 1861, 24 & 25 Victoria, c. 67, Section 23.
15 Kalhan et al., "Colonial Continuities," 128
16 Two decades earlier, in England, three treason trials—the Spa Fields Riots, 1817, the Pentridge Rebellion, 1817, and the Cato Street Conspiracy, 1820—had caused considerable juridical debate over the law of high treason, and especially its construction. The trials generally ended with restrictive construction of the law (see Steffen 2001, 145–147). In the United States, a series of treason cases were heard around the same time. For instance, see *Ex parte Bollman*, 1807, *United States v Hoxie*, 1808, and *United States v Pryor*, 1814. Also see earlier cases *United States v Lee*, 1804, and *Respublica v Malin*, 1778.
17 The Penal Code 1837, 140
18 The Penal Code 1837, 118.
19 In the 1860 Code, the word "framer" is used to refer to the authors of the 1837 Copy of the Code and probably also to the later editors. I here use it to refer to both, the authors of the earlier copy and the later editors and compilers of the 1860 Code.
20 The Indian Penal Code 1860, 2.
21 Neuman, *Strangers to the Constitution*.
22 Dinnerstein, "The Supreme Court and the Rights of Aliens."
23 The Harvard Law Review Association, "Developments in the Law: Immigration Policy and the Rights of Aliens," 96, no. 6 (April 1983): 1301.
24 Government of India Act, 1935, 26 Geo. 5 & 1 Edw. 8, c. 2 (August 2, 1935)
25 Government of India Act, 1935, Seventh Schedule List I Entry 1 and List II Entry 1 read with Part V of the Act.
26 *Niharendu Dutt Mazumdar v King Emperor*, AIR 1942 Federal Court 22.

27 *Keshav Talpade v King Emperor*, 30 AIR 1943 Federal Court 1.
28 Express Letter from Home Member to all Provincial Governments, May 1, 1943, IOR/L/PJ/8/633/196; Letter from Secretary of State to Viceroy, IOR/L/P/8/633/289.
29 The decision in *Keshav Talpade* came on April 22, and Ordinance XIV was promulgated on April 28, 1943.
30 Singh, "Clash between Indian Judiciary and Executive during Second World War," 452.
31 Ibid., 454
32 *Emperor v Benoari Lall Sharma* (1943) FCR 96.
33 The Special Courts Ordinance, No. XIX of 1943.
34 *Piare Dusadh and others v The King Emperor* (1944) FCR 61.

2 The postcolonial state of security

Introduction

We know that the newly independent states of Pakistan and India adopted much of their legal corpus from the colonial state. This adoption included several security laws, and anywhere it was not possible to adopt a specific law, its form and substance were adopted. This, for instance, was the case with the Anarchical and Revolutionary Crimes Act (1919) (ARCA), which could not be adopted for obvious reasons. However, we find its form and substance replicated in the laws made for governmental control of political opposition and agitation. We find its reflections in the Security of Pakistan Act (1952) and the Suppression of Terrorist Activities Act (1975). The major colonial laws that were adopted either in almost their original form or after amendments included the Frontier Crimes Regulations (1901), the Press (Emergency Powers) Act (1931), the Government of India Act (1935), the Defence of India Act and Rules (1939), the Enemy Agents Act (1943), and the Foreigners Act (1946). Let me briefly introduce how the colonial regime of security continued in the postcolonial state of Pakistan through these laws.

The Frontier Crimes Regulation (FCR) (1901) was adopted in its original form. The Supreme Court's decision in *Dosso* (1958) saved and extended it.[1] I will return to the FCR in Chapter 6. The Press (Emergency Powers) Act, 1931 was also adopted in almost its original form. In the early years after independence, this act was often brought into service for keeping private press and publication agencies from criticising government policies and/or supporting political opposition. The courts also only cautiously and selectively came to the help of the press. For instance, in 1949, the Lahore High Court (LHC) ruled in a number of cases that critiquing policies of the government or the Press Act itself was not to be construed as causing hatred or disaffection towards the government.[2] Similarly, the court argued a case involving a book praising the communist revolution of China, ruling it was neither seditious nor causing disaffection towards the government.[3] However, in other cases, especially relating to the ideology and/or creation of Pakistan as well as its national interests, the higher courts agreed to the government's general stance of delimiting the scope of the right to freedom of expression.[4]

For instance, in two cases, one relating to Allama Mashriqi's critique of the Islamic basis of the creation of Pakistan, the calling of the government of Pakistan as irreligious and indifferent to Islam was deemed as causing sedition, disaffection, and hatred towards the government.[5]

The Government of India Act, 1935 provided the model for incorporating the exception to the right of *habeas corpus* in the form of preventive detention. It provided for the ground of preventive detention, which should have been part of criminal (procedural) law rather than the constitutional/substantive law. Accordingly, all three Constitutions of Pakistan made provisions for preventive detention. The current Constitution (1973) makes such a provision in Article 10. One encouraging aspect, however, of the preventive detention provisions in the Constitutions was that they restricted the scope of executive's power in the existing preventive detention statutes and ordinances.

Whenever the postcolonial state was faced with the external threat of war and invasion, it invoked, almost verbatim, the Defence of India Act and Rules (1939). This happened twice, once in 1965 and once in 1971. However, on both occasions, the emergency that was imposed was prolonged beyond the period of wars. In September 1965, President Ayub Khan declared emergency, and promulgated the Defence of Pakistan Ordinance and Rules (DPO), which remained in force until the fall of his government to martial law in 1969. A couple of years later, in the wake of a war with India, the government again promulgated the DPO (1971), which remained in force through the entire democratic government of Zulfikar Ali Bhutto. At the end of his government, the emergency that had begun with the war of 1971, rather the war of 1965, continued in one form or the other—that of martial law—until 1985.

The Foreigners Act (1946) was adopted almost without amendments and remains in force to the present. This act has been instrumental in checking free movement of non-citizens, refugees, and stateless people. After independence, both Pakistan and India employed this act on the people who had migrated across the border due to partition and whose identities remained dual or difficult to ascertain. After the Afghan War of the 1980s, the act has also been extensively used to control the identity and free movement of refugees. Recently, the Foreigners Act and the Enemy Agents Act (1943) have provided basis for creating the category of enemy alien in the Protection of Pakistan Ordinance (2013) and Protection of Pakistan Act (2014) (see Chapters 4 and 6).

In the early years after independence, Pakistan had a number of security laws in force both at the national level and at the provinces. These laws were downplayed, however, by calling them "public safety" laws, as was obvious from their titles and preambles. Let us have a look at some of these laws. On October 8, 1949, the Governor General promulgated the Pakistan Public Safety Ordinance, 1949.[6] This ordinance was designed to authorise the

Central government to restrict free movement and to arrest and detain persons acting in a manner prejudicial to public safety and order in the country. The ordinance also authorised the "control of subversive associations." Moreover, it allowed the government to "control information," the press, and free expression. These powers were not limited with the expected democratic checks. For instance, the ordinance did not provide the detainee the right to be informed of the grounds of his detention or to make representation against the detention order to government. Although the ordinance did not prescribe for special tribunals, it did provide for an amended criminal procedure to expedite the trials. For example, the amendments restricted adjournment and bail during trials.

The ordinance was initially enacted for a period of one year. However, it had an interesting feature that afforded the central government the power to extend its time period, which the central government could do through simple notifications published in the Gazette Extraordinary. Accordingly, the government extended it from time to time until March 1952, when the Federal Court decided upon its status. In *Sobho Gyanchandani* (1952), the Federal Court questioned whether the government could extend the time period of an ordinance through simple notifications; in other words, the question was about conditional legislation and the delegation of power. The Chief Justice Abdul Rashid argued, "A legislature cannot delegate its powers of making, modifying, or repealing any law to an external authority. [If it does so] it would be creating a parallel legislature." The Chief Justice further said that it could delegate only those powers relating to the enforcement of law or a law's application to a specific area under certain conditions. Thus the court struck down the government notification of extension of the ordinance and also declared the relevant provision in the ordinance as unconstitutional.[7] The *Sobho* decision was a blow to the government's detention powers. However, the government responded by promulgating a fresh ordinance next day with a proviso that it would "be deemed to have taken effect on the 3rd March 1952"—the day on which the Federal Court gave its decision.[8] Moreover, the government also provided in the ordinance that any order issued under the previous ordinance would "be deemed to have been made under the provisions of this Ordinance."[9]

More or less similar to the public safety ordinance at the national level, different provinces had in force their own public safety laws. Balochistan, Punjab, and Sindh had enforced their public safety laws as early as 1947. In North-West Frontier Province (NWFP), a Public Safety Ordinance was promulgated in 1948, while in East Bengal, similar laws were enacted from 1948 onwards, as well as a Public Safety law in 1951.[10]

At the national level, a couple of months after the decision in *Sobho Gyanchandani* (1952), on May 5, 1952, the Security of Pakistan Act (SPA) 1952, was passed, which repealed the Public Safety Ordinance, 1952. This repeal also shows that the government desperately wanted to save its detention orders from judicial review. The SPA (1952) has survived the test of time and is still on the books. Since this act has remained one of the central acts of security in Pakistan, we will therefore discuss it in detail in a moment. Another important piece of legislation worth mentioning here is the second amendment to the Government of India Act, 1935. With this amendment, certain subjects, especially those of the security of the state, public safety, public order, maintenance of supplies, and services essential to society, were rearranged in the legislative lists. Accordingly, the subject of security of the state was kept in the Central List, and the other subjects in the Concurrent List, whereby provinces were empowered to make laws.[11]

Apart from these public safety laws, the government also made laws to enhance its control in the political arena. For instance, in 1949 the government passed the Public and Representative Offices (Disqualification) Act (PRODA). Although it was aimed at checking maladministration and corruption in public offices, it increased government's powers against political opposition, resistance and dissidence. A decade later this law provided the basis for Ayub Khan's Elective Bodies (Disqualification) Ordinance, (EBDO) (1959). On the other hand, to suppress serious political dissidence, for instance, as in the 1951 potential conspiracy of *coup d'etat*, the government passed a law to create special courts—the Rawalpindi Conspiracy (Special Tribunal) Act (1951).

Given the shortage of space in this chapter, I will discuss only few security laws that I think have remained central to the security regime of the postcolonial state. These laws are either still in force or have lasted for longer time periods and affected many people and resulted in registration of large number of court cases.

The Security of Pakistan Act (1952)

The SPA (1952) was one of the first major security acts introduced after independence. However, as discussed above, the government had issued two public safety ordinances before it—the Public Safety Ordinances of 1949 and 1952. The first ordinance was struck down by the Federal Court in 1952, and the second one replaced by the SPA. Initially, the SPA was also supposed to be a temporary act that would lapse in three years. However, the act was extended from time to time, such that it is still in force.[12] The SPA (1952) allowed the government to take "special measures," such as preventive detention, "to deal with persons acting in a manner prejudicial to the defence, external affairs and security of Pakistan," as well as to "the maintenance of supplies and services essential for the community." It is obvious from its "phraseology" that the act was based on the Defence of India Act (1939).

With the adoption of the Constitution (1956), the SPA (1952) became an act under the new constitutional framework. The Constitution itself provided for preventive detention as an exception to the right of safeguard against arbitrary arrest and detention (Article 7(4)). Both federal and provincial governments could make laws and issue orders for preventive detention.[13] The Constitution provided the same reasons and subjects as provided in the SPA (1952) for making preventive detention laws and orders: the defence of the state, its external affairs, and the maintenance of supplies and services. The Constitution also provided for making of an Appropriate Advisory Board which would exercise judicial oversight over all aspects of preventive detention—reasons of detention, place and conditions, and the need for extension. Bearing in mind the principle of separation of judicial and executive powers, the Constitution provided that the Board should be constituted by the Chief Justice rather than by the executive. With this provision, the appointive power of the executive—and therefore its potential influence over the appointed judges—was reduced. All cases of detention had to be judged by the Board in a period of three months, and only upon the recommendation of the Board the detention could be further extended.

Interestingly, in 1956, with the Adaptation (Security laws) Order, the objects of maintenance of supplies and services and public order were omitted from the SPA (1952). However, in the next few years, we see a shift in the focus once again on the object of public order. This shift came in the wake of Field Marshal Ayub Khan's *coup d'etat* and his taking of power. As Ayub Khan planned to stay in power for longer time than was expected, his government began to face increasing political opposition and unrest. The government was thus faced with the task of maintaining peace and order in the country rather than the tasks of defence, external affairs or security. We notice this change in a number of new ordinances and laws passed by his government. For instance, in August 1959, Ayub Khan's government issued the Elective Bodies (Disqualification) Order (EBDO). With this order, the government could disqualify a politician on reasons of misconduct, which included activities causing subversion or political instability, as well as acts of taking bribes or engaging in corruption. In December 1960, Ayub Khan's government, through the Governor of West Pakistan, issued an ordinance called the Maintenance of Public Order Ordinance (MPOO) (Ordinance No. XXXI). This ordinance was specifically meant to amend and consolidate the laws relating to preventive detention. I'll return to this ordinance in a moment. Here I want to point out that with the MPOO taking care of the object of maintenance of public order, an amendment is introduced to the SPA in 1962 to reorient its object towards the security of state.[14]

The procedure of detention under the SPA had (and still has) a number of steps that have remained subject to amendment and change. The act provided that the government could issue orders of detention for any person. In the detention order, the government was supposed to provide grounds or reasons of detention, and these grounds or reasons were supposed to be communicated to the detainee within a period of one month. But the act also provided an exception to this rule: the government was authorised to withhold any information in the public interest. In 1962, the Preventive Detention Laws (Amendment) Act reduced the time period for communication of grounds to the detainee to fifteen days. This act also advised to let the detainee know the grounds at the time of his/her detention or as soon as possible within after fifteen days. Apart from communication of grounds to the detainee, the SPA also provided for communication of the right of the detainee to make representation against the order of detention to the government. However, the act truncated this right by providing that a detainee could neither make representation in person nor hire a legal counsel to do so. The grounds of detention and the representation made by the detainee were to be placed before an Advisory Board within a period of three months. This obviously meant that the government was authorised to detain a person without the right of habeas for about three months. Unlike the provision in the 1956 Constitution, the Advisory Board of the SPA was to be set up by the government alone. However, the government was required to appoint members who were qualified for the position of a High Court judge. Thus the government could choose any lawyer with at least ten years of practice at a High Court for appointment as a member of the Board. Just as the term "advisory" suggests the Advisory Board was given only advisory authority, the Board's decision/opinion was not binding but rather advisory in nature. The government could carry on with the detention of a given person. The act required the government to review the detention order after every six months until the person was released. The government was also required to communicate its review decision to the detainee.

Maintenance of Public Order Ordinances, MPOO, 1960

On December 1, 1960, the Governor of West Pakistan, on the instruction of Ayub Khan's government, promulgated the MPOO. Since the MPOO was an ordinance requiring approval of the legislature, the government had a provision incorporated in Article 225 of the 1962 Constitution to give the ordinance permanent life. Since then, the MPOO is in force in the statutes. It has not seen many revisions, except those needed to bring it in line with the two new Constitutions—1962 and 1973.[15]

One of the political purposes of making the MPOO was to bring about uniformity in the provincial laws relating to government control—especially the control of persons and press. In its own words, the ordinance said that it was meant to "amend and consolidate the law relating to preventive detention and control of person and publications connected with the maintenance of public order." Since the four provinces of West Pakistan were administratively merged in the One Unit policy in 1954, there appeared the legal technical need for consolidating the laws of detention that were in force in these provinces. Accordingly, the MPOO replaced the individual security laws of these provinces.[16] When the One Unit plan was abandoned in 1970 and the original four provinces reconstituted, the MPOO was readopted afresh by each province.[17]

Interestingly, in this process of consolidation, the SPA (1952) was kept out, even though it also provided for preventive detention. There could be two potential reasons for this: first, that the SPA (1952) operated on central or state level, and the government wanted to continue it as an additional power tool, and second, that there was a difference in the objects of the two laws. While the object of the MPOO was the maintenance of domestic public order, the SPA's was of defence, security, and external affairs of the state.

Apart from the objects of public safety and order, the government put a softer and self-righteous veneer on the MPOO by declaring hoarding, smuggling, and dealing in the black market as cognisable offences.[18] Although these offences were already mentioned in other existing laws, the government now linked them with the notion of public safety and pubic order. By doing this, Ayub Khan's government hoped to create an impression that his laws had the element of the welfare of the people. In fact, however, the ordinance was mere tool of political control, since its central interests were preventive detention and control of the press. It was designed to deal with political resistance with an iron hand.

In 1962, Ayub Khan gave a new Constitution to the country. With the new constitution tailored to his demands, Ayub Khan began to feel strong and confident in the seat of power. At this stage, since the new constitution provided for safeguards against arrest and detention, the MPOO was also amended (1964) to bring it in line with the constitutional guarantees. Accordingly, the character of indefiniteness of the preventive detention in it was reduced to a framework of six months of detention at a time. However, Ayub Khan might not have anticipated how heavily he would have to rely on the MPOO by the mid-1960s. In the wake of a war with India in 1965, and especially the peace deal at the end, Ayub Khan began to face widespread protests, which gradually developed into an organised political movement. One of the consequences of the political movement was the law and order situation in the major cities of the country. To cope with it, the government began to rely more and more on the MPOO, the DPO, 1965, and the rules made under the Ordinance. But the more the government relied on the use of these laws the more political unrest it invited. Eventually, these laws were neither able to maintain public order and safety nor could they save his regime from collapsing.

One of the problems about the MPOO was its vague or undefined legal object. The ordinance only stipulated that it was meant to deal with persons "acting in any manner prejudicial to public safety or the maintenance of public order." However, the ordinance did not define what it meant by the terms "prejudicial," "public safety," or "public order." Such definitions would have been crucial in separating the actions legally cognisable by courts from those that could be classified as political actions. Perhaps the ordinance took these terms for granted, as they had been in use in earlier laws and the case law. For instance, the NWFP Public Safety Ordinance (1948) had defined the term "prejudicial," even though the definition was quite broad. Per the ordinance, the following actions were involved: to harm governmental relations, both external and internal, or to cause disaffection towards the government; to endanger public safety and order; to spread hatred and/or enmity among various classes of society; to disrupt integrity of the country; to associate with any political movement working against the interests of the state; or to simply cause fear and alarm among the people. In 1964, through an amendment, the MPOO added that members of proscribed organisations had to stop from performing their earlier roles, otherwise they would be considered engaging in prejudicial acts.[19]

In order to pursue the object, the MPOO provided for three kinds of powers: arrest, detention, and direction. To ensure public safety or public order, the government could arrest, detain, and/or give directions about movement and/or residence of a person. In this context, the government had to give written orders as well as specify the time period for such detention or direction. The original ordinance did not place any limit on time of detention. The preventive detention laws before the MPOO (which the MPOO consolidated) also did not place limits on time of detention or direction orders. For instance, the NWFP Public Safety Ordinance 1948 in Section 3(2) provided that

> The Provincial Government may commit any person arrested under the last preceding sub-section to such custody in such part of Pakistan and for such length of time, as the Provincial Government may, from time to time, order in that behalf.

It is interesting to notice that the NWFP ordinance did not also limit the power of territorial extent of detention; the MPOO did not approve of this. Regarding the time period of detention, an amendment was made to the MPOO in 1964 that restricted the maximum time period to six months at a time.[20] This amendment became indispensible after the adoption of the 1962 Constitution, which required restriction on the use of detention and guaranteed the right of safeguard against arbitrary arrest and detention.

The procedure of detention involved a number of procedural rights for the detainee. These rights were, however, burdened with exceptions. Unlike the earlier detention laws—for example, the NWFP Ordinance (1948)—the MPOO (1960) provided for the right of review of detention after every three months by a board consisting of a High Court judge and a senior civil servant. Second, the detainee was also entitled to be informed about the grounds of his/her detention, but only "as soon as may be" possible for the government to do so. Practically, however, it might take months before the detainee was informed and given a chance to appear before the board. A further exception to this procedural right was the provision of authority to the government to withhold any information from the detainee on the pretext of defending public interest. Third, the detainee was given the right to be heard in person, but he/she was not given the right to be represented through a legal practitioner.

This exception was perhaps based on the matter of fact that the ordinance did not liken the board to a court. Fourth, the detainee was given the right to be informed of the "opinion" of the board, but again, the government was empowered not to share the entire report or the proceedings. Lastly, the detainee could make representation to the government against the detention order; he/she could make such representation both at the first issuance of the order and after the opinion of the board. Upon considering the representation, the government could either release the detainee with or without a bond and sureties or keep him/her in detention. If, however, a person did not submit to detention, by either hiding or absconding, the government was empowered to initiate criminal proceedings against him.

Certain aspects of the rules made under the ordinance are also worth mentioning here.[21] First, detainees were to be classified on the basis of their social status into either Class I or Class II. The authority passing the order of their detention would determine their class and therefore their privileges during the period of detention as well. Second, detainees would be generally kept separate from ordinary prisoners. Third, they were allowed to maintain correspondence, but with certain restrictions. A detainee in Class I was permitted to write four letters per week, and a detainee in Class II two letters. The letters were to be written on a form (Form B), and its length was restricted to specified space. Their correspondence was "confined to purely domestic matters, or subjects relating to the welfare" of the family and friends. Any letter written by or to a detainee containing "references to communal or political or other objectionable matters" could be withheld. These rules meant that the correspondence of a detainee was kept under strict observation. Fourth, if a detainee breached any rule, then he/she could be punished by changing the confinement and/or alteration of diet for a period of fourteen days or by cancellation of any other privileges, such as regular correspondence, meeting with family, and so forth.

Apart from giving the power of preventive detention, the MPOO (1960) also empowered the provincial government to control free movement, stopping, and/or residence of any person. This power could be used on the pretext of public order, public safety, and public interest (the latter phrase being introduced by amendment in 1964).[22] Thus the provincial government could stop any suspected person from entering the province or any specific area within it as well as direct him to leave any area. Similarly, an authorised District officer could exercise this power in his/her district. The MPOO (1960), however, limited this power by providing that the government should not remove a resident from his/her province and the District officer should not remove a resident from his/her district. Second, the order had to be in writing, and the government was supposed to communicate grounds to the affected person as soon as possible. After the adoption of the 1973 Constitution, the communication time period was fixed at fifteen days at the maximum.[23] Third, the orders of control were subject to a similar review process as provided for preventive detention. However, the ordinance provided a longer life of two years to such orders.[24]

The MPOO (1960) also gave wide-ranging powers to the provincial government to control the press and publication. These powers were given in addition to the powers available under the Press and Publication Ordinance, 1960.[25] The MPOO authorised the government to stop and/or seize a printing press, a specific publication, or a newspaper, magazine, journal, or pamphlet as well as stop their entering a province or any area therein. The government could also demand for scrutiny of any potential publication or the information and/or document on which it was based. Moreover, the government could seek information about any person concerned in the communication of any information or report. The life of such an order was two months, and the affected press or person was entitled to informing of the grounds of the order, on the basis of which he/she could make representation to the government. However, no review was provided from the board against such orders, which meant that only writ petitions could be made to High Courts.

Emergency laws: the Defence of Pakistan Ordinances and Rules (1965 & 1971)

On September 6, 1965, war broke out between Pakistan and India. President Ayub Khan declared emergency in the country and, on the very same day, promulgated the DPO and the Defence of Pakistan Rules (DPR), 1965. Because of the urgency of time, the government took up the colonial defence law—the Defence of India Act and Rules (1939)—and, with minor changes, especially where the new political context had to be given, drafted the ordinance and a notification of rules under it. Although the war ended in almost seventeen days, the emergency proclamation survived until 1969. Once again in 1971, with the civil-war-like situation in East Pakistan and eventually an armed confrontation with India, the martial law government of Yahya Khan proclaimed a state of emergency and promulgated the DPO (1971) and a notification of the Rules under it. Interestingly, on both occasions of emergency, the external threat of war and invasion ended after a short period of time, but the proclamations of emergency and the emergency laws continued for a much longer time. In the case of the 1971 emergency, the new civil government of Zulfikar Ali Bhutto chose to continue the emergency. Bhutto even assumed the title of Civil Martial Law Administrator, and what is even more interesting is that on the very Independence Day that his government adopted the new Constitution of 1973, Bhutto asked the President to extend the time period of emergency in the country.

The DPO (1965) gave wide-ranging powers to the government. It provided the power to make rules on a number of subjects, including arrest and detention; free movement across borders as well as inside the country; regulation of all forms of telecommunication and transportation; regulation of markets; censorship and shutting down of press and publications; prohibition of assemblies, demonstrations, and fairs; and carrying out of searches without warrants at any private premises. The ordinance also provided for increased punishments for the scheduled offences. Moreover, if a person contravened or aided and abetted in contravening any rule, he/she could be punished with imprisonment for seven years with or without a fine. His/her property could also be seized. Similarly, if any person contravened any rule or order made under the Civil Aviation Ordinance (1960), the Arms Act (1878), the Explosives Act (1884), the Explosive Substances Act (1908), the Dangerous Cargoes Act (1953), or the West Pakistan Arms Ordinance (1965), he/she could be punished for five years. But if any person engaged or aided and abetted in the offences of waging war or carried out military operations against the state, he/she would be punished with a death sentence, transportation for life, or imprisonment for ten years.

Moreover, the government was empowered to make special tribunals without the advice of the Chief Justice. A tribunal was to consist of three members. The members were not supposed to be regular judges of a High Court. The government could appoint any person who was either qualified for appointment as a judge of High Court or had three years' experience of being a Sessions judge or District Magistrate. The government could transfer any case cognisable under the ordinance to a special tribunal. The criminal procedure was also abridged for speedy trials. Accordingly, the special tribunal could take cognisance of offences without the accused being committed for trial. It was not bound to adjourn any trial unless necessary in the interests of justice. It was also not bound to recall and rehear a witness who had already given evidence, and it could try a person in his absence given the accused had appeared once before it. Moreover, the tribunals were not supposed to write the evidence and reasoning at length, even in cases involving death or transportation for life sentences. However, an appeal could be made to a High Court in such cases involving capital sentences. In all other cases, there was no right of appeal to a superior court.

With such wide-ranging powers, the DPO (1965) eclipsed the existing security and maintenance of public order laws, especially the SPA (1952) and the MPOO (1960). Since the DPO relieved the governmental orders from the check of judicial oversight and procedural rights, the government's reliance on it increased. On the other hand, it amalgamated the objects of both the SPA and the MPOO, i.e., the security of the state and the maintenance of the local public order. Thus the government began to rely on the DPO and DPR for maintaining security and public order by extending the emergency. Soon after the war, which did not result in any gains in Kashmir against India, Ayub Khan's government began to lose popularity. At this stage, different political parties manipulated the disappointment and frustration among the people. In Lahore and Karachi, mass protests took place that initially criticised the peace deal with India but later began to criticise Ayub's entire regime, including his Constitution.

The government seemed to have had no choice but to enforce the emergency laws to restore public order. Thus a large number of arrests and detentions began under the DPO and DPR (1965). The detainees challenged their orders of arrest and detention through writ petition in the High Courts. Some of the crucial questions, from the point of view of the present study, that arose in these petitions are the following: Could Ayub Khan lawfully extend emergency, and therefore the DPO and DPR (1965), beyond the end of war and hostilities? Could the government cut down the power of superior courts to review orders of arrest and detention? During a declared emergency, what was the nature of the executive's satisfaction in issuing orders of arrest and detention under security and public order laws? Lastly, what should be the nature of grounds, the criterion of their evaluation, and their communication to the detainee?

In a number of cases, especially relating to detention under the DPO and DPR (1965), the Supreme Court cautiously answered these questions. In *Malik Ghulam Jilani* (1967), the Supreme Court made some of its most important observations, which it instructed the High Courts to follow as precedents. First, the Court indirectly accepted the government's discretion to impose and extend emergency. The Court adopted a cautious view that it could not replace its own satisfaction for the satisfaction of the executive in relation to the existence of conditions of emergency. On the one hand, this view widened the scope of the political sphere by allowing a representative body to decide upon the need to impose and/or extend emergency, but on the other, it restricted the individual's rights and liberties in the public sphere. A similar question of emergency arose much later, in 2007, when another military man in executive office, President Pervez Musharraf, proclaimed emergency—however, in this case of emergency the Supreme Court took a different view. Second, the Supreme Court in *Malik Ghulam Jilani* (1967) ruled that the executive could not curtail the judicial review power of higher courts even during a state of emergency. The Court said that all orders of the executive or (district) administration pertaining to arrest and detention could be challenged through writ petitions, and the higher courts could review them on all different accounts. This observation led to the third important question, which related to the nature of the executive's satisfaction while issuing orders of arrest and detention. The Court observed that the executive's satisfaction should be objective in nature, rather than subjective, even during an emergency. It said that mere suspicion was not enough; rather, the grounds of detention were to be reasonable and objective. In other words, they should be based on facts rather than on suspicion and/or opinions.

The Supreme Court reiterated these observations in a similar petition by Mir Abdul Baqi Baloch.[26] The case was sent back to the Karachi bench of the West Pakistan High Court with instructions to revise the judgment in the light of the decision in *Malik Ghulam Jilani* (1967). The Supreme

Court, while remanding the case back to the Karachi bench, also observed that higher courts could demand from the administration the disclosure of any document or information relating to the case, secret or otherwise. The Court further added that the higher courts could review not only the sphere of jurisdiction of the administrative authority but also the manner in which such authority is used. In another case, the Supreme Court reiterated on a couple of other procedural rights of the detainee. The court instructed to the detaining authorities that even if a security law did not provide for communication of grounds to the detainee, this did not relieve the detaining authority of its duty to provide that procedural right. Not only that, the government was instructed not to base its satisfaction on any vague and indefinite grounds but rather to "particularize the nature of activities prejudicial to the stability or integrity of the country in the grounds of detention."[27] Moreover, the Court reiterated another check on the detaining authority by asking it to clearly specify the period of detention. An order providing the phrase "till further orders" was ruled as vague and therefore illegal.

Although the Supreme Court avoided reviewing Ayub Khan's decision to extend the emergency beyond the short time period of war, he was still not satisfied with the Court's insistence upon its judicial review powers, which restricted the scope of his emergency powers. However, his government could also not antagonise the judiciary, as it was already being confronted with increasing political protests. Nevertheless, the government took the careful and nuanced step of amending the provision relating to the criteria of satisfaction of detaining authority in making arrest and detention orders under the DPO (1965). With this amendment the government changed the demand for objective satisfaction, as had been emphasised and required by judiciary, to subjective detention, as had been the case in colonial times.[28] While the amendment might seem a minor one, it had deeper consequences: on the one hand, it shifted the burden of proving *mala fide* intention on the part of detaining authority on the detainee, and on the other, it reduced the power of the higher courts to review the jurisdiction of detaining authority, the manner in which it is exercised, and the nature of grounds of detention.

The Supreme Court, however, struck down the amendment in *Begum Shorish Kashmiri* (1969).[29] The case related to a journalist and public orator, Shorish Kashmiri, who was detained under the DPR (1965). The prosecution maintained that the burden to prove the *male fide* nature of the orders was on the detainee. This meant that the prosecution had inverted the principle of innocence. The Court made an interesting technical point. While fundamental rights were suspended under emergency, the Court said that procedural rights were not suspended. The Court relied on Article 2, saying that the provision that "every person to be dealt with in accordance with law" was commensurate with the "due process" clause and its meaning in the American Constitution. In this way, the Court argued that procedural rights granted by the due process clause were also available even under emergency. Accordingly, the Court termed the principle of innocence, the requirement of reasonableness, as well as communication of grounds to the detainee as being procedural rights, which would remain available despite a state of emergency or any "exercise in futility" on the part of the government to remove them through an amendment. The Court said that the amendment contradicted the Constitution and that the government could not give itself "arbitrary, unguided, uncontrolled or naked power" beyond what was sanctioned by the Constitution.[30]

Extension of emergency and the Defence of Pakistan Ordinance and Rules (1971)

The emergency that began in 1965, continued in one form or another for the next twenty years. The DPO and Rules of 1965 only gave way to the DPO and Rules of 1971. The new democratic government of Zulfikar Ali Bhutto had gotten a taste of emergency powers and wished to continue them even after the adoption of a democratic Constitution (1973). Despite that, however, the higher courts once again played an important role in carefully defending the rights of the individual against the executive. The judiciary had initiated this approach under Ayub Khan's regime, when it struck down the amendment in the DPO (1965) regarding subjective versus objective satisfaction on the part of the administration. While Ayub Khan could not respond to the judiciary's bold decisions, Bhutto attended to it by amending the Constitution and cutting down the review powers of the higher courts. I'll return to these constitutional amendments later; here, I want to discuss some of the important cases decided by the higher courts, which ultimately led the government to make constitutional amendments.

One of the crucial cases was *Ziaur Rahman* (1973). In this case, one question related to the validation of actions taken under the martial law rule under General Yahya Khan and the civilian Chief Martial Law Administrator, Zulfikar Ali Bhutto. In the Interim Constitution of 1972, the latter added a Validation Clause in Articles 280 and 281 to bar the jurisdiction of higher courts from questioning and reviewing any orders taken during the martial law. In *Ziaur Rahman*, the Supreme Court did not agree with the exception created by the Validation Clause. The Court said that acts done under martial law and emergency would not generally be questioned, except in two crucial judicial principles: *mala fide* or *coram non judice*. The argument made in this case was later rehearsed in *F.B. Ali* (1975) and, recently, in a decision on the military courts (2015). While in practice it might have been difficult for the Court to take up and decide cases on the basis of these judicial principles, the Court's decisions nevertheless alarmed the government.

Accordingly, the government began to think of cutting down judicial review powers of the higher courts.

The government's resolve to reduce the review power of the higher courts increased further with a series of other cases from 1973 to 1976. In these cases, the higher courts gave decisions that chastised the arrest and detention powers of the executive branch and gave relief to individuals, mostly political victims. For instance, in a decision that resonated with the one made in *Begum Shorish Kashmiri* (1969), Peshawar High Court in *Fida Muhammad* (1973) warned the government about their indiscriminate and arbitrary use of powers:

> It is a misconception to think that either under the Defence of Pakistan Ordinance or the rules framed thereunder any arbitrary, unguided, uncontrolled, or naked power has been given to any authority. These provisions only confer a power, which is coupled with a duty.[31]

In the same year, Karachi High Court insisted upon certain legal principles that the courts and government should keep in mind in cases of arrest and detention. The Court said that the infringement of rights and liberties of the citizen should be "strictly construed," and any statutory interpretation should, whenever possible, favour the citizen.[32] The next year, the Lahore High Court only emphasised these principles, but in different words. The Court said the law is "extremely chary of the deprivation" of rights and liberties of the citizen.[33] Moreover, it said that the power of arrest and detention, while sanctioned by the Constitution, should be used only with discretion.[34] Praising its own role, the Karachi High Court claimed that it was due to the judiciary that citizens were able to enjoy their rights and liberties.[35] The Supreme Court further added to this by cautioning the government that the Constitution granted the jurisdiction to higher courts to defend the rights and liberties of citizens, and therefore the power of judicial review could not be "whittled down on considerations of policy or convenience."[36] This decision also showed that the judiciary had sensed that the government was bent on reducing the judicial review power of the higher courts. However, Bhutto's government went on to amend the Constitution and reduce the judicial review power of the higher courts. Despite having reduced powers, during 1975 and 1976 the judiciary was still making a modicum of effort to defend the rights of citizens. In one case, for instance, the Lahore High Court said that mere existence of a law was not enough to enable the administration to impose restraints on the liberties and rights of citizens. The Court said that the DPO (1971) suggested certain duties to be performed and protections granted by the administration before it could begin restraining rights and liberties.[37] Similarly, the Supreme Court argued, "even during the Proclamation of Emergency, the executive is precluded from taking any action which is not covered by the authority of law."[38]

Amendments to the Constitution of 1973

Just like the previous two constitutions, the 1973 Constitution also provided for safeguards against arrest and detention. In Article 10, the Constitution provided for these safeguards, which also set the limiting framework for existing statutes providing for arrest and detention: for instance, the SPA (1952), the MPOO (1960), the DPA and DPR (1971), and the Code of Criminal Procedure. The Constitution provided that a person could be detained for a period of one month. Any extension would be based on the report of the appropriate Review Board. In cases where detention orders were made under a federal law, the board would consist of three incumbent or retired judges of the Supreme Court or High Courts; in cases where detention orders were made under a provincial law, the board would consist of three incumbent or retired judges of the concerned High Court. The detainee would be given the right to make representation against his/her order as well as to be heard in person. Moreover, the detainee was provided the right to be informed of the grounds of his/her detention within one week, so that he/she could make representation.

However, Zulfikar Ali Bhutto's government, faced with a bold judiciary as well as political protests and agitation by opposition parties, reduced these safeguards. Accordingly, his government began to introduce constitutional amendments incrementally. He knew full well that any changes brought about by ordinary law would be struck down by the judiciary and therefore pushed for constitutional amendments. Thus, through constitutional amendments, he achieved both of his goals: cutting down constitutional safeguards of rights and the judicial review power of the higher courts. First came the Third Amendment in February 1975, which amended Article 10. This amendment made three major changes. First, it increased the time period of detention from one to three months. Towards the end of that period, the detention could be further extended, but only upon the recommendation of an appropriate Review Board. Second, the amendment increased the time period for communication of grounds to the detainee from one week to fifteen days. Lastly, the amendment set the maximum detention period for acting in a manner prejudicial to public order at eight months, with twelve months for "any other case," which meant those relating to posing a threat to the state, its defence, and its security. However, this maximum time period was also qualified: it could be given within any two years. The proviso meant that upon the end of two years, a person could again be subjected to preventive detention. Moreover, the amendment provided that this limitation of time period could not be claimed by a person

> ...who is employed by, or works for, or acts on instructions received from, the enemy or who is acting or attempting to act in a manner prejudicial to the integrity, security or defence of Pakistan or any part thereof or who commits or attempts to commit any act which amounts

> to an anti-national activity as defined in a Federal law or is a member of any association which has for its objects, or which indulges in any such anti-national activity.

It is obvious that the amendment drew on the SPA (1952), the MPOO (1960) and the Suppression of Terrorist Activities Act (STAA) (1975). It is also interesting to notice that like the Government of India Act 1935 (GIA), the Constitution of Pakistan, 1973, made preventive detention subject to both federal and provincial legislation. Recently, Schedule 4 of the 18th Amendment, 2010, has provided that provincial governments can legislate on preventive detention for certain additional purposes, including the maintenance of public order, supplies, and services essential to the community.[39] Another aspect worth noticing is that regarding the communication of grounds to the detainee, the Constitution had adopted the idea from the SPA (1952), which provided that the government could withhold any information from the detainee on the account of public interest.

On the other hand, some of the harsh provisions of the SPA (1952) were brought within the framework of the amendment. Those provisions that were in conflict with the constitutional provisions of Article 10 were amended. Accordingly, the Preventive Detention Laws (Amendment) Act 1975 was passed.[40] Of the important changes included in the SPA were the strengthening of the authority of the now-named "Review Board." Any extension in the period of detention was to be based on the decision of the board. The detainee was also given the right to make representation in person to the board. The board was to be set up by the Chief Justice of the Supreme Court rather than by the government, and its members were to consist of a chairman and two other judges, each of whom was (or had been) a judge of the superior courts. Moreover, the period of maximum detention was reduced from indefiniteness (in the SPA) to a maximum of eight months in cases of persons acting in a manner prejudicial to the public order or twelve months in any other case.

Apart from amending the provision relating to preventive detention, the Third Constitutional Amendment also amended the provisions of emergency in the Constitution. Originally the Constitution had provided that in a joint sitting of the Houses, a resolution could be adopted to impose emergency for a maximum of six months. But the Third Amendment removed the specific time period for emergency and said that it would continue indefinitely until a resolution was passed to end it by a majority of the total membership of the two Houses in a joint sitting. With this provision, the government enhanced its emergency powers.

Just as the government increased its detaining power through the Third Amendment, the persons affected began to seek relief from the courts. Although the courts were careful in granting relief to detainees given the overwhelming strength of government in Parliament, the government was still not happy with the role of the higher courts. In fact, the government believed the judiciary to be engaged in encroaching upon the powers of the executive and in this way creating a parallel executive. Accordingly, in November 1975, the government introduced the Fourth Constitutional Amendment and amended Article 199. The amendment stopped the High Courts from prohibiting the administration to make an order of detention as well as from granting bail to anybody detained under preventive detention law. Bhutto's government did not want the courts to stand between his government and the opposition political parties. The government was clearly using preventive detention as a tool of political control rather than as one of state security.

Bhutto's government did not stop here. It further curtailed the judicial review power of the higher courts in a more thorough way. This happened the following year, when the government introduced the Fifth Constitutional Amendment. The government revised its earlier amendment of Article 199 and provided further details. First, the amendment stopped the higher courts from prohibiting the administration from making a detention order or detaining a person after making an order if such an order had been made under a federal or a provincial law. Second, the higher courts were once again stopped from granting bail and, now, from suspending the operation of an order of custody of a person against whom a report or complaint had been made before any court or tribunal, against whom a case had been registered at any police station in respect of an offence, or who had been convicted by any Court or tribunal. Third, the higher courts were stopped from prohibiting the registration of a case at a police station as well as the making of a report or complaint before any court or tribunal in respect of an offence. Fourth, the amendment included a blanket proviso saying that the higher courts would not make "any other interim order" to provide relief to the person charged by the government. Fifth, the amendment said that all injunctions or instructions already made by the higher courts that contradicted the Fifth Amendment would become ineffective. Lastly, the judges of the High Courts were threatened by granting the government the power to transfer them for a period up to one year without their consent and without consultation of the Chief Justices concerned. Moreover, a judge of the High Court could be forcibly promoted to the Supreme Court, and if that judge refused, he/she would be deemed to have retired from his office.

The Suppression of Terrorist Activities (Special Courts) Act (STAA), 1975

Bhutto seemed discontented with his emergency powers and the Defence of Pakistan laws available thereunder. Perhaps he thought he needed more power to deal with the growing political opposition to his government. Accordingly, on February 3, 1975, he passed yet another security law—the Suppression of Terrorist Activities (Special Courts) Act (1975). It replaced a similar ordinance promulgated a year earlier.[41] The act aimed to deal with the offences of sabotage, subversion and terrorism. Although the term "terrorism" was used in the act and named as an offence, it was neither defined nor explained. Even the courts did not demand that the government define it. The act remained in force in Sindh and Punjab until the passage of the Anti-Terrorism Act, 1997 (ATA), and in the NWFP (now Khyber Pakhtunkhwa) until the passage of the Anti-Terrorism (Amendment) Ordinance, 2001.

One of the main purposes of the act was to afford the government the power to constitute special courts with exclusive jurisdiction. It is interesting to notice that similar special courts already existed (or more could be constituted) under the DPO (1971). A special court under the STAA was given similar powers as those of a session court in its original jurisdiction. Moreover, a special court could exercise the power of contempt similar to that of a High Court. The act provided that a special court would consist of only one judge. His qualifications were also not required to be high: he had to be (or be qualified to be) a judge of a High Court or have been a Session or Additional Session Judge for a period of three years. The special courts were given exclusive jurisdiction over all cases relating to a long list of offences that were prescribed in the schedule. These offences were borrowed from a number of other existing laws.[42] In 1984, a further provision was added to the act that effectively afforded the government the authority to even specify the persons to be tried in the special courts.[43]

The criminal procedure adopted under the act was also peculiar to notice. The act required that the investigation for the case be completed within fourteen days and the report then forwarded to the court. Any default or non-performance of any required procedure in preparation of the report was to be regarded as wilful disobedience on the part of the police officer. An interesting provision here was that special court was given the power to "directly take cognizance" of a case even when the case had not been sent to it.[44] Once the trial began, the court was to hear it on an everyday basis, without giving any adjournment unless it was necessary in the interest of justice. Even then, such adjournment could not be granted for more than two days. When a case was transferred from another court, the special court was not supposed to recall or rehear any witness. Moreover, the accused could be tried in his/her absence, given either that the absence was deliberate or that the behaviour of the accused was such that it impeded the course of the trial and therefore the judge needed to remove the accused from the proceedings. In cases of trial in absentia, however, the court was required to publish a proclamation in three daily newspapers, out of which two were to be in Urdu. The court was also required to appoint defence counsel for the accused. Regarding the issue of bail, the special courts were instructed to give it sparingly and only after asking the prosecution to show cause as to why such person should not be given bail. The act provided that the burden of proof would shift to the accused if he was either found in possession of an article with which he could have committed the offence or apprehended in circumstances that raised a reasonable suspicion that he had committed the offence. The appeal from a special court could be made to the High Court concerned within thirty days, and the High Court was then supposed to decide upon the appeal within three months. However, the sentence was not to be revised, nor the case transferred to any other court. About two decades later, the making of and the nature and procedure of these courts was replicated in the Special Courts Ordinance and Act (1992) and Terrorist Affected Areas (Special Courts) Act, 1992.

The use of the category of terrorism in the STAA, 1975, raises the question of its origin. My genealogical probe suggests that the category of terrorism and the STAA, 1975, exhibit clear links to the British emergency laws of Northern Ireland in the early 1970s. Two years before the passage of the STAA, the British government had passed the Northern Ireland (Emergency Provisions) Act (NIEPA), 1973. It was one of the first security laws in the post-war era that not only included a preliminary legal definition of terrorism but also provided for special courts and procedure in the United Kingdom. Later, this legal definition of terrorism was passed on to the NIEPA, 1989, and eventually, to the ATA, 2000, whereupon it came to extend over the entire United Kingdom.

The NIEPA, 1973, defined terrorism as "the use of violence for political ends, and includes any use of violence for the purpose of putting the public or any section of the public in fear." Although the NIEPA, 1973, tried to define terrorism as a distinct category, the offences that were listed were not exclusive. These offences were given in an attached schedule but had been collected from different existing laws. For example, they included arson and riot from the Common Law; setting fire to private/public buildings or other forms of property and machinery from the Malicious Damage Act 1861; causing grievous bodily harm from the Person Act 1861; causing explosion likely to endanger life or damage property from the Explosive Substance Act 1883; possessing, carrying, or using firearms and ammunition without license from the Firearms Act (Northern Ireland) 1969; and robbery and aggravated burglary from the Theft Act (Northern Ireland) 1969. In Pakistan, the STAA, 1975, came with a similar schedule, which listed offences from the penal code and several other laws such as the Explosive Substances Act, 1908; the Arms Act, 1878; the Railways Act, 1890; the Telegraph Act, 1885; the Aircraft Rules, 1937; and the Anti-National Activities Act, 1974. From these scheduled offences it is not difficult to tell that the STAA, 1975, took its legal form and phraseology from NIEPA, 1973, while its substantive content/offences came from colonial laws. Like the MPOO and the SPA, the NIEPA provided for preventive detention. In fact, in the Anglo-American security regime, NIEPA has been one of the recent foundational laws of preventive detention.

The NIEPA's object was to deal with "certain offences, the detention of terrorists, the preservation of the peace...."[45] Under this act, the Secretary of State could order to place an individual in "interim custody" for a period of twenty-eight days. Before the expiry of that period, an appointed (quasi-) judicial commission would decide on the basis of "the protection of the public" whether to release the individual from custody or to extend custody.[46] It is also worth noting that the detainee was to be served with a written statement regarding his terrorist activities only seven days before the commissioner first heard the case.[47]

The NIEPA, 1973, was amended and re-enacted in 1978, 1987, 1991, and 1996. In the last two acts, the period of "interim detention" was reduced to fourteen days, and the Secretary of State was only authorised to issue detention orders after receiving a report from a judicial adviser. What is important to notice about these acts is that the procedure of these detention laws reflected the procedure laid down in Regulation III of 1818. The following procedural steps in these acts resembled with that in Regulation III. After a person was arrested and detained for an interim period, the case is referred to an adviser within fourteen days. Here, the difference was that in Regulation III, the adviser was also the officer in charge of the custody. After referral to the adviser, the detainee was served with a written statement regarding the nature of his suspected activities. The detainee was then allowed to send written representation to the Secretary of State and/or a request that he wanted to see the adviser in person. The adviser prepared the report, taking into consideration the representation made by the detainee. The report was sent to the Secretary of State, who then made the decision on (further) detention. After making the detaining orders, he could at any time send back the case to the adviser. The detainee could also request reconsideration of the order after one year. Thus, apparently, the detention could extend for an indefinite period of time.

Martial law and military courts

Pakistan has seen at least three declared martial laws—1958, 1969, and 1977. The last of these martial laws, which lasted for longer than the others, placed considerable reliance on martial courts. General Zia-ul-Haq created hundreds of martial courts and special tribunals, which decided thousands of cases. The Supreme Court conferred legality on Zia-ul-Haq's *coup d'etat* and the resulting martial law (*Nusrat Bhutto*, 1977). However, very soon the military authorities divested the higher courts of their judicial review power and restricted their jurisdiction. Interestingly enough, only a couple of months before General Zia-ul-Haq imposed martial law, Bhutto had tried to impose it in Karachi, Lahore, and Hyderabad under Article 245 of the Constitution. The Supreme Court had struck down Bhutto's martial law as unconstitutional after giving thoughtful insight into the matter. The Court had said that in the previous two Constitutions (1956 and 1962) as well as in the Indian Constitution (Article 34), the word "martial law" was given, but it was not given in the 1973 Constitution of Pakistan. The Court thus made the point that the framers of the Constitution intended to bury martial law for good. Moreover, the Court pointed out that unlike the previous Constitutions, the present Constitution, in Article 237, did not provide for making retrospective laws validating the orders, judgments and punishments given by earlier military courts.[48]

Similarly, five years before martial law, in *Asma Jilani* (1972), the Supreme Court had denounced the imposition of the 1969 martial law. However, the following year, in *F.B. Ali* (1973), the Supreme Court, in order to curry favour with Bhutto's government, decided that martial courts set up under the Army Act, 1952, could validly try civilians who were involved in offences contained in that act. The trial of civilians in martial courts founded under the Army Act was in fact introduced by Ayub Khan, through Ordinances III and IV of 1967. In *F.B. Ali*, the Court held that these ordinances did not contravene the separation of powers doctrine or the fundamental rights guaranteed in the Constitution.

Once empowered by the Supreme Court in *Nusrat Bhutto* (1977), General Zia-ul-Haq, through an amendment to the Constitution in 1979, added Article 212-A. With this amendment, he authorised himself, as Chief Martial Law Administrator (CMLA), to establish military courts as well as special tribunals in the country.[49] The martial courts thus established had exclusive jurisdiction over all offences prescribed in martial law regulations. No other court, including the high courts, had appellate, supervisory or administrative control over the martial courts. The higher courts were thus barred to make any order, give an injunction, and/or demand a case or its report or transfer a case from a military court to any other court. In this way, Zia-ul-Haq's martial courts created a parallel judiciary. On the other hand, the martial authorities could transfer almost any case to the martial courts.

In May 1980, the powers of higher courts were further curtailed. This curtailment came in the wake of Asghar Khan's case. A full bench of the Lahore High Court was expected to deliver its verdict in the case, but before it could do so, General Zia-ul-Haq made a constitutional amendment restricting the writ jurisdiction of High Courts. Thus the higher courts were restricted in making any orders relating to the legality of martial law regulations or orders. The amendment also prohibited the higher courts from reviewing decisions made by the military courts and tribunals as well as passing injunctions to anyone acting with the authority vested in them by the martial law government. Moreover, the amendment said that these restrictions of the jurisdiction of the higher courts would be considered retrospectively. The following month, the martial law government issued Martial Law Order No. 77, which replaced the earlier Order No. 72 and further increased the jurisdiction of the martial courts. With this order, the military courts were given exclusive jurisdiction over offences of treason, subversion, sedition, sabotage, activity prejudicial to martial law, and the seducing of members of the armed forces.[50]

Special Courts of 1990s

On July 18, 1992, the Nawaz Sharif government passed two remarkable acts: the Special Courts for Speedy Trials Act, No. IX (SCA), and the Terrorist Affected Areas (Special Courts) Act, No. X (TAAA). The SCA coded two ordinances of the same title that became before it.[51] What is interesting here is the fact of matter that these Acts were enforced in addition to the already existing STAA (1975) and the MPOO (1960), which deal with more or less the same offences. The SCA and the two ordinances that preceded it aimed to address what earlier were heinous offences but were now termed as "gruesome, brutal and sensational in character or shocking to public morality or has led to public outrage or created panic or an atmosphere of fear or anxiety amongst the public." On the other hand, the TAAA aimed to address "terrorism, subversion and other heinous offences in the terrorist affected areas." Although the offences named in this act resembled those declared in the STAA (1975), in practice all these acts were dealing with offences given in the Panel Code and in a few other laws. This fact becomes clear when one looks at the list of offences given in the schedules attached to these acts. This list included offences against the state and heinous offences from the Panel Code (1860), as well as offences from the Telegraph Act (1885), the Railway Act (1890), the Explosive Substances Act (1908), the Arms Act (1878), the Pakistan Arms Ordinance (1960), the Prevention of Anti-National Activities Act (1974), and the Surrender of Illicit Arms Act (1991). In both the SCA and the TAAA, the government was empowered to add or remove any offences from the list with a simple notification.

Although the political context of both the acts was increasing sectarian and ethnic violence in the country, the TAAA (1992) was specifically directed at the metropolitan city of Karachi. This act provided the law enforcement agencies more powers than other existing security laws. It became the harbinger of the ATA (1997), especially in the giving of powers to use deadly violence and to operate without warrants for arrest, search, and detention. Moreover, the language, form, and substance used in the TAAA replicates itself in the ATA (1997). However, the term "terrorism" is not defined in this act either. The act uses the term "terrorist affected areas," which the government had the power to declare as such.

The TAAA added two full sections (4 and 5), with a number of clauses and subclauses, on the "use of force." The government was allowed to engage civil armed forces, apart from the police, to carry out operations under it. Under the "verbal orders" of the Magistrate, the police and the Civil Armed Forces could "use necessary force, even to the extent of causing death" in carrying out operations in terrorist affected areas, which were the areas, the act said, harbouring criminals, keeping hostages, involved in transporting weapons and explosives, or simply under curfew at the order of the government. Apart from the power to use deadly force, the Magistrate could give orders to arrest any person or to enter and search any premises without warrants. Interestingly, the act provided that if the Magistrate was not available, then "any police officer not below the rank of Sub-Inspector or an officer of equivalent rank in the Civil Armed Forces or a Naib-Subedar" could use the same deadly force as well as the powers of arrest and search without warrants. The act clearly put too much power in the hands of junior rank personnel without giving them sufficient training and knowledge about the consequences of the use of force.

Regarding the make-up of the special courts, under both Acts—the SCA and the TAAA—the federal government was empowered to set up special courts at any place it deemed appropriate. These special courts were to be presided over by one judge who was, or had the qualifications of, a High Court judge. The government was to appoint judges to the respective special courts after consultation with the Chief Justice of the concerned High Court. The SCA also stipulated that government would determine through notification the terms of service of the judges. The silence of the TAAA on this aspect suggested that it was left for the government to determine the length. Even the ATA (1997) had not provided for fixed tenure to judges, the idea of which was chastised by the Supreme Court in *Mehram Ali* (1998).

The special courts under both the acts were given exclusive jurisdictions. In other words, only these special courts were to deal with all cases relating to the scheduled offences in their respective territorial jurisdictions, even to the exclusion of jurisdiction of High Courts. Moreover, only they would have the power to grant or refuse bail. Under the TAAA, it was further added that a special court could try the accused for offences not scheduled in the act. Both the acts empowered the government to transfer cases from other courts to these special courts, if those cases related to the scheduled offences, as well as to transfer cases between different special courts. Both the acts also provided the special courts to "directly take cognisance" of a case that had not been sent to it yet. Furthermore, they were given the power of contempt of court similar to that of a High Court. In addition, the special courts had the power to prolong police detention/custody of an accused for ten more days after the regular detention period given in the Panel Code.

Since these special courts were supposed to ensure speedy trials, their procedure was abridged. The police was to prepare the report within fourteen days without making any technical negligence. The trial was to take place on a daily basis and to be decided within thirty days. The courts were not supposed to grant adjournments, except in the interest of justice, and that one adjournment was not to be for more than two working days. The courts were also instructed not to rehear or recall a witness or evidence. If deemed necessary by the court, the trial could also be carried out via camera. The courts were also empowered to carry out trials in summary. The SCA provided for summary trial in cases relating to false evidence, presentation, or offences against public justice. The TAAA, on the other hand, provided for summary trial in all scheduled offences punishable with imprisonment for a term not exceeding three years. Moreover, the TAAA provided for trials in absentia.

Appeals from decisions of the special courts would go to another special court, which would have appellate jurisdiction. In both acts, it was named Supreme Appellate Court. Interestingly, the government was empowered to make as many of these supreme courts as it deemed necessary. A Supreme Appellate Court was to consist of a judge of the Supreme Court and two judges of a concerned High Court. These judges were to be nominated by the government after consultation with the concerned Chief Justices. An appeal could be made within seven days after the decision in a special court, and was to be disposed of by the Supreme Appellate Court within thirty days.

An important feature of these acts was the power of the government to determine the "manner, mode and place" of punishment. The government could exercise its discretion "having regard to the deterrent effect" of the execution of the sentence. This provision created the possibility of public executions and/or hangings. Accordingly, the Supreme Court took *suo moto* notice of this provision in the acts.[52] The Court said that public hanging violated the dignity of man as guaranteed in Article 14 of the Constitution. Moreover, the Court said it violated Article 7 of the Universal Declaration of Human Rights in Islam. (A group of leading Muslim scholars had prepared this declaration and published it in 1980.)

From a historical point of view, special courts created under these acts were set up on the pattern of tribunals from the colonial era and those in Northern Ireland. For instance, we can recall that the 1939 Act provided for a three-member tribunal, while later, in the Enemy Agents Act, 1943, the tribunal's strength was reduced to one. The NIEPA, 1973, also provided for a one-member court. Similarly, Acts IX and X provided for a one-member tribunal. Moreover, the 1939 Act had provided that the members should be qualified for the position of high court judge, session court judge, additional session court judge, district or additional district magistrate. These acts, and later, the Anti-Terrorism Act, 1997, required similar qualification.

Similarly the DIA, 1939, had authorised special courts to try all prescribed and any other offences that the government placed before them. The NIEPA (Section 10), 1991, had also authorised special courts to try both scheduled and non-scheduled offences directed to them by the government. Moreover, it is worth mentioning that Northern Ireland's Special Powers Act, 1922, had provided in Section 2(4) that all kinds of offences were subject to special courts. The clause said:

> If any person does any act of such a nature as to be calculated to be prejudicial to the preservation of the peace or maintenance of order in Northern Ireland and not specifically provided for in the regulations, he shall be guilty of an offence against those regulations.

Just as in these acts, the 1992 Act (Section 11) and, later, the 1997 Act (Section 17) of Pakistan authorised special courts to try both scheduled and non-scheduled offences.

Furthermore, just as the DIA, 1939, enjoyed the "overriding effect" on all other laws, including the penal code, the Pakistani acts also provided a similar provision. Interestingly, special courts set up under the 1939 Act also enjoyed some sort of overriding effect or precedence over all other lower courts and the Pakistani special courts were also given such precedence.[53] Hence, a case proceeding in a special court would assume precedence over any other case against the same person in any other lower court. And like Section 9 of the 1939 Act, the Pakistani acts also authorised government to "transfer" cases from a lower ordinary court to a special court. Moreover, like the DORA and DIA, the 1997 Act authorised summary trials, and a year later, the Pakistan Armed Forces (Acting in Aid of Civil Power) Ordinance allowed for setting up military courts with jurisdiction over civilians. In summary, trials offenders could be punished with imprisonment for up to two years.[54]

Certain basic elements of the trial procedure of Pakistani special courts were modelled on both the colonial DIA, 1939, and Enemy Agents Ordinance, 1943. For instance, a judge could order the exclusion of the public from the trial and carry it out via camera. The accused could be tried in his/her absence.[55] A special court was not bound to adjourn the expedited proceedings except in exceptional circumstances, and if so, for only a few days. The court was also not required to recall or rehear witnesses in the event that the composition of the court changed or that the case was transferred to another special court. Offences against the state remained non-bailable except on the order of a high court after receiving guarantees. The appeal against the judgment of a special court was to be made to a high court.[56] The burden of proving oneself innocent was laid on the accused in cases where he was found in an affected area where firearms were used or found in possession of firearms.[57]

Conclusion

At the end of this chapter, I want to highlight how there took place a subtle shift in the object of security laws from that of defence to security and, eventually, to preventing terrorism. I have observed that in the DIA, 1939, the object was defence, and it was clearly declared in the preamble. The concern for security was always present, but on the other hand, it was not central. It is in the SPA, 1952, that we notice the shift from the object of defence to that of security. And the shift from the object of security to that of preventing terrorism comes at a later stage in 1975 with the passage of the STAA. The latter shift at this stage, however, was only rudimentary, as its primary context was that of local party politics and not of state security. Therefore, despite the use of the category of terrorism, the focus remained much on the suppression of acts of sabotage and subversion. It should be noted that terrorism was not even defined in the STAA (until Anti-Terrorism (Amendment) Ordinance, 2001). Instead, a list of "scheduled offences" was provided, and these offences were collected from the penal code. Moreover, they resembled the scheduled offences of the ARCA, 1919. In other words, the offences that were once termed anarchical and revolutionary crimes were now termed as terrorism. The act also provided for special courts and procedure, which were also modelled on the DIA, 1939, and the ARCA, 1919.

Notes

1 *State v. Dosso*, PLD 1958 SC 533.
2 *Abdullah Malik v. Crown*, PLD 1949 Lahore 212; PLD 1949 Lahore 282.
3 *Sher Muhammad v. Crown*, PLD 1949 Lahore 511.
4 Khan, *A History of the Judiciary in Pakistan*, 20.
5 *Abdur Rahman Malik v. The Crown*, PLD 1950 Lahore 234; *Ali Muhammad Khadian v. The Crown*, PLD 1952 Lahore 573.
6 Ordinance No. XIV of 1949.
7 *Sobho Gyanchandani v. The Crown*, PLD 1952 FC 29.
8 The Pakistan Public Safety Ordinance (VI of 1952). It was promulgated on March 4, 1952 and published in the Gazette on March 5, 1952. See Section 1(3).
9 Section 18(1).
10 These provincial laws included: Baluchistan Public Safety Regulation (No. I of 1947); Sindh Maintenance of Public Safety Ordinance, 1947; West Punjab Public Safety Act, 1947; Punjab Special Tribunals Act (XVIII of 1947); NWFP Public Safety Ordinance, 1948; West Punjab Public Safety (Amendment) Ordinance, 1948; East Bengal Government Ordinance Temporary Enactment and Re-enactment Act (XII of 1948); Baluchistan Public Safety Regulation (I of 1949); West Punjab Public Safety Act (XVII of 1949); East Bengal Preventive Detention Ordinance (VI of 1949); East Bengal Government Temporary Re-enactment Act, 1951; East Bengal Public Safety Ordinance, 1951; Baluchistan States Union Public Safety Regulation, 1954; and East Pakistan Public Safety Ordinance, 1958. Also see Hussain, "Pakistan," 181.
11 Second Amendment to the Government of India Act (1935). See ibid, 180–181.
12 One of the latest petitions against detention under SPA heard by IHC was in 2015 (see PLJ 2015 Islamabad High Court 347). Earlier in 2003, Deputy Attorney General Sher Zaman Khan, in a case, informed the Lahore High Court that the Security of Pakistan Act 1952 was still on the statute book. Dr. Ahmad Javed Khwaja and his family members were detained under this act. "LHC Told 1952 Security Act Still in Force."
13 Entry 18 of the Federal List and Entry 5 of the Provincial List in the 5th Schedule empowered the respective government to make laws and issue orders of preventive detention.
14 Preventive Detention Laws (Amendment) Act, 1962, Section 2(1). Also see Hussain, "Pakistan," 181.
15 The following major amendments have been made to it: the West Pakistan Maintenance of Public Order (Amendment) Ordinance, 1962 (XXX of 1962); The West Pakistan Maintenance of Public Order (Amendment) Ordinance, 1964 (XVII of 1964); the Punjab Laws (Adaptation) Order, 1974 and Adaptation of Laws Order 1975 of other three provinces; the Punjab Maintenance of Public Order (Amendment) Act, 2009 (II of 2009); the Punjab Maintenance of Public Order

(Amendment) Act, 2015 (XVI of 2015); the Punjab Maintenance of Public Order (Amendment) Act, 2016 (XLV of 2016); and the Punjab Maintenance of Public Order (Amendment) Act, 2017 (XX of 2017).

16 In Article 28, the ordinance provided for amending the Baluchistan Public Safety Regulation, 1947, and the Baluchistan States Union Public Safety Regulation, 1954. It also repealed the following laws: (a) the Bahawalpur State Public Security Act, 1944, (b) the North-West Frontier Province Public Safety Act, 1948, (c) the Punjab Public Safety Act, 1949, (d) the Khaipur Public Order and Detention Act, 1954, and (e) the Sind State Prisoners Regulation, 1827.

17 The province of Punjab readopted the MPOO (1960) in 1974 and the other provinces together in 1975 through Laws Adaptation Orders in each province.

18 In 1998 the Punjab government made the offences prescribed in the Drugs Act 1976 as cognizable offence under the MPOO (1960) through an amendment (Act I of 1999).

19 The West Pakistan Maintenance of Public Order (Amendment) Ordinance, 1964 (XVII of 1964).

20 Ibid. However, if a District level officer made the order then it was good only for one month. The Governor of West Pakistan issued a notification (No. 3-104-H-Spl-I/64) in this regard on February 27, 1965. See also PLD 1992 Pesh. 107.

21 The West Pakistan Public Order Detenu Rules, 1962. Notification No. 8-41-H-Spl-1/57 dated: May 8, 1962.

22 The West Pakistan Maintenance of Public Order (Amendment) Ordinance, 1964 (Ordinance No. XVIII).

23 The province of Punjab has fixed the maximum time limit to fifteen days through the Punjab Maintenance of Public Order (Amendment) Act 2009 (Act No. II). Other provinces also follow this maximum time limit since it is in line with Article 10(5) of the Constitution. However, the courts have emphasized that communication of grounds should be made much earlier than that, preferably on the same day. See PLD 1966 SC 286; PLD 1967 Pesh. 195; PLD 1988 Kar. 237; 2001 Y.L.R. 1097.

24 An order made by the provincial government was good for two years, but the one made by a district officer was good for only one month. The Governor of West Pakistan issued a notification (No. 3-104-H-Spl-I/64) in this regard on February 27, 1965. See also PLD 1992 Pesh. 107.

25 Ordinance No. XV of 1960. In this ordinance the government provided for making a Special Bench of the High Court, which would hear all appeals. In 1963 provincial ordinances were issued on the same pattern.

26 *Mir Abdul Baqi Baloch v. Government of Pakistan*, PLD 1968 SC 313.

27 Khan, *Constitutional and Political History of Pakistan*, 196.

28 Ayub Khan's government amended the clause 3(2)(x) through Ordinance No. 2 of 1968. The amended section said that "the sufficiency of the grounds on which such opinion as aforesaid is based shall be determined by the authority forming such opinion." Also see Newberg, *Judging the State*, 104.

29 *Government of West Pakistan v. Begum Agha Abdul Karim Shorish Kashmiri*, PLD 1969 SC 14.

30 Also Compare Newberg's view on this case. Newberg, *Judging the State*, 104.

31 *Fida Muhammad v. Province of NWFP through Home Secretary, Peshawar*, PLD, 1973, Peshawar 156.

32 *Liaqat Ali v. Government of Sind through Secretary, Home Department*, PLD 1973 Karachi 78.

33 *Maulana Abdus Sattar Khan Niazi v. The State*, PLD 1974 Lahore 324.

34 *Begum Nazir Abdul Hamid v. Pakistan (Federal Government) through Secretary Interior*, PLD 1974 Lahore 7.
35 *Zafar Iqbal v. Province of Sindh and two others*, PLD 1973 Karachi 316.
36 *Khan Muhammad Yusuf Khan Khattak v. S. M. Ayub and two others*, PLS 1973 Supreme Court 160.
37 *Chaudhary Zahur Ilahi v. Secretary to Government of Pakistan*, Ministry of Home and Kashmir Affairs, PLD 1975 Lahore 499.
38 *Federation of Pakistan v. Ch. Manzoor Elahi*, PLD 1976 Supreme Court 430.
39 Before the amendment, both federal and provincial governments exercised the power to legislate on the subject of preventive detention. The 4th Schedule, modelled on the 1935 Act, provided the federal government with the authority to legislate on preventive detention for defence and security issues. (See Federal Legislative List Part I, Entry I.)
40 Act 44 of 1975.
41 The Suppression of Terrorist Activities (Special Courts) Act, 1975 (No. XV of 1975). It received presidential assent on February 1–3, 1975, published in Gazette Extraordinary. The act repealed the Suppression of Terrorist activities (Special Courts) Ordinance, 1974 (No. XVIII of 1974). It was amended a number of times in 1984, 1987, 1995, 1996, and 1997.
42 These laws included: the Panel Code (1860), the Explosive Substances Act (1908), the Arms Act (1878), the West Pakistan Arms Ordinance (1965), the Pakistan Arms Ordinance (1960), rule 43 of the Defence of Pakistan Rules (1971), the Railway Act (1890) the Telegraph Act (1885), the Aircraft Rule (1937), and the Prevention of Anti-National Activities Act (1974).
43 Ordinance XI of 1984. The Ordinance said, "Provided further that the Government constituting a Special Court may, by notification in the official Gazette, direct that the Special Court shall have jurisdiction to try only such person who have committed scheduled offences as may be specified in the notification."
44 Section 5(3) as amended by Act V of 1990. The Quetta court suggested the reason of this provision was "to have a check on Police" to stop it from exercising its "whims and wishes" in sending a case. NLR 1995 Criminal Quetta 539.
45 It is worth noticing that these offences that are classified as scheduled offences were given priority or overriding effect over non-scheduled offences, just as anti-terrorism laws and trials enjoy overriding effect over other laws and trials. (Sections 2 and 3 read: "Where an indictment contains a count alleging a scheduled offence and another count alleging an offence which at the time the indictment is presented is not a scheduled offence, the other count shall be disregarded.")
46 Schedule 1 Part II Entry 11 sub-entry 3.
47 Schedule 1 Part II Entry 13.
48 *Darvesh M. Arbey, Advocate, v. Federation of Pakistan*, PLD 1977 Lahore 846.
49 Constitution (Second Amendment) Order 1979. President's Order 21 of 1979. PLD Central Statutes 567.
50 Khan, *A History of the Judiciary in Pakistan*, 209.
51 The Special Courts for Speedy Trials Ordinance (No. XXXVIII of December 4, 1991) and the Special Courts for Speedy Trials Ordinance (No. II of April 2, 1992). The two Acts were passed on the same day on July 18, 1992 and published in the Gazette Extraordinary on the same day on July 22, 1992.
52 Suo Moto Constitutional Petition, 1994 SCMR 738.
53 Act IX Article 5 stipulates: "The Special Court shall have the exclusive jurisdiction to try a case…and no other Court shall have any jurisdiction or entertain any proceedings…."

54 The 1998 amendment for setting up military courts was, however, struck down by the Supreme Court in *Liaquat Hussain* (1999) as unconstitutional.
55 Compare Section 10(5) of 1939 Act and Section 13 of Act X of 1992. In *Mehram Ali* (1998) the Supreme Court held that the procedures of the special courts should follow the established criminal procedure in order to ensure justice. Hence, in 1998 an amendment removed this provision.
56 Originally appeals went to an appellate tribunal whose decision was deemed final. But in *Mehram Ali* (1998) the Supreme Court struck down that provision as constructing a parallel court system. The government amended the provision (Section 25 of 1997 Act) and allowed appeals to be made to High Courts. Compare with sec. 13 of 1939 Act, which allows appeals to High Courts.
57 This section corresponds to Section 7(1) in the NIEPA 1973. In Section 20(1) it was provided that the onus of proving that a person was not collecting information on the police or armed forces lay on the person.

3 The Anti-Terrorism Act, 1997

Introduction

In 1997, when Nawaz Sharif returned to power for a second time, Pakistan was in the grip of violence. Sectarianism was at its peak with target killings taking place throughout the country, but especially in the metropolitan city of Karachi. Karachi and its neighbouring city of Hyderabad were faced with the violent ethnic strife involving Muhajirs, Sindhis and Pathans. Moreover, these cities were faced with small armed gangs who were involved in so-called gang wars as well as street crimes like stealing, extortion, bank robbery, and kidnapping for ransom. This deteriorated law and order situation was adversely affecting the social life and business of the metropolitan city of Karachi.

Soon after his election, one of the first steps Sharif took was the passage of the Anti-Terrorism Act (ATA) 1997. This act was much more comprehensive than the security laws of 1991 and 1992, which Sharif's first government had passed as discussed in the previous chapter. The government thought that the regular courts were not providing speedy justice, and the police (and other LEAs) were not equipped with sufficient powers to cope with the growing menace of terrorism. Thus Sharif's government thought there was a need for identifying certain offences that constituted terrorism and could be tried in special courts with speedy criminal procedure.

The legal backdrop of the Act was the Mehram Ali case (1998). Ali, who belonged to an armed wing of the *Tehreek e Nifaz e Fiqa e Jafaria* (TNFJ) had killed two prominent leaders of another armed sectarian organisation, *Sipah e Sahaba Pakistan* (SSP), in a bomb attack. The case went to a regular criminal Session Court in the province of Punjab, where it proceeded at a slow pace. To protest against the killings of their leaders, the followers of SSP carried out processions in Islamabad, the capital city, as well as in other parts of the country, which resulted in destruction of public property and arson. After this incident, the confrontation between the two armed sectarian organisations increased, resulting in more violence.

It is important to note that when the ATA (1997) was passed, the international War on Terror had not yet begun. Therefore, the focus of the act was limited to local terrorism—the nature of which was mainly sectarian, ethno-national strife and street violence. Geographically speaking, it concentrated more in urban areas, than on the border or the tribal areas. Therefore, the kind of terrorism we know today is quite different from the terrorism of 1990s. Again, it is different from the kind of terrorism or the way it was conceived in 1970s through the Suppression of Terrorist Activities Act (STAA) (1975). This early form of terrorism (of the 1970s) was (or would be today thought as) a misnomer, as it was based more on political agitation and disruptive political activities of the then opposition political parties. This conception of terrorism has, however, not survived in the legal security regime, especially with the repeal of the STAA. Moreover, the recent security laws have incorporated special explanatory notes clarifying that political or religious demonstrations, as well as any peaceful rallies, would not be brought within the new definition of terrorism.[1]

Just as the international War on Terror began in 2001, the scope of the ATA (1997) in Pakistan took a new turn. However, although the attention of the state on local terrorism did not diminish, it was now increasingly seen as an epiphenomenon of international terrorism. The ATA (1997) was thought to be a crucial legal instrument to deal with international terrorism. Because the Supreme Court had lessened its bite (in *Mehram Ali* 1998), the military government of General Pervez Musharraf in 2001, a couple of weeks before the 9/11 terrorist attacks, introduced amendments to the act to enhance powers of the law enforcement agencies (LEAs) and the special courts. With the passage of time, more and more amendments were introduced in the act, which I discuss at some length in the following.

Terrorism

In the previous chapter, I briefly pointed to how the offence of terrorism came along in the criminal justice system of Pakistan. I pointed to its two sources: (a) international—the British emergency laws for Northern Ireland and an ATA of the United Kingdom and (b) local—the colonial wartime laws, especially the Defence of India Acts and Rules, as well as their postcolonial manifestations, especially the security acts of the early 1950s. In one way or other, both sources have British origin, which at the minimum, belies the argument made by an eminent professor, Charles Kennedy, that the West is a latecomer in introducing anti-terrorism laws, and that, therefore, it should learn from Pakistan.[2]

While the political concept of terrorism was in debate internationally as well as in Pakistan for quite a few decades (for instance, in the United Kingdom since the 1960s with the political strife in Northern Ireland, and in Pakistan since the 1970s with the introduction of the STAA) there was hardly any widely accepted and systematic definition of terrorism that could have been accepted in International law and public law in Pakistan.

This lack of definition was a hurdle to making anti-terrorism laws in Pakistan. A Pakistani High Court in a decision (2004) pointed to this difficulty in the following words:

> Currently no definition of "terrorism" is available in the customary international law. "Terror" as a manifestation of horror, shock or disgust, is known to human society and civilization since times immemorial, but "terrorism" as an "ism" or an articulated pattern of thought and activity, is relatively of a recent origin... "Terrorism" in this context has to be understood as a species different and apart from terror, horror, shock, fear, insecurity, panic or disgust created by an ordinary crime.[3]

Until 2001, Pakistan's criminal justice system didn't provide a definition of terrorism, although at least four laws relating to terrorist activities—the Suppression of Terrorist Activities Act 1975, the Special Courts Ordinance 1991, the Terrorist-Affected Areas (Special Courts) Act 1992, as well as the ATA, 1997—had been passed by then. In the legal regime of security, terrorism was only thought as "terrorist activities," and therefore, not a consistent and systematic political ideology—an "ism." These terrorist activities, in fact, comprised different offences already available in the Panel Code (1860) and certain other acts. The purpose of these earlier laws was not to define and explain terrorism as separate species of crimes but rather to ensure speedy trials with abridged criminal procedure. The lack of focus on terrorism as an offence in itself was perhaps because by then terrorism had not seen the growth of organisations or taken an organised form, at least in Pakistan. In other words, terrorist organisations with full-fledged agenda, ideology, purpose and financing had not yet begun to impact Pakistan. The Anti-Terrorism (Amendment) Act of 2001, for the first time, gave a comprehensive legal definition to the concept and offence of terrorism in Pakistan.

Let us note that the word "terrorism" was used for the first time in the ATA (1997). Before the ATA, the phrase "terrorist activities" was in use, and it was used in the STAA (1975), even though it was not defined or explained there. The terrorist activities, rather, provided therein as consisting of a collection of offenses from already existing laws: for instance, the Arms Act, 1878; the West Pakistan Arms Ordinance, 1965; the Railway Act, 1890; the Telegraph Act, 1885; and the Anti-National Activities Act, 1974. What was critical about the STAA was that it did not distinguish between political agitation and terrorist activities—or perhaps the government deliberately left this grey area undefined to target opposition political parties. We see that Bhutto's government had the National Awami Party (NAP) banned and tried its leader, Khan Abdul Wali Khan, in a special court for the offence of engaging in anti-state activities. The word "terrorist" and the phrase "terrorist activities" were once again used in the early 1990s in the two laws passed by Nawaz Sharif—the Special Courts Ordinance/Act (1991/1992) and the Terrorist-Affected Areas (Special Courts) Act, 1992. However, the phrase was not defined even in these laws.

When the ATA (1997) was passed, it also used the phrase "terrorist act" (instead of terrorism) and defined it in Article 6 in the following words:

> Whoever, to strike terror in the people, or an any section of people, or to alienate any section of the people or to adversely affect harmony among different sections of the people, does any act or thing by using bombs, dynamite or other explosive or inflammable substance, or firearms, or other lethal weapons or poisons or noxious gases or chemical or other substances of a hazardous nature in such a manner as to cause the death of, or injury to, any person or persons, or damage to, or destruction of, property or disruption of any supplies or services essential to the life of the community or display firearms, or threaten with the use of force public servants in order to prevent them from discharging their lawful duties commits a terrorist act.

It is worth noticing that this definition is strikingly similar to the one given about ten years before by a law in India called the Terrorist and Disruptive Activities (Prevention) Act 1985 and 1987.[4] However, this definition of the ATA (1997) would undergo significant changes over the next few years.

In April 1999, through an ordinance, the Sharif Government introduced the offence of "civil commotion" to the list of terrorist acts.[5] This offence was earlier provided in the Pakistan Armed Forces (Acting in Aid of Civil Power) Ordinance (PAFO) (1998), which had also provided for trial of civilians in military courts set up in Karachi. Although the PAFO was revoked, the offence of civil commotion survived. The civil commotion was defined in the following words:

> [...] creation of internal disturbances in violation of law or intended to violate law, commencement or continuation of illegal strikes, go-slows, lock-outs, vehicle snatching/lifting, damage to or destruction of State or private property, random firing to create panic, charging *bhatha* [protection money/extortion], acts of criminal trespass, distributing, publishing or pasting of a handbill or making graffiti or wall-chalking intended to create unrest or fear or create a threat to the security of law and order[...]

Towards the end of the year, the new military government of General Pervez Musharraf amended the ATA (1997) for a second time. Through this amendment, the government added several offences from the Panel Code in the ATA. These included abetment and/or concealing of a design for an offence, criminal conspiracy, waging of war, kidnapping, banditry, and hijacking.[6] However, the following year, in July 2000, the government made another amendment to the act and removed the offence of civil commotion (Section 7A) and the punishment for it (Section 7B) from the ATA (1997).[7] But interestingly, a year later, on August 15, the government felt the need to reintroduce the offence of civil commotion, which it did through an ordinance,[8] and later, in 2005, the government significantly increased the punishment for it.[9]

However, some of the major changes in the ATA (1997) came only in August 2001, as I said earlier. The government introduced an amendment to redefine terrorism. This time "terrorism" itself was defined (and not the phrase "terrorist acts"). Secondly, as I have referred to in the previous chapter the new definition of terrorism was based on the British ATA, 2000. For a quick comparison of the two definitions, let us juxtapose them. The Pakistani definition says:

> In this Act, "terrorism" means the use or threat of action where:
>
> a the action falls within the meaning of subsection (2), and
> b the use or threat is designed to coerce and intimidate or overawe the Government or the public or a section of the public or community or sect or create a sense of fear or insecurity in society; or
> c the use of threat is made for the purpose of advancing a religious, sectarian or ethnic cause.

While the British definition says this:

> In this Act "terrorism" means the use or threat of action where—
>
> a the action falls within subsection (2),
> b the use or threat is designed to influence the government or to intimidate the public or a section of the public, and
> c the use or threat is made for the purpose of advancing a political, religious or ideological cause.

It is quite clear that the Pakistani definition followed almost verbatim the British definition of terrorism. However, some changes were made in clauses (b) and (c) to suit the local political context involving sectarian and ethnic dimensions. Similarly, the addition of the terms "coercion" and "overawe" came from the local context of security and panel laws. Interestingly, their addition came at the cost of grammatical construction of clause (b). When viewed closely and in comparison with the British definition, it becomes evident that while the British definition uses the term intimidation for the public, the Pakistani definition does not use it as such. Similarly, in the Pakistani definition, all three terms ("coercion," "intimidation," and "overawe") do not seem to relate well with "the public." The terms "coercion" and "overawe" are normally used in relation to government—as evident in the British definition.

Let us also have a look at the definition of terrorism in the United States at that time. The Patriot Act, 2002, defined terrorism by making an amendment in the United States Code, Title 18, Section 2331. With this amendment the definition of terrorism in the United States came closer to that of the British definition. The Code provided that terrorism consisted of "activities that...involve violent acts or acts dangerous to human life that are a violation of the criminal laws of the United States or of any State." Moreover, it includes those acts that "appear to be intended (i) to intimidate or coerce a civilian population; (ii) to influence the policy of a government by intimidation or coercion; or (iii) to affect the conduct of a government by mass destruction, assassination, or kidnapping..." Section 411 of the Patriot Act further provides in the definition the acts of "indicating an intention to cause death or serious bodily injury," "to prepare or plan a terrorist activity," and "to solicit funds or other things of value."

One of the interesting dimensions of the American juridical debate on the War on Terror worth noticing is that it does not distinguish between terrorism and acts of war, which are often used interchangeably. For instance, in the aforementioned definitions, certain criminal offences are classified as terrorism. On the other hand, the same offences are categorised, as in the National Defense Authorization Act (NDAA) (2011) as "hostilities against the United States or its coalition partners" (Section 1031).[10] And more clearly, US Senator John McCain, who was one of the sponsors of NDAA, in support of the act argued: "...those people who seek to wage war against the United States will be stopped and we will use all ethical, moral and legal methods to do so."[11] It is quite obvious from this unresolved relationship between terrorism and acts of war that the shift from the law of high treason to that of the criminal code in the United States also remains incomplete.

In Pakistan, in 2009, the definition of terrorism in the ATA (1997) was once again expanded. This time, the expansion came in the wake of the religious vigilantism of students of the Red Mosque in Islamabad. Through an Ordinance (No. XXI), which was later codified as an Act in 2013 (No. XX), the government made a number of amendments. First, it amended subsection 1 of Section 6 to expand the purpose of a terrorist action. The scope of the new purpose would now include intimidation and terrorising social sectors, media, the business community, and security forces, as well as damaging and looting property. Second, it amended subsection 2 of Section 6 to provide that property might include government premises, official installations, schools, hospitals and private property. Third, in the same subsection in clause (g), the amendment provided that "taking the law in own hand" and private "award of any punishment by an organization" would be considered as a terrorist action. Fourth, the amendment added two new clauses, (o) and (p), to subsection 2. In these clauses, armed resistance and dissemination of unauthorised ideas or preaching through private FM radio stations were declared as terrorist acts. These two clauses obviously came in the backdrop of the armed conflict in Swat valley, where

Tehreek-e-Nafaz-e-Shariat-e-Mohammadi and the Taliban had launched an armed resistance against the state. The use of a private FM radio channel was part of this resistance led by Maulana Fazlullah. He preached *jihad* (armed resistance), recruited foot soldiers, and raised funds through his private FM channel. In 2013, when this ordinance was adopted as an act, it was, however, clarified that a religious rally or a peaceful demonstration would not be considered a terrorist action. Lastly, it warned office bearers of all banned organisations from regrouping and/or remaking the organisation with any new name. If they contravened the provisions, their passports could be taken away, bank accounts frozen, and arms licences cancelled.

After all amendments, the new expanded definition of terrorism in the ATA (1997) mentions the following offences:

> a) it involves the doing of anything that causes death; b) it involves grievous violence against a person or grievous bodily injury or harm to a person; c) involves grievous injury to property; d) involves the doing of anything that is likely to cause death or endangers person's life; e) involves kidnapping for ransom, hostage taking or hijacking; f) incites hatred and contempt on religious, sectarian or ethnic basis to stir up violence or cause internal disturbance; g) involves stoning, brick-batting or any other form of mischief to spread panic; h) involves firing on religious congregations, mosques, imambargahs, churches, temples and all other places of worship, or random firing to spread panic, or involve any forcible takeover of mosques or other places of worship; i) creates a serious risk to safety of the public...; j) involves the burning of vehicles or any other serious form of arson; k) involves extortion of money [bhatta] or property; l) is designed to seriously interfere with or seriously disrupt a communications system or public utility service; or n) involves serious violence against a member of the police force, armed forces, civil and armed forces, or a public servant.

This new definition has also settled as to what the criterion of terrorism is: whether it is the heinous actions (*actus reus*) or the purpose of it (*mens rea*). To this aspect I will return shortly. Here, I want to point to the procedural nature of the act. The fact that the ATA collects offences already available in the Panel Code and other security laws and subjects them to special criminal procedure makes it more a procedural law than a substantive one. The Supreme Court, in a decision in 2001, also commented on this matter: "[...] although this act to some extent contains the substantive law [...] it is procedural in nature."[12] One of the consequences of its procedural nature, however, is that the substantive rights of the subjects/accused persons could remain unaffected.[13]

In March 2013 the definition of terrorism in the ATA (1997) further expanded to cover international terrorism, and to incorporate the financial angle to it—money collection, financing, and laundering.[14] This amendment came under pressure by an international forum called the Financial Action Task Force (FATF). As a member country, Pakistan was asked to make provisions in its anti-terrorism laws to deal with international terrorism and (money laundering resulting in) financing of terrorism. Accordingly an amendment was made in Section 6(b), which also provided that action, or threat of action, against any foreign government or population or an international organisation would also be considered terrorism. Moreover, the definition of the word "terrorist" was amended to include persons taking actions of "facilitation" and "funding."

Courts on the definition of terrorism

The question as to what constitutes terrorism has remained a matter of recurrent interest on the floor of higher courts. After the passage of the ATA (1997), it became a challenge for the courts to settle the test or criteria for determining what actions constitute terrorism. There were a number of factors that remained a matter of interest for the courts in determining terrorism. These included heinousness of the actions, purpose, gravity, effect or consequences, and design or plan. As in *Basharat Ali* (2004) the Lahore High Court (LHC) noted:

> The resume of legislative developments in the field of terrorism in Pakistan shows that with different laws and definitions of terrorist act or terrorism the emphasis has been shifting from one criterion to another including the gravity of the act, lethal nature of the weapon used, plurality of culprits, number of victims, impact created by the at an effect of fear and insecurity brought about or likely to be created in the society by the action.[15]

On the other hand, the act also provided a list of offences or actions, as I have quoted previously, that were to be considered as terrorism. This list increased further in subsections 3 and 5 of Section 6, which provide for the possibility of including in the definition of terrorism any actions that involved the use of firearms and explosives or actions benefiting a proscribed organisation. The LHC also acknowledged in the same decision the fact that courts were not employing any consistent test in determining what was terrorism until the new definition came along in 2001. In Court's own words,

> One cannot help noticing that the cases pertained to offences committed for private purposes with no motivation to destabilize the society at large were all adjudged by the Supreme Court to be cases of terrorist acts or terrorism on the basis of a presumptive and speculative quantification of the effect that the relevant actions could have created in the society.

With the new definition, terrorism came to consist of two parts: the actions (*actus reus*) and the purpose (*mens rea*). The definition gives precedence to the *mens rea* part of terrorism. As the Lahore High Court explained in a case,

> ...after stumbling through various approaches in that regard the Legislature in our country has finally hit upon a definition of terrorism which is not only closest to its real meaning but the same is also in accord with the international perceptions about the same. The earlier emphasis on the speculative effect of the act has now given way to a clearly defined *mens rea* and *actus reus*...Thus, it is no longer the fear or insecurity actually created or intended to be created or likely to be created which would determine whether the action qualifies to be termed as terrorism or not but it is now the intent and motivation behind the action which would be determinative of the issue irrespective of the fact whether any fear and insecurity was actually created or not.

The Court also indicated that courts might take some time to understand this settlement in favour of the *mens rea* element:

> The mind-set inherited in the background of the Summary Military Courts, Speedy Trial Courts, and Special Courts for Suppression of Terrorist Activities, which were different Courts constituted at different stages in the past for separate and special handling of offences of grave nature, may take some time to be dispelled and it may take a while to appreciate and realize that an act of 'terrorism' is not just a grave offence but it is a class and specie apart...

The Court defined terrorism as a

> preplanned and organized system of intimidation. Its requisite and attributes are that such act and its effects are made known to the people and widely circulated with exaggeration. It is neither hidden nor disguised. It means an act which is committed with the sole object to terrorise the people and to [make them] feel insecure.[16]

Generally, in deciding a terrorism case, an Anti-Terrorism Court (ATC) is supposed to look at both the elements. However, courts have to ensure that all actions must have the purpose and/or design as well as the conscious taking of action/offence. In one decision, the Lahore High Court ruled, "Test to determine whether a particular act is 'terrorism' or not is the motivation, object, design or purpose behind the act and not the consequential effect created by such act."[17] Similarly, the Karachi High Court decided, in another case, "Physical harm to the victim is not the sole criterion to determine the question of terrorism, as motive should be the key word or the objective of the act."[18] These decisions and a number of other decisions have emphasised the difference between purpose and consequences of action, and they have settled that the purpose, rather than the consequences, is crucial.[19] However, the courts have not entirely excluded the possibility of considering consequences as immaterial—as in one case, about a violent dispute during an election, in which the Lahore High Court said,

> Election dispute could not be termed as a personal dispute...Terror so created in election disputes, would create in election disputes, would create feeling of insecurity among public at large and a wave of panic and fear would persist in the area.[20]

In other cases, on the other hand, the courts have also emphasised the gravity of an incident as a consequence, to which I will return shortly. In yet another decision, the same court reemphasised the purpose element:

> To create fear or insecurity in the society through a crime is not by itself terrorism unless the motive or the design or the *actus reus* or *mens rea* pre-exists for creating such fear or insecurity in the society. A private crime resulting in fear or insecurity as a by-product, a fall out or an unintended consequence of fright etc., cannot be termed as an act of terrorism.[21]

The Peshawar High Court extended the purpose by inference in a case in which a huge quantity of illicit arms and ammunition were being transported. The court said, "Only conclusion which could be drawn was that such transportation involved serious risk to safety of public which was already under wave of extreme terrorism."[22]

It is also worth pointing out in the ATA (1997) that unlike the British definition the *mens rea* element is composed of two further elements: the purpose and the design. Generally, both the elements can count towards making a strong terrorism case. However, the act has split the two elements in such a way that courts can require any one of them along with *actus reus* to take cognisance. For instance, in *Asghar Ali Mubarak* (2016), the court said that since there is "or" between the two elements, any of the two would suffice in a case of terrorism.[23]

The other component of terrorism is gravity of the action. The courts have defined it as that part of action that measures the "tendency to create" sense of terror, fear, panic, and/or insecurity in the people or a section of it.[24] In 2003, the Lahore High Court placed emphasis on the word "serious" in the definition of terrorism in Section 6. The court said, "Not every disruption of or interference with the duties of a public servant or every coercion, intimidation or violence against a public servant" could be considered as an act of terrorism. The court said that Section 6 "speak[s] of 'serious interferences,' 'serious disruption': 'serious coercion or intimidation' or 'serious violence' against a public servant. The word 'serious' has been defined by S.2 (w) of the said Act to mean 'dangerous to life or property.'"[25] However, the following year in another case the court also clarified that: "Mere gravity, heinousness, gruesomeness or shocking nature of any offence, committed in pursuance of personal enmity or in settlement of personal vendetta is not by itself sufficient...." In other words, the court inferred that the purpose of an action was more important than the gravity of it. In this line of argument, the Supreme Court decided in a case that if the purpose was to spread terror but "actual terror [was] not caused," such an act would still be considered as an act of terrorism as long as it had terrorist intentions.[26] The Supreme Court added that it is "not necessary that the force must have been used immediately after the threat."[27] However, the Supreme Court also observed, "It is the cumulative effect of all the attending circumstances which provide tangible guidelines to determine the applicability or otherwise of subsection (b) of Section 6."[28]

Another crucial aspect of the offence of terrorism to notice is that it is considered to have been committed against the state. An important consequence of this aspect is that an individual victim cannot claim to have reached a compromise with the offender. Quetta High Court in a decision said that under the ATA "private complainant or the legal heirs of the deceased, had no right to compound the 'scheduled offence' as those offences were mainly against the state and not against individuals." Moreover, the court said, "Not providing the right to compromise the offence by legal heirs of deceased, was neither violation of Islamic Injunctions, nor of any fundamental rights."[29]

While the *mens rea* element is generally essential to establish a case of terrorism, the ATA (1997) has provided two exceptions to it: first, if an offence leads to the derogation of an international convention to which Pakistan is a party—the Fifth Schedule to the act gives nine such conventions (Section 6, subsection 3-A); and second, if the offence involves "use of firearms, explosives or any other weapon" (Section 6(3)). In this latter case, the establishing of terrorism purpose mentioned in 6 (subsection 1-C) is not needed, which relates to

> advancing a religious, sectarian or ethnic cause or intimidating and terrorizing the public, social sectors, media persons, business community or attacking the civilians, including damaging property by ransacking, looting, arson or by any other means, government officials, installations, security forces or law enforcement agencies.

Hence it is a curious provision. Since much of terrorism in Pakistan has involved, in one way or other, the use of firearms and/or explosives, it seems then that it depends on ATCs whether they choose to bring a specific action involving firearms and explosives under Section 6(3) or decide it under Section 6(1).

Subjects of the ATA (1997)

For quite some time, until 2001, the major subjects of the anti-terrorism laws were only individuals or citizens. In 2001, the Musharraf government introduced an amendment whereby "organisations"—terrorist organisations—also became subject to the act. The amendment declared that an organisation "concerned with terrorism" would be declared as a terrorist organisation, and could therefore be tried and punished. The phrase "concerned with terrorism" was explained as preparing, participating, committing, encouraging and/or assisting an act of terrorism, or stirring up disorder by inciting hatred or malice on sectarian, ethnic or religious grounds, presenting those who commit acts of terrorism as heroic persons, and not expelling them from their ranks, or being otherwise involved in terrorism. In January 2002, Musharraf's government declared in an ordinance that even if one person of an organisation was found involved in terrorism, the entire organisation or network would be responsible and would be subject to the law.[30]

Although unlike the STAA (1975), the ATA (1997) did not aim to target political agitation of the opposition political parties in 2002, when the Political Parties Order was passed, political parties became an indirect target. For instance, Section 3 of the Political Parties Order 2002 prohibited political parties from: "c) promoting sectarian, regional, or provincial hatred or animosity; d) bearing a name as a militant group or section… or e) imparting any military or paramilitary training to its members or other persons." Section 4 also required that every political party maintained an official manifesto ("constitution") and Section 15 provided for the dissolution of a political party if it was found to be "foreign-aided" or was found "indulging in terrorism." If a political party were dissolved because of its involvement in the aforementioned actions of terrorism, then the members of that party could not hold any political office for a minimum of four years. They could also be subjected to criminal prosecution if warranted.[31]

After the Swat valley operations (2008–2009), the government began to become tough on suspected organisations. As I mention earlier, through the Ordinance of 2009, which was later adopted as Act XX of 2013, the banned organisations were not allowed to reconstitute themselves through new names. They could be punished for terrorism, their offices could be closed, their passports could be withdrawn, and their bank accounts frozen. The government also began to trace sources of financing of suspected organisations. In 2013, the government declared that money-laundering activities resulting in financing of banned organisations would amount to terrorism.

The use of force

The ATA authorised the LEAs to use force to secure compliance (Section 5). This use of force included the power to fire upon a suspect and cause grievous injury or death. However, the Act enjoined upon the LEAs to use only "necessary" power, and only after giving "sufficient warning." But what constitutes necessary power and sufficient warning is left for the officers to decide and the internal inquiry committees of the concerned LEA to review. The courts might also exercise their jurisdiction over incidents of the use of force, because the use of lethal force impinges upon the scope of Article 9 of the Constitution, which guarantees protection of life and liberty to citizens. However, their decision would rely on sufficient amount of evidence available to them, which is collected by the LEAs themselves. Most of such incidents do not come up to courts for trials and are, therefore, likely to be covered up through the provisions of indemnity and internal inquiry committee reports.

The provision for the use of lethal force has been one of the most debated provisions of the act. The authorisation of the use of lethal force has remained a critical and controversial provision, and it has been amended a number of times as well. In *Mehram Ali* (1998), the Supreme Court laid down some important principles to be heeded by the LEAs in the use of force. First, the law enforcement agencies could not use this power for any ulterior or other purposes. The Court gave a "note of warning to all concerned" LEAs that in case power was "misused for ulterior purpose or even otherwise is abused, person responsible for the same would have to face the consequences." Second, the Court advised that the power to fire upon a person should be used only when the police force was fired upon by that person. Third, the Court criticised and struck down the provision in the ATA (1997) that a person who "in all probability is likely to commit" a terrorist act could be fired upon. The Court said:

> An officer of any of the above forces under the present provision can kill any person, if he considers that in all probability the former is likely to commit a terrorist act or scheduled offence. The formation of opinion as to the probability or likelihood of commission of offence will vary from person to person as it depends on subjective satisfaction. There is no check or guideline provided for the exercise of the above power conferred by the above provision. The aforesaid provision in its present form is not sustainable. The same may be amended and it may be provided that the officer can fire upon an accused person if he has been himself fired upon by him.[32]

Accordingly, the government amended the act and the words "in all probability is likely to commit" were removed from Article 5(2)(i).

The following year, the Supreme Court made another landmark decision in *Jamaat-i-Islami, Pakistan*.[33] In this case, the Court made at least four significant points. First, the Court said that the right to use force "is to be exercised as a preventive measure and not to be made basis for launching an attack for retaliation, lest it would be tantamount to legalizing alleged police encounters/extra-judicial killings in the garb of exercise of power...."

Second, the Court said that "police personnel cannot exercise the right of private self-defence more than what has been directed in the above sections," i.e., the sections from 99 to 106 of the Pakistan Penal Code. Third, the Court said that the authority to use fire or kill was not proportionate to punishments given in the Act for several offences. Therefore, when a person was committing an offence that was punishable by a lesser punishment than death sentence, how could it be justified that the power of shooting be exercised against him? In Court's own words,

> Furthermore, all the offences mentioned in the Act are not punishable with death, but are also punishable with imprisonment for life or with rigorous imprisonment for various terms. It is incumbent upon the police force to act so as to enforce Article 9 of the constitution, given in Chapter 1 thereof, which provides that no person shall be deprived of life or liberty save in accordance with law rather than to violate the same and expose himself to criminal prosecution.

Lastly, the Court took the moral Islamic argument against the possibility of indiscriminate use of power.

> Such a course can never be countenanced in a civilized society, particularly, in Pakistan, where Islam is the State religion. It would also militate against the Objectives Resolution forming substantive part of the Constitution under Article 2-A…

Later in August 2001, through an ordinance (No. XXXIX), Musharraf's government incorporated in the act the advice of superior judiciary that the power to fire should be used only when a terrorist fires first. However, Sharif's government, in June 2014, removed this provision with Act No. VI. This latter act instead provided that the use of force to fire would be used as a last resort. Moreover, only an officer of grade 17 or a magistrate could give such orders. All cases that resulted in grievous injury or death would, however, be reviewed by an internal committee of the police or any other involved security agency. It needs to be noticed that after the decision of the Supreme Court in *Mehram Ali* (1998), the government had also incorporated a provision in the act requiring the officers responsible in cases of use of deadly force to justify their actions in writing for suspecting and taking action against a person or a premise. In the *Jamaati Islami* case (2000) the Court also struck down a provision in Article 5(2)(i) which allowed the use of lethal force against persons who are suspects of terrorism but not committing an offence at the time of encounter with the LEAs. The court said:

> It also provides that it shall be lawful for any such officer, or any superior officer to use force, or to order the firing upon any person or

> persons against whom he is authorised to use force in terms thereof. The above provision is violative of Article 9 of the Constitution, which guarantees that no person shall be deprived of life or liberty save in accordance with law.[34]

Here, I want to point to another interesting kind of power available to the LEAs. This power consisted of cordoning off of areas (for instance, an entire *mohalla*, a block of a city, or a village) for the purpose of search, arrests, and investigation. An area could be cordoned off for fourteen days, and the period could be further extended as well. With this power, the LEAs can cordon off entire sectarian or ethnic communities and carry out operations within. In the summer of 2011, the Rangers killed a young man in Karachi. He was suspected of stealing in a local park. The area was under semi-curfew (cordoned) and the Rangers were on the patrol. The young man was brought to the Rangers personnel. One of the personnel shot him in the leg, apparently to punish him. However, after shooting, they left him on the ground bleeding, crying, and imploring. The young man bled to death. Interestingly, a private TV crew was nearby and they recorded the incident on camera. Soon the news began to flash on local TV channels about the incident, showing this video clip. The video clip also became viral on social media. The Supreme Court took a *suo moto* action of the incident, questioning the use of force by the Rangers. Later, in its decision, the Court explained that the use of force in the incident was not the necessary force warranted in Article 5 of the ATA.

> [The m]anner in which death of [the] deceased had occurred clearly indicated barbarism because once he had been overpowered, as it was evident from the video clips, he was not to be fired upon in any case and at the best the Rangers personnel could have handed him over to the police, if there was an allegation of his being involved in the commission of some offence, but Rangers had no authority to open fire uopon him under S.5(2)(i) of the Anti-Terrorism Act, 1997.

In this case, the Rangers personnel did not stand a chance to cover up the incident or hide behind the indemnity clause and/or the internal committee report. The LEAs have often used the provisions for indemnity and internal committee report to defend their actions. However, in such cases where incidents get video recorded, those provisions cannot help them much. It is worth pointing out that the courts have often emphasised the restricted scope of indemnity clauses saying that "legal provisions might not be permitted to be made liberally in favour of forces" when the "forces were constitutionally and legally mandated to jealously *safeguard* the lives, liberty and property of the subjects" (emphasis mine).[35]

Preventive detention

As I have discussed in the previous chapter, the broader regime of preventive detention is regulated within the framework of the Constitution (1973). In Article 10, which guarantees safeguard against arbitrary arrest and detention of citizens, an exception is made to provide for preventive detention. This exception allows for quite broad Constitutional framework of preventive detention in terms of powers and detention periods. For instance, the Constitution provides for preventive detention up to one year, and if someone is adjudged to be involved in anti-national activities, then he/she could be detained beyond one year. However, the Courts have ruled that such period should not be for more than three years. Moreover, if someone is adjudged as an enemy alien then he/she could be detained indefinitely. Within this Constitutional framework operate various security laws, which practically regulate the preventive detention regime. These laws include the Security of Pakistan Act, 1952; the Maintenance of Public Order Ordinance, 1960; the Suppression of Terrorist Activities Act, 1975 (repealed); the ATA, 1997; the Actions in Aid of Civil Power Regulations, 2011; and the Protection of Pakistan Act, 2014 (ended 2016). For the federally and provincially administered tribal areas, there is a separate regime of detention possible under Articles 245 and 247. This article provides for taking emergency measures and making regulations for preventive detention in the tribal areas.

Interestingly, neither the Constitution nor any other security law, including the ATA (1997), defines what preventive detention is.[36] The higher courts have, however, placed some meaning on it in case law. For instance, in one case, an Indian Court said that preventive detention meant

> detention of a person without trial and conviction by a court, but merely on suspicion in the mind of an executive authority... Preventive detention is thus preventive, not punitive, in theory...[It is aimed] at curtailing his liberty, with a view to preventing him from committing certain injurious activities in future.[37]

Preventive detention aims to check "anti-social and subversive elements from endangering the public safety and security of the state."[38] One of the reasons as to why it has not been defined in statutes is that the preventive detention laws tend to be procedural in nature. They provide for practical steps to be taken for detaining individuals rather than debate the substance behind the procedures and/or detention. On the other hand, it is also interesting to notice that the provisions of preventive detention in the Constitution are criminal procedural law provisions and, therefore, their appropriate place is the Panel Code or the Criminal Procedure Code rather than the Constitution.

It is important to mention that preventive detention can assume a number of forms. The ATA suggests four different kinds of orders that could be passed against a terrorism suspect. First, the act provides for proscription of a terrorism suspect (Section 11-EE). Second, the act provides for surveillance of a terrorism suspect (Section 11-EE). Third, the act provides for (preventive) detention (Section 11-EEE). Lastly, the act provides for detention for inquiry (Section 11-EEEE). All these orders restrict an individual's liberty in one way or another. The provision for proscription of a suspected person was introduced in 2014 (Act VII, 2014). This section was, however, originally added to the ATA in 2002 with the title of "Security for Good Behaviour." Then, it was a brief subsection, providing only for enlisting suspected persons in the Fourth Schedule. However, in 2014, it was amended and given a new title: "Proscription of Person." Moreover, a detailed explanation was added to it to give procedural steps for proscription. Accordingly, this subsection now provides for two types of restrictions on an individual's liberty: restriction on movement (proscription) and surveillance. Through an order of proscription, a suspected person can be restricted from visiting any public place, office, institution, or any other declared place. He/she could be confined to a specific vicinity and regularly report to the concerned police station. For ensuring good behaviour or compliance, he/she could be asked to execute surety bonds and deposit money. It is worth noticing here that almost similar powers are available to the LEAs under the MPOO (1960).

The surveillance of suspects was provided by Musharraf's second Anti-Terrorism (Amendment) Ordinance, issued on November 16, 2002. It was meant to observe persons suspected of associating with terrorist organisations. The provisions of surveillance were incorporated in subsection 11-EE. Accordingly, if the government suspected a person of associating with a terrorist organisation, then it could put his name on the list prepared under the Fourth Schedule, and thereafter that person would remain under surveillance. However, for proscribing or placing under surveillance, the government had to rely on certain prerequisites, which included "concrete material and cogent reason" that satisfied a "reasonable person."[39] The proscribed person and the person under surveillance were allowed to appeal before the government within one month. The LEAs could keep the person under surveillance, or in proscription, for up to twelve months. Actually, however, this period could be extended up to three years.[40]

Detention procedure

It is important that we point to the procedure involved in detention under the ATA (1997). There are four steps in the procedure. In the first step, the government (both the federal and provincial) is required to notify that the name of the suspected person is put on the list maintained under Section 11-EE and the Fourth Schedule. Within three days, the information about the notification is communicated to the person named.[41] The second step involves registration of a First Information Report (FIR) against the person. However, the registration alone of a case against the person is not sufficient to detain him/her.[42] In the third step, the government passes a detention order against the person. The government is also supposed to communicate the grounds of detention to the person well in time. These grounds should not be "mere apprehensions" of the police or a LEA, but rather "physical involvement or participation" that could build objective satisfaction.[43] The fourth step provides to the suspected person the right to make representation before the government.

In 2007, a higher court ruled in a case that if the Home Secretary of the Punjab Government was the authority passing the detention orders, then he/she could not hear the representation made by the detainee. Arguing that nobody could be judge of his own cause, the Court said that the representation should be made to the Secretary Law.[44] Procedurally, once the representation of a detainee is declined, he can then use his constitutional right to lodge a writ petition in a High Court. The superior courts have also maintained in a number of cases that the prosecution or the LEAs could not withhold from them any information, no matter how secret it was. The Courts instead maintained that whether any specific piece of information was secret or privileged was the discretion of the courts to determine.[45]

At this point, I would like to expend some space on the linkages of Pakistan's preventive detention regime with the Western regimes. One of the recent foundational laws of preventive detention in the Anglo-American security regime is NIEPA, 1973. The object of the act was to deal with "certain offences, the detention of terrorists, the preservation of the peace...."[46] Under this Act, the Secretary of State could order to place an individual in "interim custody" for a period of twenty-eight days. Before the expiry of that period, an appointed (quasi) judicial commission would decide on the basis of "the protection of the public" whether to release the individual from custody, or to extend it.[47] It is also worth noting that the detainee was to be served with a written statement regarding his terrorist activities only seven days before the commissioner first heard the case.[48]

The Northern Ireland Emergency Provisions Act (NIEPA), 1973, was amended and re-enacted in 1978, 1987, 1991, and 1996. In the last two acts, the period of "interim detention" was reduced to fourteen days, and the Secretary of State was authorised to issue detention orders only after receiving a report from a judicial adviser. What is important to notice about these acts is that the procedure of these detention laws reflected the procedure laid down in Regulation III of 1818. The following procedural steps in these acts resembled those in Regulation III. After a person is arrested and detained for an interim period, the case is referred to an adviser within fourteen days. Here, the difference was that in Regulation III, the adviser was also the officer in charge of the custody. After referral to the adviser, the detainee is served with a written statement regarding the nature of his suspected activities. The detainee is then allowed to send a written representation to the Secretary of State and/or a request that he wants to see the adviser in person. The adviser prepares the report, taking into consideration the representation made by the detainee. The report is then sent to the Secretary of State, who makes the decision on (further) detention. After making the detaining orders, he can, at any time, send back the case to the adviser. The detainee can also request for reconsideration of the order after one year. Thus, apparently, the detention could extend for an indefinite period of time.

In 2001, the United Kingdom's Anti-Terrorism, Crime and Security Act (ACS), provided for the detention of non-citizens. Under Section 23, non-citizens could be indefinitely detained without trial. With a certificate from the Home Secretary, a non-citizen could be detained and at once become "a suspected international terrorist." However, this provision of indefinite detention turned out to be inconsistent with Article 5 of the European Convention for the Protection of Human Rights and Fundamental Freedoms (ECHR), 1950. In December 2004, the House of Lords in *A v. Secretary of State for the Home Department* held that Section 23 was illegal on two grounds: first, that it exhibited a disproportionate response to what was "strictly required by the exigencies of the situation" and thus infringed on Article 5 of the ECHR; and second, that it violated the right of all human beings to be free of discrimination as enshrined in Article 14 of the ECHR. Clearly, the Lords were of the opinion that the section discriminated without a rational and objective justification between citizens and non-citizens. The government responded by passing an amendment—the Prevention of Terrorism Act (PTA), 2005. The PTA, 2005, provided for two types of "control order"—the derogating and non-derogating control orders. The derogating control orders could be issued to control individuals who posed a serious risk to public safety. By the order of a high court, they could be placed under house arrest for a period of six months, which could also be extended. The non-derogating control orders imposed a combination of restrictions—for instance, curfew, electronic tagging, restriction on association, search of residence, and/or restriction on the use of telephone and Internet. These orders could extend up to twelve months and could be renewed.

Apart from detention-without-trial and control orders, there have been two other legal routes for detention in the United Kingdom. One was called "pre-charge detention" and was provided in the Terrorism Act, 2000. Under it a person could be held for forty-eight hours. In 2003, the Criminal Justice Act increased pre-charge detention to fourteen days. Then, in 2006, the Terrorism Act further increased the period to twenty-eight days. Another route provides for much shorter periods of time, specifically for the purpose of questioning and body search at borders, ports, and airports. This type of detention, which reflected stop and search detention under NIEPA, is allowed for a maximum of nine hours.

In the United States, detention without trial is one of the legal instruments available to the executive, especially in cases where there is a lack of substantial evidence necessary for trial. Both citizens and non-citizens can be placed under preventive detention.[49] Moreover, it is not constrained by law, whether international or local, or by judicial oversight. This type of preventive detention, along with the deployment of armed forces in civilian areas, is reminiscent of detention-without-trial and military deployment in Northern Ireland. The Bush administration claimed that human rights law did not apply "to the conduct of hostilities or the capture and detention of enemy combatants" because such matters were "governed by the more specific laws of armed conflict."[50] It was convinced that preventive detention was the exclusive subject of the executive.

At the beginning of the War on Terror, it was declared in a Presidential Military Order on November 13, 2001, that citizens of the United States would not be subject to preventive detention. For citizens, there existed another law—Article III of the Constitution. The subjects of the November 2001 military order were the members of al-Qaeda or those who had "engaged in, aided or abetted, or conspired to commit, acts of international terrorism." Although citizens of the United States were declared not to be the subject of the November Order, covertly, they remained so. They could be detained, sent on rendition, or could be permanently incapacitated. For instance, in *Hamdi* (2004) the detainee remained in detention for over three years before the Supreme Court took up his case. The prosecution did not charge him of "espionage, treason, or any other crime under domestic law."[51] Two justices, Stevens and Scalia, in the plurality decision, held that the US Constitution required that Hamdi be "entitled to a habeas decree requiring his release unless (1) criminal proceedings are promptly brought, or (2) Congress has suspended the writ of habeas corpus."[52] The criminal proceeding meant the proceeding of high treason. Justice Thomas, on the other hand, held that the President of the United States had the power to "unilaterally decide to detain an individual if the Executive deem[ed] this necessary for the public safety even if he [was] mistaken."[53] Although the plurality decision in *Hamdi* granted him the right of habeas, the passage of NDAA, 2011, has once again withdrawn that right from citizens. Accordingly, those American citizens who have been "covered persons" can be denied the right of habeas.[54]

Special courts and criminal procedure

The special courts, and the special criminal procedure by which they operate, are not anything new in the ATA (1997). They have been set up during emergencies, and we know that emergencies have been imposed many times in Pakistan. One of the reasons for providing special courts in the ATA (1997) was to avoid inordinate delays. For instance, the higher courts have themselves warned against delays in criminal and terrorism cases:

> Inordinate delay in imparting justice is likely to cause erosion of public confidence in judicial system on the one hand and on the other hand it

> is bound to create a sense of helplessness, despair, feeling of frustration, and anguish apart from adding to their woes and miseries.[55]

Another reason for setting up special courts and special procedure was given by the general principle that a "departure from the rule of procedure, which caused no prejudice and injustice to [an] accused, there is no necessity to undo such order."[56] This legal reasoning has by then attained the form of generality, such that it has often supported the legality of the executive's making special procedures in criminal justice.

On the other hand, the creation of special courts has always been challenged in higher courts as well. One of the reasons for such challenging has been the fear of creating a parallel judicial set-up to the one that already exists. This fear is not only entertained by bar councils, media, and human rights activists, but also by the superior judiciary. Whenever the executive has created special courts outside the appellate jurisdiction and supervisory oversight of the superior judiciary, they have been struck down or brought within the hierarchy of the regular judiciary. In this way, superior judiciary has maintained the separation of powers doctrine by not allowing the executive to perform judicial function or (to become the judge of its own cause).

The fear of superior judiciary about the executive's usurpation of judicial power has its history. The executive has often shown its intention to control special courts and to keep them outside the appellate and administrative control of the Superior judiciary. For instance, the special courts created under the ATA were initially kept outside both appellate jurisdiction and administrative control of the superior judiciary. The ATA instead created an appellate court of similar jurisdiction as of the High Court. Thus the ATA did not allow appeals to the superior judiciary. Moreover, initially judges of the special courts were not given fixed tenure of job. They could be picked and removed by the government.

Another example that we can give is that after the passage of the ATA and the making of special courts, the government passed Pakistan Armed Forces (Acting in Aid of the Civil Power) Ordinance (PAFPO) (1998), which created special military courts. Since military comes under the executive's control through the Ministry of Defence, such courts technically were outside the hierarchy and administrative control of the superior judiciary. The Supreme Court, therefore, struck them down by saying:

> Provision of Pakistan Armed Forces (Acting in Aid of the Civil Power) Ordinance, 1998, in so far as these allow the establishment of Military Courts for trial of civilians charged with the offences mentioned in S.6 and Schedule to the said Ordinance, are unconstitutional, without lawful authority and of no legal effect.[57]

However, the superior judiciary has almost never taken the view that special courts cannot be created. Rather, in a number of decisions it has ruled that special courts with special criminal procedure could be created for reasons of emergency, efficiency, and the interest of justice, as well as for ideal reasons of inexpensive and expeditious justice as provided in the Constitution (Article 37). In a decision in 1998 involving the question of creating special courts under the ATA, the Supreme Court said:

> Efficiency in the Courts is serious national problem, an expression of greater public concern than even the threat of war. Article 37(d) of the constitution of Islamic Republic of Pakistan, 1973, enjoins upon the State to ensure 'inexpensive' and 'expeditious justice'. Thus visualized, speedy resolution of civil and criminal cases is an important Constitutional goal, as envisaged by the principles of policy enshrined in the Constitution. It is, therefore, not undesirable to create Special Courts for operation o with speed but expeditious disposition of cases of terrorist activities/heinous offences have to be subject to constitution and law.[58]

Interestingly, the creation of special courts has also been challenged on an Islamic basis. However, the Supreme Court has again taken the view that special courts, with speedy justice dispensation on the basis of expedited criminal procedure, are exactly what Islam teaches. The court said:

> There is no bar under the Constitution or the law for setting up more than one Special Courts and if the competent Legislature has so enacted, Court cannot question its wisdom as jurisdiction of the Court is limited only to finding out as to whether any provision of the Constitution or the Islamic injunction has been violated by enacting this law. There is nothing in the Anti-Terrorism act, 1997 which goes against the Islamic Principles of administration of justice which are not only sacred but are also very dear.[59]

Development of the special courts under the ATA

The ATA provided for creating special courts for trying all the offences given in the act. The act provided that the government could create as many courts as it deemed necessary and also determine the place of their sitting, duration and jurisdiction.

In the wake of the decision in *Mehram Ali* (1998), the government issued the Anti-Terrorism (Amendment) Ordinance (1998). The ordinance granted tenure of office for two years (which was later extended to two and half years in November 2002) to the judges of ATCs. The ordinance disbanded the special Appellate Tribunals and provided that appeals from the special courts would go to the respective High Courts. Moreover, the ordinance also placed restrictions on trials in absentia. An ATC trying a suspect in absentia was required to publish in at least three national dailies, out of which one must be an Urdu language newspaper. The court was also required to appoint a defence counsel for the accused, and the latter (or on his behalf his relatives) could also choose a defence of his own choice. However, in 1999 another ordinance was passed that took back this right of choosing defence of his own choice.

In *Liaquat Hussain*, the Supreme Court decided that an ATC should hear one case at a time in order to expedite the disposal of cases. Although this recommendation was incorporated in 1999, it was only with the proviso that if a given case did not proceed further, then more than one case could be assigned to an ATC. Thus within a year the number of cases began to pile up. According to one report, there were about 451 cases pending before Sindh ATCs.[60] This also meant that the courts were unable to dispose of cases within the given time of one week per case.

On December 2, 1999, Musharraf's government established two new special courts—one at LHC and another at KHC. Each of these courts had both original and appellate jurisdictions. They were to be headed by a High Court judge, they had the power to "transfer, claim, or readmit any case within that province," and they would hear appeals from lower ATCs.[61] After the 9/11 terrorist attacks in the United States, the anti-terrorism legal regime began to take precedence over the regular criminal courts. Within a couple of months, eleven new ATCs were set up in the North-West Frontier Province (NWFP, now called Khyber-Pakhtunkhwa) and four in the province of Sindh. With that, there were then forty-one ATCs in total working in the country. However, the government had decided to close five ATCs before the events of September 11—two in Baluchistan and three in Punjab—owing to the "lack of terrorism cases."[62]

In January 2002, Musharraf's government wished to set up ATCs with increased number of judges—from one to three—with the proviso that one of the judges must be a "military person." His government explained that the inclusion of a military judge was meant to expedite the disposal of cases. His government also provided that all cases that were stuck in the old ATCs were to be moved to these new courts, which would work unimpeded until November 30, 2002.

In November 2004, President Musharraf's government amended the ATA 1997 to give the right to appeal to the victim or his legal heirs against the acquittal of an accused by an ATC in the High Court. Accordingly in Section 25, two subsections, 4A and 4B, were added. Earlier, only the government could appeal against the decision of an ATC. Now the victim and his legal heir could also appeal. This was a unique feature added to the criminal procedure—now, if the government didn't pursue the case further in a High Court, then the victim or his family would be able to do so. By giving this right, Musharraf's government wanted to eliminate the possibility of leniency that could be shown on the part of the police, the prosecution, or the Attorney General's office to a suspected terrorist.

The 2004 amendment made two more crucial changes. It provided for the confiscation of passports of persons convicted under the ATA (1997). Secondly, it increased the punishment for the offence of aiding and abetting any act of terrorism from fourteen years to life imprisonment. The following year, Musharraf's government further increased punishments for all types offences given in the ATA. Where an offence was earlier punishable for five years, it was now punishable for ten years (Section 7B). Similarly, those punishable for fourteen years went up to life imprisonment (Section 7C), those for seven went up to ten years (Section 7D), those for six months went up to two years (Section 7G–I), those for three went up to five years and those for one went up to five years.

In 2005, the second amendment to ATA was made, which provided for a special bench in each High Court consisting of at least two judges to hear appeals arising from ATCs. The special bench was bound not to give more than two consecutive adjournments, and after such adjournments, if the defence counsel did not appear, the Court might appoint a state counsel for the accused. Before this amendment, the courts could give adjournment if "necessary in the interest of justice" but an adjournment was not to be for more than two days. It is interesting to notice that the case for not giving adjournments in terrorism-related cases first came in the Suppression of Anti-Terrorist Activities Act, 1975. This act had provided that courts should not grant adjournments unless they were "necessary in the interest of justice." Moreover, it was provided that even if the accused absconded, the court could continue with the proceedings in absentia, given that the accused had once appeared before the court.

In 2014, Act VI made a change in the criminal procedure. Earlier, if an ATC was not able to decide a case within seven days, the ATC was supposed to write to the Administrative Judge of the concerned High Court. With the change, the ATC is now required to write to the Chief Justice of the concerned High Court.

Jurisdiction

The territorial extent of the jurisdiction of an ATC is prescribed in Article 12 of the ATA (1997). The government is authorised to set up ATCs in each province and the Islamabad Capital Territory and determine the territorial extent of their jurisdiction. Generally, an ATC will take cognisance of a terrorist offence that takes place in its territorial jurisdiction unless the government sends it to another ATC for reasons of safety of witnesses, of prosecution, or for ensuring fair trial. The provision relating to ensuring fair trial is broad enough to allow the government to transfer almost any case from one ATC to another. The act, however, also provides in explanation of the Article 12 that the other ATC to which a case is transferred must be one having territorial jurisdiction for more than one area.

The jurisdiction of an ATC in relation to the nature of offences is quite broad as well. The ATA (1997) provides that an ATC can take cognisance of all scheduled offences and terrorist actions mentioned in various articles. And I have already mentioned earlier, not only were Articles 6, 7 and 11 amended several times to increase the number of cognisable offences, but the Scheduled list was also enlarged by incorporating a number of offences from the Panel Code. Apart from that, the courts have ruled that aiding, abetting, and conspiracy in relation to all these offences was also "exclusively triable" by ATCs.[63] Moreover, an ATC can take cognisance of an offence connected to or incidental to a scheduled offence of the ATA (1997).[64] It is also worth mentioning that an ATC determines on the basis of an FIR or any other evidence submitted by the prosecution whether or not an offence in question is a scheduled offence and, therefore, the sole jurisdiction of an ATC.[65] Only upon revision of the decision by a High Court can a case be sent back to a regular court.

Regarding the extent of powers, the jurisdiction of an ATC is that of a Session Court. It also exercises powers of the court of Magistrate, which is that it can take immediate cognisance of an offence reported in writing by the police.[66] An ATC can, in fact, be more powerful than both a Session Court and a Magistrate Court, especially in cases that fall within the jurisdiction of the ATA. Since ATA has been given overriding effect on all other laws for the time it is in force, courts created under other laws have to yield to the jurisdiction of the ATCs (when cases can be tried under ATA and any other law). This provision became critically contentious when it came to offences relating to juveniles. A number of pleas were brought to different high courts asking for trial in the juvenile courts, which were created under the Juvenile Justice System Ordinance 2000 because juveniles required special attention, care, and protection. However, the courts have consistently pointed to the technical/procedural difficulty of the overriding effect of the ATA over all other laws. The courts have thus decided that ATCs could try juveniles.[67] However, this allowing of ATCs to try juveniles is partly based on the political fact of involvement of minors in terrorism, especially in cases of suicide bombing.

In one interesting case, an argument was made that ATCs get their jurisdiction on the basis of the nature of offence committed, while juvenile courts on the basis of age of the offender—therefore suggesting that the superior judiciary had a choice, and in this way it could choose the latter. However, the court maintained its earlier precedence of the overriding effect of the ATA over all other laws.[68] Nevertheless, the superior judiciary has in at least one case decided that the punishment (life sentence) prescribed in the juvenile ordinance should be given precedence over the punishment (death sentence) in the ATA. The court rejected the plea for issuing death sentences to juvenile.[69]

Although an ATC exercises the same powers as a Session Court, it cannot in practice grant bails. Since the trial is supposed to be carried out on a day-to-day basis, and since adjournments are hardly allowed, it makes sense that the granting of bail is restricted. A High Court ruled in 2001 that

> Powers under S.30(4) of the said Act being not analogous to Ss. 497 & 498, Cr.P.C., therefore powers vested in Special Court relating to bail were to be exercised with utmost care and caution in reasonable, justified and judicious manner keeping in view the intention of the Legislature.[70]

In the same year, an Ordinance was passed to remove subsection 30(4).[71] Now the offences under the ATA (1997) are practically considered as non-bailable.

One point of jurisdictional concern for the ATCs relates to the question how they could respond to petitions of *qisas* (or acceptance of blood money by the legal heirs of the victims). A high court decided that although *qisas* is an Islamic right of the legal heirs of a victim, it is granted through courts in the interest of justice. Such right is available when the crime is of a private nature—between two individuals not involving the state. But in cases of terrorism, the actions are considered to be done against the state, because the purpose is to target larger sections of society with the aim of creating fear and insecurity. Therefore, courts could not grant the right of *qisas* in cases of terrorism to legal heirs of individual victims. Furthermore, the court ruled that such denial of right of *qisas* is not against the spirit or injunctions of Islam, nor of the constitution.[72]

At this stage, I want to once again point to the Anglo-American context for comparative purposes. In the United States, after 9/11, one of the first steps that the Bush Administration took was to set up military tribunals. The November 13 Order, 2001, sanctioned special tribunals for terrorists. The Secretary of Defense appointed "one or more military commissions." The Defense Secretary also determined where the commissions might "sit at any time and any place" as well as designated attorneys for prosecution. The tribunals were given "exclusive jurisdiction with respect to offenses by the individual" who would not be allowed to "seek any remedy" in any US or foreign court. The tribunals were given the authority to award punishments, "including life imprisonment or death." After the commission made a decision, the record had to be directed to the President or the Secretary of Defense "for review and final decision."

However, the Supreme Court's decision in *Hamdan* struck a blow to the military tribunals.[73] The Supreme Court held that the rules and procedures of the tribunals violated the Uniform Code of Military Justice and the 1949 Geneva Convention. According to the Supreme Court, the rules and procedures should be those of a court martial "insofar as practicable." Justice Stevens held that in Hamdan's case, the military tribunal violated Common Article 3 (CA3) of the Geneva Convention, which applied to "armed conflict not of an international character occurring in the territory of one of the High Contracting Parties." The article prohibits

> ...the passing of sentences and the carrying out of executions without previous judgment pronounced by a regularly constituted court affording all the judicial guarantees which are recognized as indispensable by civilized people.

As the court invoked CA3, it apparently resulted in a juridical conundrum. The conflict was international, as the Bush administration claimed. But it did not involve two states, as the CA3 required. Evidently, al-Qaeda was not a contracting party. Then the conundrum was whether "civilised people" would yield similar judicial guarantees to those who were not civilised or who did not engage in "civilised warfare". The court believed they should, but the administration believed they should not.

As a response to the decision in *Hamdan*, and, in fact, the increased judicial reviews by the courts, the administration moved Congress to pass the Military Commission Act, 2005. The act prohibited invocation of the Geneva Convention in American Courts and stripped the courts of jurisdiction to hear *habeas corpus* applications of the non-citizens in Guantanamo.[74] It is worth noticing that for aliens there is no guaranteed right of habeas in all these states under discussion—the United States, the United Kingdom, and Pakistan.

Evidence

Although the ATA (1997) provided for speedy disposal of cases (i.e., within seven days), it did not say much about how evidence could be examined and cross-examined in such a short period of time. On the other hand, the superior judiciary increased this difficulty by ruling in a number of cases that the appraisal of evidence should follow the standard requirements of the Criminal Code.[75] This meant that the appraisal of evidence under the ATA (1997) had to take care of the Law of Evidence (1984), the Criminal Procedure Code (1898), and the Fair Trial Act (2014). The ATA (1997) also allows evidence collected from digital data of cell phones, telephones, emails, and social media accounts as admissible, which should also be appraised through forensic within this short time period. However, to help expedite the process, the government set up a research cell in anti-terrorism departments to test digital data as well as undertake data-mining.

Moreover, the judiciary has also stressed upon determining the quality of evidence rather than the quality of it.[76] This emphasis upon the regular procedure of appraisal and quality of evidence leads to three different kinds of evidence: (a) "wholly reliable", (b) "halfly reliable" or partially reliable, and (c) "unreliable." The wholly reliable evidence does not need corroborative evidence, while the partially reliable does need corroborative evidence.[77] The superior courts have also advised that in the case of partially reliable evidence, the (trial) courts need to be dynamic and pragmatic, such that they keep in mind all the facts and circumstances and ignore any minor technical lapses made by the investigating agencies.[78]

The courts have also often divided evidence in two other categories: (a) substantive or direct evidence and (b) corroborative or indirect evidence. The substantive evidence, if wholly reliable, does not need further evidence or testimonies. It includes ocular evidence of a witness. The corroborative evidence, on the other hand, is supporting and/or confirming evidence, which adds weight and strength to the partially reliable substantive evidence. It includes testimonies, facts and/or circumstances, and forensic reports. Without substantive or direct evidence it often becomes difficult to convict a suspect.[79] For instance, in a number of cases the courts have rejected corroborative medical/forensic evidence in absence of substantive evidence as not enough for conviction.[80] In one case, the Supreme Court has said,

> Even if in the present case such DNA report was admitted into evidence and relied upon, it would in no manner be sufficient to connect the necks of the accused person with the commission of the crime when the bulk of other evidence against them was found to be unbelievable.[81]

Similarly, the courts have decided that a piece of corroborative evidence based on an email could not be taken as substantive.[82]

To build a successful case, the prosecution needs to present evidence carefully and systematically such that each piece of information contributes to making the case beyond reasonable doubt. For instance, a superior court has advised: "Men could lie, but circumstances would not; [however, if] circumstances could mislead, courts were required to exercise great care and caution in considering each and every piece of evidence and ensure that it would lead to one single conclusion and exclude any other possibility except that of the guilt of accused."[83] Thus the appraisal of evidence involves a number of steps: the evidence should be direct and/or substantive; any corroborating evidence and factual circumstances should be consistent with the direct evidence; and the whole statement of witnesses should be assessed and cross-examined, with the entire process leading to one single conclusion, which is beyond reasonable doubt. The courts have emphasised that any successful prosecution needs to be built on quality evidence rather than quantity of evidence.[84] In a moment, I illustrate the significance of systematic appraisal of evidence under the ATA (1997) by discussing a recent case of child rape and murder.

However, an interesting feature of the ATA (1997) is that by prescribing a regular criminal procedure, it does not suggest inverting the burden of proof principle as the Foreigners Act (1946) and the STAA (1975) did. Another such aspect relates to the onus of the prosecution and defence. The courts have maintained that the initial onus does not lie upon the accused.[85] Similarly, the courts have maintained that "mere suspicion, [no matter] however grave, cannot take [the] place of evidence...."[86] The 1975 Act had provided that if an article/instrument was found in possession of the suspect, then he would be considered to have designed to commit the act unless he could prove otherwise. In this way, the Act had partially inverted the principle of innocent unless proven guilty. Prior to the 1975 Act, this inversion had already been done in the Foreigners Act 1946, wherein it was provided that the individual would have to prove his identity and innocence rather than the state needing to establish it. In the case of Foreigners Act, it was aimed at foreigners, but with the 1975 Act, however, it became directed at citizens.

Zainab case (2018)

At the beginning of 2018, a case of child rape and murder in the district of Kasur, Punjab, caught the attention of both electronic and social media. The incident created shock, fear, and anger among the people around the country, but especially in Kasur, Punjab. What added to the fears of the people was the fact that the police were unable to find, identify and arrest the culprit for several weeks. Finally, when he was identified through a DNA identification test, there arose questions about the ability of the police and prosecution to get him convicted. On the one hand, the people were outraged and wanted to see the accused punished as soon as possible, but on the other, the Punjab government was faced with the challenge of getting the accused convicted under the ATA (1997), which employs the regular law of evidence. In the trial court (ATC), the government had been able to get the accused convicted in just four days of rigorous day-to-day hearings. The ATC sentenced the accused to death. However, the case now goes to the Lahore High Court, where the questions of law, criminal procedure, and due process will be debated. The case will also be placed in the backdrop of earlier precedents. The major questions that the court will have to look into include: (a) whether the action (*Actus Reus*) fall within the scope of the ATA (1997), (b) whether the purpose (*mens rea*) was to cause terror and insecurity, (c) whether there was design to intimidate the public, (d) whether the corroborative evidence draws a complete picture beyond reasonable doubt, and (e) whether due process was granted to the accused. Although the action, consisting of murder and rape, falls within the definition of terrorism in the ATA (1997), what might be challenging to prove are the purpose and/or design of the terrorist act. The accused is said to have committed several child rapes and murders before as well, so the defence might argue that his actions have personal sexual and psychological instincts behind them, rather than the political motives of spreading fear and insecurity. It is true that the consequence of his action spread intense fear, insecurity, and anger, but then, the higher courts have set precedents that instruct that the element of consequences and gravity are not so material. In order to get the decision of the trial court upheld by the High Court, the prosecution will have to present fully reliable evidence. However, we know that neither direct evidence in the form of eyewitnesses nor any other substantive evidence is available. What is available is corroborative forensic evidence found from the scene of crime (for instance, the jacket of the accused) and medical evidence consisting of the DNA test. Other pieces of the evidence are also corroborative, which will need careful and systematic presentation along with forensic and medical evidence to make a case beyond reasonable doubt. Any discrepancy at stage will make the case weaker.

Why ATCs could not deliver

Although ATCs were set up to provide speedy justice in cases of terrorism, they could not remain speedy in the long run. One of the reasons for this was that their dockets became cluttered with cases of ordinary criminal nature. The prosecution in these criminal cases either could not distinguish well between cases of terrorism and cases of ordinary criminal nature, or they just wanted to take the shorter route. The difference was about the object of the offence. Terrorism cases were those whose goal was to spread fear, terror, and insecurity in society. In other words, although the offences mentioned in the ATA (1997) were almost the same as in the Panel Code—for instance, murder, arson, kidnapping, drug trafficking and so forth—the motive of these offences in the case of terrorism had to be indirectly aimed at causing terror, fear, and insecurity in the society at large. Thus this practice of taking the shorter route resulted in cluttering of dockets of ATCs. On the other hand, there was no mechanism at the filing-of-case level where court registrar or court's attorney could distinguish cases of terrorism from cases of criminal nature. The burden of finding or proving the object hence fell on the ATCs. And they could prove the object only after rehearsing the process of hearing the case. According to one report, about seventeen thousand cases were under trial in different ATCs throughout the country by the end of 2014, and a big number of these cases (85%) were estimated to be of ordinary criminal nature.[87]

Notes

1 In the Protection of Pakistan Act (2014) and the Army (Amendment) Act (2015) it has been provided clearly that political protests and peaceful civil processions will not be classified as terrorism. I will return to this point in the next chapter.
2 Kennedy, "The Creation and Development of Pakistan's Anti-Terrorism Regime, 1997–2002," 411.
3 *Basharat Ali v. Special Judge, Anti-Terrorism Court-II, Gujranwala*, PLD 2004 Lahore 199.
4 Section 3(1) of India's The Terrorist and Disruptive Activities (Prevention) Act 1985 reads:

> whoever with intent to overawe the Government as by law established to strike terror in the people or any section of the people or to alienate any section of the people or to adversely affect the harmony amongst different sections of the people does nay act or thing by using bombs. Dynamic or other explosive substance or inflammable substances or firearms or other lethal weapons or poisons or noxious gases or other chemicals or any other substances (whether biological or otherwise) of a hazardous nature in such

a manner as to cause, or as is likely to cause, death of, or injuries to, any person or persons or damage to, or destruction of, property or disruption of any supplies or services essential to the life of the community commits a terrorist act.

5 Ordinance No. XIII, August 27, 1999.
6 The Anti-Terrorism (Second Amendment) Ordinance, 1999 (December 2, 1999).
7 Ordinance No. XXIX of 2000.
8 Ordinance No. XXXIX of 2001.
9 The offences that were punishable for six months imprisonment were now to be punished for five years and that of five years by ten years.
10 The phrase is also used in the Military Commissions Act, 2005. The act speaks of those persons who have either engaged in hostilities or have "purposefully and materially supported hostilities" against the United States and its allies.
11 McCain, "Remarks by Senator John McCain in Support of the Conference Report of the National Defense Authorization Bill."
12 *Mumtaz Ali Khan Rajban v. Federation of Pakistan*, PLD 2001 SC 169.
13 *Mehram Ali v. Federation of Pakistan*, MLD 1998 1411.
14 Act XIII of 2013.
15 *Basharat Ali v. Special Judge, Anti-Terrorism Court*, PLD 2004 Lahore 199.
16 *Ibid.*; *Jahangir Akbar Awan v. State*, PLD 2000 Karachi 89.
17 *Basharat Ali v. Special Judge, Anti-Terrorism Court-II, Gujranwala*, PLD 2004 Lahore 199.
18 *Hazoor Bakhsh v. State*, PLD 2008 Karachi 487.
19 See *Tariq Hakim v. the State*, 2011 YLR 19 Lahore.
20 *Asadullah v. Muhammad Tariq and 2 others*, PLD 2006 Lahore 651.
21 YLR 2013 Lahore 92.
22 *Ayub Khan v. the State*, 2009 MLD 793.
23 *Asghar Ali Mubarak v. Special Judge, Anti-Terrorism Court*, 2016 P. Cr. L. J., 1108.
24 *Michroo v. State*, 2015 YLR 2617 Karachi; *Jahangir v. State*, 2011 YLR 2330 Lahore; *Soorat Khan v. Anti-Terrorism Court, Sibi and 7 others*, PLD 2010 Quetta 52; *Sarfaraz v. Special Judge Anti-Terrorism Court Bahawalpur and 3 others*, 2005 MLD 1096 Lahore.
25 *Taj Muhammad. Judge Anti-Terrorism Court and another*, PLD 2003 Lahore 588.
26 *Muhammad Amjad v. The State*, PLD 2003 SC 704. On the other hand, Karachi High Court has ruled that "the criteria to judge was the gravity of offence; and its modus operandi, whether (or not) it created a sense of fear or insecurity in the society." 2011 P. Cr. L. J. 1370 Karachi.
27 *Mumtaz Ali Khan Rajban v. Federation of Pakistan*, PLD 2001 S. C. 169.
28 *Muhammad Amjad v. The State*, PLD 2003 SC 704.
29 *Gul Muhammad v. The State*, PLD 2012 Quetta 22.
30 The Anti-Terrorism (Amendment) Ordinance, 2002.
31 Kennedy, "The Creation and Development of Pakistan's Anti-Terrorism Regime, 1997–2002," 407–408.
32 *Mehram Ali v. Federation of Pakistan*, PLD 1998 SC 1445; Also see *Jamiat-Islam Pakistan through Syed Munawar Hassan v. Fedeartion Of Pakistan*, PLD 2000 SC 111.
33 *Jamiat-Islam Pakistan through Syed Munawar Hassan v. Fedeartion Of Pakistan*, PLD 2000 SC 111.
34 Ibid.
35 *Ghulam Abbad v. Mushtaq Ahmed*, 2014 YLR 201.
36 A point can be made that the Actions (in Aid of Civil Power) Regulations, 2011, have defined internment. However, this definition comes in a limited context

of army operations. Thus the definition of internment is given in the following words:

> ...restricting any person to a defined premises during the period the counter-insurgency operation is ongoing in order to incapacitate him from committing any offence or further offences under this Regulation or any other law, for securing peace in the defined area.

S.R.O. 11 (6)P/L/2011, § 2(g).

37 *State of Tamil Nadu v. Senthil Kumar and another*, AIR 1999 SC 971.

38 *Government of East Pakistan v. Rowshan Bijaya Shaukat Ali*, PLD 1966, SC 286; *Khawaja Mureed Hussain v. Government of the Punjab, Home Department, Lahore and 6 Others*, 2013 P. Cr. L. J., 312.

39 PLD 2011 Lahore 1451; 2013 P. Cr. L. J., 312.

40 *Muhammad Yousaf Farooqi v. Government of Punjab*, 2012 P. Cr. L. J., 905; 2013 P. Cr. L. J. 312.

41 The Court declared the detention order of a suspect because his name was not first included in the list created under Section 11-EE and the Fourth Schedule (Shaheena Nargis v. District Officer Police, 2006 P. Cr. L. J. 33).

42 *Abdur Rauf v. Chief Commissioner*, PLD 2006 Lahore 111.

43 *Sakina Mai v. Government of Punjab*, 2007 P. Cr. L. J. 956.

44 *Ameera Khanum v. Government of Punjab*, 2007 P. Cr. L. J. 527.

45 *Sakina Mai v. Government of Punjab*, 2007 P. Cr. L. J. 956; *Abdur Rauf v. Chief Commissioner*, PLD 2006 Lahore 111.

46 It is worth noticing that these offences that are classified as scheduled offences were given priority or overriding effect over non-scheduled offences, just as anti-terrorism laws and trials enjoy overriding effect over other laws and trials. (Sections 2 and 3 read: "Where an indictment contains a count alleging a scheduled offence and another count alleging an offence which at the time the indictment is presented is not a scheduled offence, the other count shall be disregarded.")

47 Schedule 1 Part II Entry 11 sub-entry 3.

48 Schedule 1 Part II Entry 13.

49 In *Hamdi* the Supreme Court held that the AUMF conceded to the President the power to detain US citizens captured on battlefield (542 *Hamdi* 507, 517). The NDAA 2011–2012 has recently codified the detention without trial of American citizens apprehended anywhere in the world, including in the United States. Section 412 of the Patriot Act authorizes the Attorney General to detain foreign nationals he/she certifies as terrorist suspects without a hearing and without a showing that they pose a danger or a flight risk.

50 Response of the United States to Request for Precautionary Measures—Detainees in Guantanamo Bay, Cuba, July 2002, 41 I.L.M. 1015, 1020–21 (2002).

51 *Hamdi v. Rumsfeld 2004*, 542:540.

52 *Hamdi v. Rumsfeld*, 542 US 507, 573 (Supreme Court 2004), 542:573.

53 Ibid., 542:590.

54 NDAA Section 1031. A "covered person" is one

> 1 ...who planned, authorized, committed, or aided the terrorist attacks that occurred on September 11, 2001, or harbored those responsible for those attacks.
> 2 ...who was a part of or substantially supported al-Qaeda, the Taliban, or associated forces that are engaged in hostilities against the United States or its coalition partners, including any person who has committed a belligerent act or has directly supported such hostilities in aid of such enemy forces.

55 *Shahid Hussain v. the National Accountability Bureau (NAB)*, 2015 P. Cr. L. J. 883.

56 *Nazeer alias Wazeer v. the State*, PLD 2007 SC 202.
57 *Liaquat Hussain and others v. Federation of Pakistan*, PLD 1999 SC 504.
58 *Mehram Ali v. Federation of Pakistan*, PLD 1998 1145.
59 *Mehram Ali v. Federation of Pakistan*, 1998 MLD 1411.
60 Kennedy, "The Creation and Development of Pakistan's Anti-Terrorism Regime, 1997–2002," 401.
61 The Anti-Terrorism (Third Amendment) Ordinance, 1999 (December 2, 1999).
62 Kennedy, "The Creation and Development of Pakistan's Anti-Terrorism Regime, 1997–2002," 405.
63 *Muhammad Rasool v. the State*, PLD 2012 Quetta 122.
64 *Zahida Rizvi v. The State*, 2011 YLR 1319.
65 *Faisal Iqbal v. The State*, PLD 1998 Lahore 371.
66 NLR 2005 Cr. L. J. 158.
67 *Muhammad Rasool v. the State*, PLD 2012 Quetta 122; *Qamar Hussain Shah v. The State*, PLD 2006 Karachi 331; *Meraj Hussain v. Anti-Terrorism Court*, 2007 P. Cr. L. J., 1011; *Ketno v. Judge, Anti-Terrorism Court*, 2005 MLD 353.
68 *References by Judge Special Court II* (Criminal References Nos. 32 and 33 of 2005), 2006 P. Cr. L. J. 921.
69 *Nematullah v. Abdul Kahar*, 2006 YLR 1036.
70 *Muhammad Shareef v. State*, 2001 YLR 900.
71 Ordinance No. XXXIX of 2001.
72 *Gul Muhammad v. the State*, PLD 2012 Quetta 22.
73 *Hamdan v. Rumsfeld*, 548 US 557 (Supreme Court 2006).
74 Section 7 of the MCA 2005 amended Section 2241 of United States Code 28 ousting the jurisdiction of courts. Also see the Detainee Treatment Act, 2005, which apparently strips the jurisdiction of courts. It should be noted that the Patriot Act, 2002, had originally restricted *habeas corpus* jurisdiction of courts in cases relating to non-citizens. However, on certain procedural requirements the courts did exercise review.
75 For instance, in one case the judiciary said:

> Law does not make any distinction in the matter of appreciation of evidence in a case under Anti-Terrorism Act, 1997 or under normal criminal law. Credibility of witnesses has to be measured with the same yardstick, whether it is an ordinary crime or a crime striking terror society. Law does not make any distinction either in leading evidence in its assessment. Rule is one and the same, that is intrinsic worth of testimony and fact.

Nadeem v. State, 2014 P. Cr. L. J. 374 FSC.
76 *Bao Saleem v. The State*, 2008 MLD 647; *Sahibzar v. The State*, 2003 P. Cr. L. J. 699; *Saleem Khan and others v. The State and others*, 2001 P. Cr. L. J. 503.
77 *Imran Ashraf v. The State*, 2001 SCMR 424.
78 *Ibid*; *Ghulam Hussain v. State*, PLD 2007 SC 71.
79 *Ali Muhammad v. State*, 2011 YLR 3055.
80 *Azhar Hussain v. State*, PLD 2003 Lahore 217; *Muhammad Yusuf v. State*, 2012 YLR 1992.
81 *Azeem Khan and another Vs. Mujahid Khan and others*, 2016 SCMR 274.
82 *Qurban Ali and another v. The State*, 2007 P. Cr. L. J. 675.
83 *Suleman v. the State*, 2012 YLR 2395.
84 *Bao Saleem v. the State*, 2008 MLD 647; *Sahibzar v. The State*, 2003 P. Cr. L. J. 699; *Saleem Khan and others v. The State and others*, 2001 P. Cr. L. J. 503.
85 *Tariq Hakim v. the State*, 2011 YLR 1580.
86 *Jaffar Mehmood v. State*, 2016 YLR 846.
87 Hashim, "Army Courts to Try Pakistan Terror Suspects."

4 Expansion and entrenchment of the legal regime of security

Introduction

Pakistan has seen gradual increase in terrorism over the past two decades. In the early years of the War on Terror (2001–2004), there took place hardly any terrorist incidents worth attracting the State's attention. The Tehreek-e-Taliban Pakistan (TTP) only began to emerge in the years 2004 and 2005, especially after the first drone attack in the country. This drone attack targeted a *jirga* (tribal meeting consisting of elders) between State representatives and local tribal supporters of the foreign and Afghan Taliban in South Waziristan. Feeling betrayed by the clandestine drone attack, the foreign and local militants began to reorganise themselves in order to start a violent campaign against the Pakistani state. For the next couple of years, the TTP kept on growing and spreading throughout the Federally Administered Tribal Areas (FATA). In 2005, the government took initial steps to quell the fledgling TTP, but it failed. Eventually, the government signed a peace deal with them, which gave them room to further thrive and spread. In 2007, when the government carried out a military operation at the Red Mosque in the capital city of Islamabad to clear it of alleged storing of weapons and hiding of militants, the TTP, along with various other smaller religious armed organisations, found reason to propagate their agenda and speed up their campaign of violence. The following year, the Taliban, facilitated by the *Tehreek-e-Nafaz-e-Shariat-Mohammadi* (TSNM), began to infiltrate the Swat Valley and managed to take control of it. Their takeover of the valley forced the government to launch a large-scale military operation there. Although the Taliban was pushed out of the valley, they were not defeated or finished; they just moved to other border areas, especially to North Waziristan, where they reorganised themselves. From there, they kept launching terrorist attacks until 2014.

After the operation in the Swat Valley, several smaller operations were carried out in various parts of the FATA and Provincially Administered Tribal Areas (PATA) as well as in other parts of the country, especially in Karachi. With these military operations and the retaliations from the Taliban, the incidence of terrorism in the country began to dramatically rise. During these military operations, the Armed Forces arrested and detained thousands of suspects who were placed in internment centres set up in various parts of the FATA. Initially, the Armed Forces handed over a number of suspects to prosecution departments of the police to try them in the Anti-Terrorism Courts (ATCs). However, the Armed Forces were frustrated to see that the courts were unable to ensure high rates of convictions, especially because of the requirements of evidence and the standard criminal procedure. The acquittal of suspects, and the slow pace of the criminal procedure through various stages in different courts, did not meet the expectation of the Armed Forces in their efforts against terrorism. To address this frustration, the government in 2011 issued two regulations—the Actions (in Aid of Civil Power) Regulations (AACPRs). These regulations legally allowed the Armed Forces to set up internment centres and detain suspects for the duration of military operations. During the internment, the Armed Forces could also engage in interrogation of suspects to prepare detailed charge sheets against them.

By 2013, when Nawaz Sharif was elected for a third time to government, the country was faced with the highest level of terrorism and violence ever seen in history. According to the Global Terrorism Index report, in terms of the impact of terrorism, Pakistan was ranked second in the world in 2011. About 910 terrorist incidents took place and caused 1468 fatalities and 2459 injuries.[1] In the next two years, the graph of terrorism rose even higher. In 2013, Pakistan ranked third on the Global Terrorism Index, with 1933 terrorist incidents causing 2345 fatalities and 5035 injuries. According to the report, "terrorism increased significantly in Pakistan in 2013, with a 37% increase in deaths and 28% increase in injuries since 2012."[2] The report further said:

> More than 500 cities in Pakistan had at least one terrorist incident in 2013, with two or more incidents occurring in 180 cities. Of all attacks 16 per cent occurred in the largest city of Karachi in the south. However, the majority of attacks occurred in the north closer to the border with Afghanistan. This includes cities such as Peshawar, Quetta and Jamrud, which combined, had more attacks than Karachi.[3]

According to another source, civilian deaths in 2012 and 2013 were more than 3000 each year, including 732 casualties of security personnel in 2012 and 676 in 2013.[4] However, the number of terrorist groups decreased from twenty-nine groups in 2012 to twenty-three in 2013.[5] It is also worth mentioning here that some of the most violent terrorist incidents took place immediately after Sharif's election. For instance, in July 2013, a suicide bomber attacked a funeral at the Police Line in Quetta. The attack resulted in the deaths of forty people, mostly security personnel. The next month, a church was attacked in Peshawar by two suicide bombers, killing eighty-seven people and injuring many more.

In the backdrop of this growing wave of terrorism, the newly elected government of Nawaz Sharif introduced the Protection of Pakistan Ordinance (PPO). About a month later, Raheel Sharif was appointed the new Army Chief. He would later take the decision of carrying out a large-scale military operation, named *Zarb-e-Azb*, in North Waziristan in June 2014. It is primarily after this operation that the level of terrorism began to plummet in the country. According to the Global Terrorism Index report (2015), Pakistan saw its highest decrease in terrorism-related deaths from 2013 to 2014:

> Whilst Pakistan saw a seven per cent reduction in incidents and a 25 per cent reduction in deaths from 2013 to 2014, the country still has the fourth highest number of deaths from terrorism in the world. There were 1,760 people killed from terrorism in Pakistan in 2014.[6]

However, towards the end of the year (2014), the Taliban once again launched several attacks. Among these was the deadliest-ever attack, on a school in Peshawar and which killed about 150 children. The cold-blooded killings of school children shocked the people across the country and impelled the government to revise its security policy. Accordingly, a National Action Plan (NAP) was put together to expand both legal and physical security infrastructure. In the NAP it was declared that the government would set up military courts for speedy trials of terrorists. Apart from creating military courts, the Sharif government decided to lift the moratorium on the execution of death sentences. The government wanted to enable the military courts not only to award death sentences but also to execute them within shortest possible time. In this way, the government envisaged a strategy to create deterrence effect on the minds of terrorists.

It is in this backdrop of growing terrorism that more security legislation was passed, which led to further expansion and entrenchment of the legal regime of security in the country.

What is entrenchment?

Before we discuss the expansion and entrenchment of security laws in Pakistan, it is an imperative to define our understanding of the term entrenchment. First I present the general understanding in the legal scholarship, and then I present my own understanding as I employ in this chapter. From the point of view of law, entrenchment, or more specifically, legislative entrenchment, refers to the practice of lawmaking by which laws (or certain provisions in it) are made difficult to amend and repeal. There are two broad types of legislative entrenchment—qualified/unqualified and symmetric/asymmetric. The qualified entrenchment seeks certain qualifications or conditions—for instance, a special procedure for altering law. The unqualified entrenchment is absolute, and it does not allow alteration in the law in any circumstance.[7] On the other hand, a symmetric entrenchment means explicit and direct, while asymmetric entrenchment means indirect and implicit introduction of prohibition of alteration of law.[8] In constitutional theory, the concept of entrenchment has generated considerable debate about its legitimacy, legality, and utility,[9] and we know that most constitutional democracies provide for certain entrenched provisions, doctrines, rights, and duties.

In this chapter, I engage the concept of entrenchment as a backdrop to highlight two related tendencies towards entrenchment in the security laws of Pakistan: that (a) politically, security laws show the tendency to outlive the necessity (e.g., the War on Terror) that bring them into force, and (b) legally, they tend to seek their place in constitutional law (or statutes), and thereby create a more permanent legal status. Once entrenched—both politically and legally—the permanence of the security law is established by references to either different articles of the Constitution or to constitutional court cases. Another way the government affords them permanence and constitutionality is the direct cover through a constitutional amendment. In this way, security law gets not only legislative entrenchment, but also judicial entrenchment, such that the judiciary is not be able to strike them down.

Expansion and entrenchment

The Actions (in Aid of Civil Power) Regulations, 2011 (AACPR)

From 2007 to 2011, the War on Terror in the FATA and PATA went on without proper constitutional sanction. About a dozen military operations were carried out in different parts of the FATA and the PATA. During these operations, hundreds of suspected terrorists (both tribal men and aliens) were detained, investigated, with some also handed over to the police and other LAEs and/or produced before the ATCs. As the operations went in the tribal areas, there arose the question about their legality and proportionality, especially regarding the use of force, massive indefinite detentions, and practices of investigation. In June 2011, the government responded by invoking the emergency Article 245 of the Constitution, which provides for calling the Armed Forces in aid of civil authority.[10] The government thus issued two identical notifications through the offices of the President and the Governor (KPK) under Article 247, which authorises the government to make regulations for the "peace and good government" of tribal areas. The notifications provided retrospective legality to all the operations carried out since February 1, 2008.

What is significant about the AACPRs is that they brought the FATA and the PATA under the anti-terrorism legal regime for the first time. Although the War on Terror had been going on in these border territories since 2004, there was hardly any legal framework determining the legal contours of the war. Apart from this territorial expansion of the anti-terrorism legal regime to the border territories, the AACPRs also envisaged expansion of its legal terrain, i.e., certain new legal aspects were added to elements of the use force, detention and criminal procedure.

Since the military operations involved a wide range of force used—from firearms to heavy artillery and air strikes—the AACPRs had to cross the earlier limit on the use of force set in the ATA (1997). However, the basis for the use of force in the AACPRs was the doctrine of necessity, which was same as in the previous anti-terrorism laws. Similarly, the principle of proportionality in the use of force provided in the AACPRs was the same as in the ATA (1997). But the AACPRs (for the first time) provided for collateral damage, evacuation or displacement of people, and the loss of life of vulnerable persons. These new aspects, which related more to the law of war, seemed to tip the earlier equation of proportionality (between the offence and the use of force) given in the ATA (1997). Moreover, the AACPRs provided that in cases of misuse of force, an inquiry would be made, but only within the "hierarchy" of the Armed Forces. In the ATA (1997), although the clear provision was about an internal inquiry, there was also possibility of external judicial inquiry. Moreover, the ATA (1997) did not stop the higher courts from taking *suo moto* actions. On the other hand, in the case of the AACPRs there was only provision for internal committee inquiry of the Armed Forces or in the case of civilian officers misusing power by a civilian bureaucratic inquiry at the order of the Governor. In this way the courts were barred from exercising their jurisdiction.

One of the primary powers given to the Armed forces and other LEAs under the AACPRs was the power of long-term detention without trial. In various operations the Armed Forces had detained hundreds of terrorism suspects. However, there was no legal framework to regulate their detention. Thus the AACPRs were issued to fill this gap. Although the basic model envisaged for detention in the AACPRs resembled that of the constitutional model of preventive detention in Article 10, it went beyond that in terms of giving powers to the LEAs. For instance, in Article 10, preventive detention can be maintained for a maximum of ninety days at a time unless further extended by the Advisory Board, while in the AACPRs, it could be maintained for 120 days, and could be further extended as well. In fact, terrorism suspects could be kept in detention as long as military operations went on and the AACPRs were in place. It was also provided in the AACPRs that the prosecution of detainees would begin only after the operations ended. Moreover, under the AACPRs, an individual could be arrested anywhere in Pakistan and could be sent to a detention centre in the FATA or the PATA as long as the detaining authority was satisfied that the individual or the offence he/she committed related to the tribal areas. It is also interesting to notice that until the promulgation of the AACPRs, the Constitution's preventive detention model had not extended to the FATA and the PATA. Now, with the AACPRs, its more severe form extended to them. Furthermore, the AACPRs provided that a tribal subject could be apprehended and detained if it was "expedient for peace." The AACPRs provided for an "Oversight Board" to keep oversight of the procedure and conditions of detention. This Oversight Board was, however, not of judicial nature or involved judges of higher courts. Rather, it consisted of two military officers and two civil officers.

Although the AACPRs did not make any new special courts, they could engage the tribal quasi-judicial institution of *jirga* under the FCR and the ATCs. In this way, the AACPRs indirectly brought the tribal institution of *jirga* and the colonial law of the FCR under the umbrella of the legal security regime. What is pertinent to notice about *jirga* and the FCR is that they do not have well-developed rules about criminal procedure or evidence collection and admissibility. Moreover, suspects also lose the right to appeal to higher courts. The AACPRs, by providing for two different court systems—the FCR *jirga* and ATCs—effectively increased the government's control of the trial of terrorism suspects.

In the matter of evidence, the AACPRs provided for two types of evidence as well. One type was the evidence collected during detention, which is prepared in the form of a report or a *challan* and admissible in courts. This type of evidence was similar to the one given in the ATA (1997). However, the second type of evidence was different. It consisted of testimony given by a member of the Armed Forces or any other authorised official, which was to be considered as conclusive evidence against a suspect. This new form of evidence defied the Law of Evidence (1984) as well as the provisions of evidence in the earlier security laws.

Another legal aspect of the AACPRs worth noticing relates to the punishments it prescribed. This aspect becomes crucial given the second type of evidence, i.e., testimony of an officer admissible under it and the abridged criminal procedure of the FCR and the ATCs. The AACPRs allowed for a death sentence. It should also be noticed that the death sentence was not (or has never been) provided in the FCR. The AACPRs created the possibility of awarding a death sentence or other high punishments based on testimony and abridge criminal procedure. On the other hand, it is also interesting to notice that one of the major offences in the AACPRs is the same old offence of the waging of war or taking up arms against the state. Although this offence is not coterminous with the offence of terrorism as defined in the ATA (1997) and explained in the case law (see Chapter 3), it could now be tried under the FCR *jirga*. However, it is doubtful at best if the FCR *jirga* could understand this offence, given its long history in the Panel Code and case law on the one hand, and the lack of experience and understanding of it on the part of *jirgas* on the other.

Lastly, I want to point to how the AACPRs restricted the jurisdiction of the higher courts. Although the tribal areas have remained outside the territorial jurisdiction of the higher courts since the colonial times, the promulgation of the AACPRs produced the hope of getting relief from the higher courts. Accordingly, writ petitions were lodged in the Peshawar High Court. In one petition filed in 2014, it was argued that the Armed Forces were called in Khyber Agency in 2008. They had remained stationed there since then (even to the present day, March 30, 2018). Several operations were carried out and finished, but the forces were never called back. It was further argued that during these operations, excessive force was used to demolish houses, shops and other buildings as well as to arrest, detain and even kill innocent tribal people. Moreover, the petitioner argued that no compensation was given even in deserving cases, because there was no mechanism in place for identification of such cases. Thus the petitioner requested the High Court to set up a judicial inquiry and hold responsible those who violated the use of force, as well as to order for provision of compensations. The Court, however, expressed its jurisdictional incapacity to provide relief to the petitioner. The Court said:

> Thus in view of the peculiar backdrop of the facts of the case, there is double restriction imposed by the Constitution in exercise of the Constitutional jurisdiction of the High Court: firstly in view of the general bar contained in Article 247(7) of the Constitution regarding the matter relating to FATA and secondly, special restriction is imposed by Article 245(3) of the Constitution relating to the areas where Armed Forces are acting in aid of civil power. Thirdly, petitioner has made a prayer for constitution of judicial commission which does not come within the jurisdictional domain of the High Court, nor the High Court can direct the Armed Forces to lift the curfew from a particular area because it pertains to the strategy of war in the field which may not be controlled nor formulated by the courts. Rather it is the job of the field commanders who according to circumstances and situation prevailing in the field may evolve and implement the same.[11]

The Protection of Pakistan Act (2014)

In October 2013, a few months after his election to government, Nawaz Sharif promulgated the PPO. It was designed on the recommendations of an advisory committee set up earlier by him to amend the ATA (1997). The committee was set up in the wake of a massive paramilitary operation going on in Karachi. Upon the recommendations of the committee, seven amendments to the ATA 1997 were made to expand the scope of anti-terrorism laws (Act XX, 2013). Apart from that, the committee also made recommendations relating to reinforcing state security against potential "enemy aliens." These recommendations eventually resulted in the PPO, 2013. There was also speculation that the government gave the ordinance because it feared that the Supreme Court would question in its soon-to-be-given decision in *Muhabat Shah*, about the unauthorised removal of thirty-five internees from an internment centre in Malakand by the Armed Forces.[12]

On January 22, 2014, a second ordinance was issued to amend the 2013 Ordinance to further expand its legal scope. The second ordinance came with a Statutory Regulatory Order (SRO) from the Interior Ministry, which made it retrospectively in force since December 5, 2013. Finally, on July 9, 2014, the two ordinances were codified in an act called the Protection of Pakistan Act (PPA), 2014. Later, as the government feared that the Supreme Court might put the Act to judicial review, it gave the act constitutional cover under the 21st Amendment (2015). Thus, after the amendment, the Supreme Court had no choice but to uphold the PPA as constitutional.[13]

From the object of the PPA (2014) it seems that it was designed to achieve what two different (sets of) laws achieved in colonial times—the Defence of India Act 1919—and later, 1939—on the one hand and the Foreigners Act 1864 on the other. The broader dimensions of the PPA—the offences, the powers of the law enforcement agencies, special criminal procedure, and punishments—resemble closely that of the DIA 1919 and 1939. I have already pointed to how the latter colonial acts had also provided legal language and substance to security laws made in the post-independence time period—for instance, the Security of Pakistan Act, 1952, the Pakistan Defence Regulation (1965), and the Suppression of Terrorism Act, 1975.

Ostensibly there are two types of defined subjects in the PPA (2014): (a) enemy aliens and (b) militants. The original ordinance, the PPO (2013), had provided for one clear subject, the enemy alien. But within a year, three more subjects were introduced with the passage of two more laws—the Protection of Pakistan (Amendment) Ordinance (PPAO), 2014, and the PPA, 2014. These subjects were (a) the enemy combatant, (b) the militant, and (c) the citizen. The incorporation of the last of these subjects—that is, the citizen—has been an indirect consequence of the subject of militant. The category of enemy combatant, which was introduced in the PPAO (2014), was dropped from the later act—the PPA (2014).

The primary subject of the Protection of Pakistan laws was the category of enemy alien. This category was introduced for the first time in the PPO (2013), even though it was already available in Article 10(9) of the Constitution of 1973. It was, however, not defined in the Constitution. The definition of the category of enemy alien in PPO (2013) was worded in the following terms: an enemy alien was a person who (a) failed to establish his/her Pakistani citizenship, and (b) was found engaged in any of the offences of waging war, insurrection, and/or depredation. This definition of enemy alien was complicated in the PPA (2014). In this act, it was indirectly defined through the category of the militant. We will return to this complication in a moment. At this stage, I want to shed some light on the genealogical provenance of the category of enemy alien.

The definition of the category of combatant enemy in the PPAO (2014) comprised at least two main dimensions—identity of the individual and involvement in offences. First, a combatant enemy could be just "any person," unlike the enemy alien, who had to be an alien. Second, such a person should be involved in (a) raising of arms or waging war or in aiding and abetting of the same, (b) threatening of the security and integrity of the state, (c) committing or threatening to commit a Scheduled Offence, and/or (d) involved in depredation.

The category of combatant enemy was substituted with the category of militant in the PPA (2014). As mentioned earlier, the definition of the former category was retained from PPAO (2014) to define the latter category in PPA (2014). The definition was, however, broken down into five clauses, and some new phrases were added to it. For instance, in clause (c) of Section 2(f), two new phrases—"advocating" and "encouraging"—were added to define the act of engagement in an offence. Apart from that, a new offence of "violent struggle" was introduced. These new phrases and the offence of violent struggle were neither defined in the act, nor any other previous security law, nor in the case law. Hence it remained for the superior courts to define and fix the meaning of these new additions. With these additions, the scope of the Protection of Pakistan laws widened even beyond that of the ATA, 1997.

On the other hand, the Protection of Pakistan laws provided for a double burden of proof—one relating to proving (national) identity, the other to proving non-involvement in any scheduled offence. The first type of the burden of proof required an individual to prove his/her identity as a citizen of Pakistan—or of any other country—or to prove to have a different international legal status. The second type of the burden of proof required the individual to produce evidence to dispel the charge made against him/her by law enforcement agencies. In both cases, by placing the burden of proof on the individual, the Protection of Pakistan laws have inverted the principle of *innocent unless proven guilty.* Interestingly, this inversion was made in the face of clear decisions by higher courts to the contrary. For instance, in 2012, the Supreme Court, in *Suo Moto* Case No. 5 said:

> Indeed it is the cornerstone of the administration of justice in this country that all people, whether they appear to us innocent or guilty, are entitled to the due process of law and are to be deemed innocent until proven guilty after a fair trial.[14]

Apart from the court decisions, a provision for fair trial was introduced recently in the Constitution. In 2010, this provision was added by incorporating Article 10(A) in the Constitution through the 18th Amendment. This article requires that "for the determination of his civil rights and obligations or in any criminal charge against him a person shall be entitled to a fair trial and due process." Defining the scope of this article, the higher courts have explained that "regardless of the nature of allegations, every accused will be entitled to the due process of law and will be presumed innocent until proven guilty."[15] The courts have also made clear that these entitlements will be in both substantive and procedural laws.[16] This latter clarification is important because most of (or much part of) security laws is procedural in nature (see also this book's Introduction and Chapter 3).

In the PPA (2014), the government did not provide the rationale for inverting the principle of burden of proof. It should also be noticed that even in the ATA (1997), this principle was not derogated from. However, we can trace the root of this inversion, which I think goes back to the colonial law of the Foreigners Act, 1946, and its preceding version of 1864. In this act, Section 9 clearly provided that it was upon the individual to prove his/her national identity or international legal status. The act furthermore provided in Section 8 that if an individual was not able to prove his/her identity, and it was also difficult for the administration to ascertain the identity, then the central government would provide him/her with certain identity/nationality. For this purpose, the government would take into consideration his "appearance," which could include physical, ethnic, and/or cultural characteristics. Once a certain identity was accorded to the individual, such decision was final and could not be challenged in any court. However, if the individual did not agree to the given identity, then it was upon him/her to prove the alternate identity. Interestingly, in Section 10, the act provided the government the discretion to exempt any (foreign) individual or group of individuals from the application of this act.

One of the controversial aspects of the Protection of Pakistan laws related to the use of lethal force sanctioned in it. The law enforcement agencies under Section 3 of the PPO and PPA could shoot to kill an individual suspected to be an enemy alien or militant. This power to shoot had earlier been provided under the ATA (1997); however, it soon came under restrictions required by the higher courts, which I shall discuss soon. But, interestingly, we find that the power to kill was not provided in the Foreigners Act 1946, even though this act was the basic act that dealt with aliens.

Let me point out that Section 3 of the PPA, which provided for the use of lethal force, was not an original or new section. Rather, it was a copy of Section 5 of the ATA, 1997, as amended in 2004 and 2014. (However, some minor changes were introduced in it before the copy-paste was done.) First, the rank of police officer who could order to fire was reduced from BPS-17 (ATA) to BPS-15 (PPA). It also needs to be pointed out that in the Terrorist Affected Areas (Special Courts) Act (1992), this power was to be exercised by the Magistrate. Second, the provision to set up an internal inquiry was supplemented with a judicial inquiry in the PPA (2014). Lastly, following the amendment in the ATA through the Act VI of 2014, it was provided in the PPA 2014 that the power to fire would be used in the last resort.

It is worth noticing that the higher courts had placed some checks on the abuse of use of power under the ATA (1997). For instance, in a number of cases, the superior courts ruled that it was illegal to fire on an individual suspected of "likely to commit an offence even in all probability" unless he/she fired on the LEAs first. The courts have further ruled that the use of such power without certain checks could violate Article 9 of the Constitution, which made it a duty of the state to protect its citizens, as well as the guidelines provided by the Supreme Court in *Mehram Ali.*[17] In another case, the Lahore High Court ruled that in cases where this power was "misused for ulterior purpose or even otherwise [was] abused, [the] person responsible for the same would have to face the consequences."[18] An exemplary case in this connection was that of a young man killed by the Rangers in Karachi. While on routine duty, the Rangers apprehend the young man suspected of engaging in local theft and robbery. A group of half a dozen personnel first manhandled him, and then one of them shot him in the leg. The young man was badly injured. The Rangers personnel did not take him to a nearby hospital after injuring him, and therefore the young man bled to death. A private TV crew, which happened to be somewhere nearby, recorded this incident on camera, and later provided the video clip to local news channels. As the video clip showed the graphic scene of killing, it shocked the people across the country. The Supreme Court took a *suo moto* action of the incident. In its decision punishing the personnel, the Court noted that the young man was already overpowered, and hence there was no threat from him of causing harm anymore. Accordingly, the act of firing on him was beyond the scope of the powers accorded to the Rangers under Section 5 of ATA (1997). The Court also argued that the action was "negation of Article 9 of the Constitution." The Court further added that the incident was an act of "barbarism." In the Court's own words,

> Present was a classical case of highhandedness of the law enforcing agencies. Senior functionaries of both the agencies instead of feeling sense of responsibility and showing uprightness and honesty, were concealing the facts while appearing before the court.[19]

Although the Supreme Court intervened to correct a grievous incident of abuse of power, it did not intervene in a similar incident at a checkpoint in Kharotabad, Balochistan. In this incident, a group of aliens were fired at and killed. I'll return to this case in Chapter 6.

In Section 3 of both the PPO (2013) and PPA (2014)—the section providing for the use of force—it was provided that LAEs could arrest a suspect and search any building or premises without a warrant. Such arrests and searches could be made, the laws provided, if there was reasonable suspicion or credible information that a person had committed, or was about to commit, a scheduled offence. Here, in this section, the phrase "about to commit" was coterminous with the scope of the phrase "preparation to commit," which obviously increased the discretion of LEAs in the use of force.

On the other hand, the phrase "credible information" added in the PPO (2013) and the PPA (2014) was a new phrase. Unlike the phrase "reasonable suspicion," which reflected the requirement of objective satisfaction criteria beyond reasonable doubt, the phrase "credible information" did not carry the same meaning. It would be on the higher courts to fix the meaning of this phrase. However, apparently it seems that the purpose of introducing this phrase was to give cover to the use of force and make different types of evidence acceptable in cases of arrest and search. However, it is also significant to notice that "credible information" could be used only to effect arrest and search, but not to fire to kill (as it was used and defended in the Kharotabad incident).

The Protection of Pakistan laws also gave the power of detention. In the PPO (2013), it was mentioned that the order of detention of an enemy alien was to be written by the Secretary of Interior, or an officer of not below the rank BPS-21 who was specially designated for this purpose. For comparative purpose, we can notice that the legal structure of the provision in the PPO (2013)—especially the requirement that the Secretary Interior should issue orders of detention—was similar to the structure of detention laws in colonial times and the present anti-terrorism law in the United Kingdom. However, this requirement was lowered in the subsequent laws—the PPAO (2014) and PPA (2014). These laws instead provided that such orders could be issued by "the government," which meant it could be delegated to officers of lower ranks.

The detention powers given in the Protection of Pakistan laws were partially a response to the higher courts' challenge to the LEAs in cases of the "missing persons." In 2013, the Supreme Court in *Muhabat Shah* held that enforced disappearances included the unacknowledged and unauthorised removal of detainees from internment centres and that "no law enforcing agency can forcibly detain a person without showing his whereabouts to his relatives for a long period." The Protection of Pakistan laws and the AACPRs tried to give legal cover to secret detentions, transfer of detainees from one detention centre to another, and, in certain situations, non-disclosure of the grounds of detention. Moreover, the provision in the PPA (2014) that during detention, an internee could be handed over to the police or any other LEA for investigation purpose created the room for indirect disappearance (Section 6.3).

Another feature of the Protection of Pakistan laws was the creation of Prosecution Agency. Obviously the Armed Forces and the government were not satisfied with the performance of the prosecution department of the police. The prosecution departments were not well trained, especially in dealing with terrorism cases, and also lacked equipment and infrastructure like forensic laboratories. They also faced the issue of separation of powers and responsibility within different police departments—operations, investigation, and prosecution. Thus, in order to carry out speedy and effective prosecution, the Protection of Pakistan laws provided for setting up an "independent" Prosecuting Agency. A prosecutor general would head the agency, and he/she would be of forty-five years or more of age, and would have the experience of not less than ten years as an advocate at a High Court. The prosecutor general would issue instructions and guidelines for investigation and prosecution. However, this valuable provision could not materialise.

The Protection of Pakistan laws tried to give discretion to the executive to withhold information from the detainee. We know that similar provisions were also given in the Security of Pakistan Act (1952), the Maintenance of Public Order Ordinance (1960), and the Defence of Pakistan Rules (1965 & 1971). In the PPO (2013), an amendment was introduced through PPAO (2014) to provide for the power of withholding information from courts. The government explained that the purpose was to ensure the safety of detainees and prosecuting teams. The withholding of information under the PPO and the PPAO was possible because the subjects were not citizens, but enemy aliens or combatant enemies against whom the Constitution (and the Foreigners Act, 1946) gave discretionary powers to the Executive. In the PPA (2014), however, it became difficult to withhold information from courts because now citizens were also made subject to the law. Therefore, the provision was brought in line with the earlier decisions of the higher courts in the act.

The Pakistan Army (Amendment) Act 2015

On December 16, 2014, a small group of terrorists armed with automatic weapons and explosives attacked an Army Public School in Peshawar, Khyber-Pakhtunkhwa. The attack left more than 150 children dead, along with some teachers and school administration staff. The cold-blooded killings of schoolchildren shocked the entire country. It posed a question of the ability of the government and the Armed Forces to curb terrorism and ensure security. The Prime Minister rushed to Peshawar to meet the bereaved families as well as to chalk out a new strategy to fight terrorism. After a week-long meeting and negotiations with major political parties of the country, the Prime Minister, in a televised address, announced the twenty-point NAP.

Among the most important points of the NAP was the government's resolve to set up military courts, which would expedite the process of trying suspected terrorists. The NAP also allowed the Armed Forces to execute death sentences of the convicted terrorists. Other important points included the government's resolve to activate the National Counter Terrorism Authority (NACTA) to carry out operations against armed militias, counter hate speech and extremist material, stop financing of terrorist organisations, ensure that proscribed organisations did not re-emerge, establish a counterterrorism force, and take steps against violence in the name of religion. Moreover, the government envisaged taking practical steps for the registration of *madrasas*, stopping glorification of terrorists in the media and social media, and bringing around political reforms in the FATA and Baluchistan. The NAP obviously set forth a big agenda and made high promises to the people. However, today, four years later, we notice that much of the promises could not be achieved. This could also be guessed from the fact that the second meeting on the NAP took place only after nineteen months, when another shocking attack took place in Quetta on a lawyers' gathering, killing more than fifty people.[20]

For the purposes of this study, what interests us in the NAP is the resolve to create military courts. Within a month of announcing the NAP, the Sharif government passed two major acts—the Pakistan Army (Amendment) Act and the Constitution (21st Amendment) Act—to introduce military courts in the country. These acts authorised military courts to try civilians who claimed to or were known to belong to a terrorist organisation "using the name of religion or a sect." The courts were set up for two years ending on January 6, 2017.[21] However, by the end of two years, the government passed another set of amendments to extend the life of military courts for two more years. It is also worth noticing that the two acts were passed within the same day—i.e., on January 6, 2015—in both the houses of the Parliament. The next day, the President gave assent to the acts. This speed in the lawmaking procedure indicates how the government chose to dispense with adequate debate on the parliamentary floor on the details of these acts. Instead of the debate, political negotiations between the government and the opposition took place, especially during and after the All Parties Conference.

Although the immediate reason behind taking this drastic step of setting up military courts was the school killings in Peshawar, the long-term reason was the increasing frustration of the Armed Forces with the criminal procedure of the ATCs. Because this procedure followed due process, it often resulted in acquittal of terrorism suspects. The conviction rate in the ATCs was also quite low. Second, the ATCs were clogged by a massive number of cases that did not relate to terrorism but rather to ordinary murder, drug and arms trafficking, kidnapping, and so forth. By the time the army courts were introduced, there were around 17,000 cases under trial in ATCs. About 85% of these cases were not related to terrorism.[22] Thus the military courts were set up with the expectation to achieve a higher conviction rate, and interestingly, they did yield a 90% conviction rate. However, this became possible only by letting go the principle of due process and criminal procedural checks.

It is pertinent to note that the military courts were set up immediately after the passage of the PPA (2014), which had also envisaged special courts with speedy criminal procedure. However, for some reason, the government was not able to set up the PPA courts. In fact, the government's interest in the PPA courts dwindled with the possibility of setting up military courts. The government perhaps thought that, like ATCs under the ATA (1997), the PPA courts might also fail to achieve an increased conviction rate and become cluttered with cases of ordinary criminal nature. Moreover, since these courts would be headed by civilian judges, and therefore be subject to the oversight of superior courts, they might not be as so effective.

When seen in the long-term view of history, the setting up of military courts was not anything novel. The military courts were set up under both martial law governments and civilian governments. One of the first major court decisions, which brought the question of constitutionality of military court trying civilians, was in *F.B. Ali* (1972). In this case, the Supreme

Court decided that martial courts set up under the Army Act (1952) could validly try civilians who were involved in offences given in the Act. The Court's decision was based on approval of Ayub Khan's two ordinances—Ordinances III and IV of 1967—that had authorised the trial of civilians in martial courts. The Court reviewed the constitutionality of the ordinances and decided that they did not contravene the separation of powers doctrine (i.e., separation of the judiciary from the executive) or the fundamental rights guaranteed in the Constitution. This decision laid the legal foundation for justifying the creation of military courts for trying civilians. However, four years later, when Zulfikar Ali Bhutto imposed martial law in Karachi, Hyderabad, and Lahore and set up martial courts under it, the Lahore High Court struck them down.

Towards the end of the 1990s, the second government of Nawaz Sharif also tried to introduce military courts in Sindh, especially Karachi. After establishing the governor's rule in the province by dismissing the elected government, the Sharif government called in Armed Forces under the ordinance Pakistan Armed Forces (Acting in Aid of Civil Power) Ordinance, PAFO, on November 20, 1998. The ordinance gave the military authorities the power to try civilians. An officer at the rank of Brigadier or higher assigned the task to set up courts could "convene as many courts as may be deemed necessary to try offenders." The Ordinance also gave the Armed Forces the authority to create an appellate court, which would take appeals. In other words, appeals could not be made to civilian higher courts. Moreover, the government could transfer any cases from a regular criminal court to a military court.

What was remarkable about the military courts was that they were given the power to award death sentence. Apart from that, the ordinance also provided for the offence of "civil commotion" and made it punishable up to seven years. This offence was once part of the security regime of the colonial state. What was new about this offence now was that it was made "particularly subject to implementation by military courts," even though when "many of the activities defined as 'crimes' [in it] could also be interpreted as 'normal' political behavior."[23] Interestingly, the offence survived even when the ordinance could not, it and was incorporated in the ATA (1997).[24] On January 30, 1999, about a month and a half later, the ordinance was extended to the whole of the country. It was also amended once again to provide the power to try "absconders" in absentia in the military courts. However, in less than a month, on February 22, 1999, the Supreme Court struck down the ordinance in *Liaquat Hussain* (1999) as against the letter and spirit of the Constitution.

Now, about a decade and a half later, the third government of Nawaz Sharif once again introduced military courts. This time, however, the government also introduced a constitutional amendment to protect it from the judicial review of the Supreme Court, and a similar fate as that of the PAFO (1998). Let us have a look at the setup and procedure of the military courts created under the Army (Amendment) Act, 2015. These military courts are clearly different from the ATCs, as well as from regular criminal courts, in several ways.

First, the process and/or criteria for the selection of cases to be sent for military trials are not clear. While a military court can take cognisance of a case only when the Federal Government sends the case to it, the criteria upon which the government exercises its discretion for selecting cases are, however, not laid down. What is known is only the initial process: the provincial apex committees, comprising civil and military officials, select cases of individuals charged with terrorism-related offences and send them to the Ministry of Interior, which prepares a final list of cases and sends it to the military courts. Second, the location and timing are not known, and public access to these courts is denied. Even family members, media, and community organisations are not granted access. In fact, no one knows where and/or when the courts sit and trials take place. Third, detainees are not provided with detailed written charge sheets. They remain unaware of the grounds of the charges against them. Fourth, judges of the military courts are regular officers of the Armed Forces, who remain subject to their command and hierarchy. They do not enjoy security of tenure. Moreover, they do not have—or need to have—legal knowledge or training. A military court is composed of three to five serving officers of the Armed Forces.[25] A law officer of the Judge Advocate General branch of the Army advises the military courts, but he has no decision-making authority.

Fifth, just as in the ATA (1997) and the PPA (2014), the government can transfer any terrorism case from any other court to a military court. In such a case, there is no requirement for reappraisal of evidence in the military court. In other words, if the evidence were acceptable in the previous court, it would be acceptable in the military court as well. This means that evidence provision under other security laws—for instance, the SPA (1952), the ATA (1997), AACPRs (2011) and PPA (2014)—are indirectly made acceptable in the military courts. Moreover, many of the convictions could be based on confessions or self-incrimination. Sixth, in order to protect witnesses and others who are associated with a case in a military court, their identities are kept secret. Seventh, there is no right to public hearing in military courts. In the ATA and the PPA, there was discretion given to the judge to deny the right of public hearing to anyone or any group of people or to hear a trial via a camera. But in the case of these military courts, such right is denied from the beginning. Eighth, the court is not bound to provide a written and reasoned judgment or to keep detailed record. Ninth, there is no right to appeal against the judgment of a military court to a High Court or the Supreme Court. Appeals can be made only to a military appeals court, whose decision is final. A military appeals court is presided over by "an officer not below the rank of Brigadier." The Chief of Staff of the Army, or any other officer appointed by him, also sits in the appellate court.[26] Just as in the case of the military courts of first instance, the appeals court also does not require any special legal qualifications from their judges; rather, they remain subject to regular command and control. Similarly, a judge advocate belonging to the Judge Advocate General's Department of the Army may attend hearings, but he will not have a decision-making role. The military appeals court has the power to reduce or increase the punishment awarded by the military courts of first instance. Lastly, defendants are denied copies of detailed judgment.

The subjects of the military courts are individuals who belong to or are affiliated with a terrorist organisation "using the name of religion or a sect." In other words, the subjects are both aliens and citizens belonging to either an international terrorist organisation or a local sectarian armed group. The need for specifically mentioning terrorist organisations using the name of a religion or sect was to clarify that those organisations that are considered as nationalist, separatist, or as political parties would not be made subject to the military courts. The offences that are cognisable are certain acts of violence and terrorism: specifically, attacking military officers or installations; possessing, storing, or transporting explosives, firearms, suicide jackets, or other articles; using or designing vehicles for terrorist attacks; causing death or injury; creating terror or insecurity in Pakistan; and waging war against the state. Some of the offences are directly copied from the PPA (2014), whose courts could not become operational. These include crimes against minorities; killing, kidnapping, extortion, attacks, or assaults on government officials, members of the judiciary, foreign officials, tourists, media personnel, social workers, or other important personalities; destruction of or attacks on energy facilities, gas or oil pipelines, aircrafts and airports, national defence materials and institutions, and educational institutions; and illegally crossing national boundaries "in connection with" any of the aforementioned offences. Generally speaking, the list of offences in the Army Amendment Act (2015) also resembles that of the ATA. The latter act, on the other hand, borrowed offences from the Panel Code as I describe in the first chapter. The central or the oldest defined offences in this list were the Offences against the State, such as, for instance, the waging of war against the State. This category was available in the Panel Code, and before that, in the very first Regulations (for instance, Regulation X of 1804) of the colonial security state of India in the early 19th century.

It is also worth noticing that the Pakistan Army (Amendment) Act (2015) contains a proviso relating to its overriding effect over all other security and criminal laws in force. In other words, if any other law in force comes in conflict with the amended Army Act, then the latter will override the former. This has particularly led to a controversial conflict with the Juvenile Justice System Ordinance, JJSO (2000). The JJSO (2000) provides juvenile courts exclusive jurisdiction to try individuals below eighteen years of age and prohibits the death sentence of minors. Because some detainees have claimed to be minors at the time of their arrest or their involvement in the offence, the Army Act comes in direct conflict with the JJSO. In this regard, the case of

Haider Ali is worth noticing. Haider Ali's mother claimed, in an appeal filed in Peshawar High Court, that her son was arrested in 2009, when he was a student of class 10 and was only fourteen years old. He remained in secret, indefinite detention for six years before his family came to know, through the military press (ISPR), that he had been found guilty of involvement in "heinous offences relating to terrorism." A military court had sentenced him to death. Haider Ali's mother challenged her son's conviction and sentence on the basis of his juvenility as well as on the fair trial requirements. The Peshawar High Court, however, dismissed her petition on the basis of the overriding effect of the Army Act over all other laws for the time being in force.[27]

An important aspect about trial of minor in military courts relates to Pakistani State's commitment to certain international conventions. Pakistan has ratified certain international conventions on the rights and safety of minors that are apparently violated by the military courts' convictions and executions of minors. The ratification of such conventions mean that Pakistan generally agreed to the broader principles enshrined in these conventions, as well as the specific provisions in pursuance of those principles. For instance, Pakistan has ratified the International Covenant on Civil and Political Rights, ICCPR (2010), the Convention on the Rights of the Child, CRC (1990), and the UN Standard Minimum Rules for the Administration of Juvenile Justice, UNSMRAJJ (Beijing Rules). These conventions not only provide the fair trial guarantees but also additional protections and care. The CRC provides that trials of minors should proceed without delay and final judgment should be delivered within six months, parents should be present in every step of the trial and there should be independent scrutiny of the methods of interrogation including the presence of a lawyer and parents. On the other hand, the UN Draft Principles Governing the Administration of Justice through Military Tribunals provide that given the concern for protection, safety, and well-being of the child "in no case…should minors be placed under the jurisdiction of military tribunals."[28] It should also be noticed that death sentences are absolutely prohibited in cases of minors under both Pakistan's criminal laws and international conventions. The CRC, in its Article 37(a), and the ICCPR, in its Article 6(5), strictly prohibit death sentences for minors.

The high rate of confession, or self-incrimination, suggests that the interrogation methods employed by the Armed Forces are different from those available to the police and judiciary. There are speculations that they resort to physical and psychological torture. On the other hand, we know that Article 14 of the Constitution clearly prohibits the use of statements extracted as a result of torture to be presented as evidence for self-incrimination. Similarly, an international convention—the Convention against Torture and Other Cruel, Inhuman or Degrading Treatment or Punishment—to which Pakistan is a signatory prohibits torture and degrading treatments to individuals. A couple of cases are worth mentioning here. On January 2010,

Muhammad Ghauri went missing. He was student of the Islamic International University. The Commission of Inquiry on Enforced Disappearances was requested to look for Ghauri. The Supreme Court also took notice of his disappearance and directed the Inspector General of Police, Islamabad, to locate him. For three years, the IG office and the intelligence agencies kept denying any information about his whereabouts. However, in 2013, they admitted that Ghauri was at an internment centre in the FATA. Although Ghauri's whereabouts became known, he was neither released nor were the charges against him disclosed. In January 2016, his parents suddenly came to know through the media that their son had confessed to his offences and, therefore, was sentenced to death by a military court. Ghauri's father rushed to the Lahore High Court and filed a writ petition, but it was dismissed. Similarly, another detainee, Qari Zahir, confessed to his offences and was therefore sentenced to death. However, his family claimed in a writ petition to the Peshawar High Court that he was forced to put his thumb impression on a piece of paper that he could not understand. The Peshawar High Court dismissed their petition.

By 2016, a total of eleven military courts were set up across the country. Three of these courts were set up in the Punjab, three in KPK, two in Sindh, and one in Baluchistan. In a press statement, the Pakistan Army's Inter-Service Public Relations (ISPR) said that the government had sent to military courts a total of 275 cases of suspected terrorists by the end of 2016. The military courts tried 274 of these cases and awarded death sentence to 161 and imprisonments of different terms (mostly life) to 113. Moreover, the press statement said that the Armed Forces also executed death sentences of at least forty-eight civilians.[29] What is alarming to know about these convictions was the fact, divulged by the press statement, that 135 out of 144 convicts had confessed to their offences. This confession rate is higher than 90%.[30] On the other hand, the International Commission of Jurists (ICJ)—a collection of sixty jurists from around the world—have critiqued the military courts of Pakistan in the following words:

> ...the government and military authorities have failed to make public information about the time and place of their trials; the specific charges and evidence against the convicts; as well as the judgments of military courts including the essential findings, legal reasoning, and evidence on which the convictions were based.[31]

The ICJ has also noted that suspects tried by military courts remained in military custody at all times, even after the magistrate recorded their confessions. Being subject to long-term detention shows that the suspects would have remained susceptible to direct and indirect torture, coercion, and psychological pressure. Some of these suspects were detained under the AACPRs as far back as 2010 and kept in internment centres in the FATA before they could be brought before the military courts. Another aspect the

ICJ highlighted was of two convicts who were under the age of eighteen at the time of commission of the offence and/or at the time of arrest. The ICJ warned about the legality of the military courts in the following words:

> Pakistan has a legal duty to protect its people against terrorist attacks, and where terrorist attacks occur, a duty to investigate, prosecute and bring perpetrators to justice. However, for counter-terrorism measures to be effective in the long term, they must be lawful and also be seen to be legitimate. The experience from around the world has shown that departure from ordinary legal procedures and safeguards in the name of fighting terrorism is counterproductive, as it feeds and fuels the very violence it is meant to curtail.[32]

In the NAP, which had proposed to set up military courts for two years, the government had promised to bring about necessary "reforms in criminal courts system to strengthen the anti-terrorism institutions," as a long-term measure. Once such reforms were done, the government promised there would be no need for setting up of military courts again. Although the government could not bring about promised reforms in the criminal justice system, it nevertheless drafted a bill—the Criminal Laws (Amendment) Act, 2016—with the object to "root out the evil of terrorism with exemplary deterrence." The bill added a new connotation to the meaning of terrorism: "inciting religious, sectarian or ethnic hatred." This type of terrorism would be punishable with one to three years of imprisonment. The bill also provided that convictions could be made on the basis of "modern techniques." The use of such modern techniques or evidence collected through electronic gadgets was previously left to the discretion of the court as to whether or not to accept such evidence. Interestingly, the bill also made acknowledgement of neglect and violation of duty on the part of law enforcement officers. For such neglect and violation, the bill prescribed an increase of punishment from one year to three years of imprisonment. After a couple of incidents of lynching in different parts of the country, for the first time the government identified lynching as an offence of the type terrorism. The government therefore suggested providing it in the ATA 1997. The bill, however, did not address those weaknesses in the criminal procedure that were made as justifications for setting up military courts. These weaknesses include prolonged delays in trials, lack of adequate protection to witnesses, lack of adequate security for judges, and lower conviction rates.

The PPA and the Army (Amendment) Act lead to entrenchment

The PPA 2014 and the Army (Amendment) Act (2015) are good examples of entrenchment of the legal regime of security. In both cases, the government feared that the Supreme Court might strike them down. Therefore, the government went a step above the ordinary legislation and passed a constitutional amendment (21st Amendment) in 2015 to give constitutional cover to the two acts. There was also the fear of political/parliamentary opposition against the acts. It was due to the fact that the political parties suspected that their leadership or followers might be made target of the PPA and the military courts. Their fear and suspicion was due to a history of such victimisation of political parties. For instance, under the Suppression of Anti-Terrorist Activities Act (1975) the government targeted several opposition political parties. Moreover, in Karachi, the Motahida Quomi Movement (MQM) party often claimed victimisation at the hands of the Rangers. When the government gave assurances, as well as made explanatory notes in both these laws, these suspicions and fears among the opposition subsided. After this, they joined hands with the government in the passage of these laws. It is interesting to notice that the laws were passed without any negative vote. The two parties that criticised these laws at least initially, the Pakistan Tehreek-e-Insaf (PTI) and Jamiat Ulema-e Islam (Fazl ur Rehman) (JUI(F)) only abstained from voting rather than casting votes against the amendments.

Although the government was able to rally support of political parties for the military courts, it feared that the Supreme Court might not be convinced. The Supreme Court had, in the past, declared military courts incommensurate with the separation of power doctrine in the Constitution and had struck them down. For instance, in *Asma Jilani* (1972) and *Darvesh Arbey* (1977), the Court had declared martial law and martial courts unconstitutional.[33] Again in 1999, in *Liaquat Hussain* the Court struck down the PAFO (1998) and declared military courts unconstitutional.

In the present case of the Army Amendment Act (2015) and the 21st Constitutional Amendment Act (2015), the Supreme Court received several petitions challenging the constitutionality of these acts. By January 27, 2015, when the Supreme Court's three-member bench took up the petitions, the number of these petitions had risen to about fifteen. Because the question involved determining the limit of legislative powers of Parliament, the Supreme Court also took up other sixteen petitions against the 18th Amendment and grouped them together in one case. After reviewing all thirty-one petitions, the three-member bench of the Court, headed by Justice Anwar Zaheer Jamali, requested the Chief Justice to set up a full bench (a seventeen-member bench) of the Court to hear the case. Accordingly, on April 3, 2015, the full bench of the court is put together. The bench first ordered to put off the death sentences given to six suspected terrorists by the new military courts until the case was decided.

A lengthy debate began on the floor of the Supreme Court about the constitutionality of the military courts. The question of constitutionality further stretched to include the question relating to the power of Parliament to introduce such amendments in the Constitution that conflicted with other substantive articles—especially Article 4 and articles relating to the

Fundamental Rights and the jurisdiction of Courts or to the basic structure of the Constitution. Thus it also became a question of whether there is something as basic structure of the Constitution, which the Parliament could not touch. In a detailed judgment of around 900 pages, recording the opinions of all dissenting judges, the Supreme Court decided by a majority of eleven to six, turning down the petitions that challenged the setting up of military courts. The majority opinion of the Court said that it had no judicial review jurisdiction over a constitutional amendment. Second, there was no implicit or explicit check on the sovereign powers of the Parliament to make any constitutional amendments. This meant that the Parliament could amend any part of the Constitution, even those parts or provisions thought as the basic structure. The Court ruled by a majority that the introduction of military courts was constitutionally and legally valid. Justice Azmat Saeed authored the majority opinion and reasoned that (a) trials before military courts met principles of criminal justice, (b) the constitutional scheme allowed deviation from standard procedure in exceptional cases, and (c) the amendments only authorised military trials for terrorists, who deserved different treatment. However, the court added that it retained the power to review any decision of a military court on the basis of *mala fide* and *corum non judice*. In other words, the Court could review a decision of a military court if the case in question involved bad intentions on the part of government while sending the case to a military court, or by the military court in its decision, or the case was beyond the jurisdiction of the military courts as specified in the Army Amendment Act.

On the other hand, the six judges who dissented had different opinions. For them, the military trials of civilians were against the principles of justice, fair trial, and independence of judiciary. They argued that the introduction of military courts was "super-imposed on the Parliament, as they were not based on the Will of the Parliamentarians, but of the heads of the Parliamentary parties." In this line of opinion, they further stated that Parliament was made to accept the doctrine of necessity upon which these courts were allowed. Interestingly, this doctrine was normally employed in the past by the judiciary itself in cases legalising military *coups d'etat* and military courts. Furthermore, they reasoned that according to the Constitution, the Armed Forces worked under the Executive branch, and therefore, military courts violated the now well-established principle of separation of executive and judiciary. Similarly, they pointed out that the principle of separation of executive and judiciary is violated by encroachment upon the jurisdiction of courts to determine the nature of cases, or their administrative jurisdiction to determine to which court it should be sent. The present amendment allowed the government to determine as to which cases should be forwarded to the military courts. On the other hand, they suggested that if the government took measures to improve the ATCs, the prosecution, and the evidence collection and presentation, then there might not be a need for setting up military courts.[34]

Notes

1 "2012 Global Terrorism Index," 16.
2 "Global Terrorism Index 2014," 20.
3 "Global Terrorism Index 2014," 20.
4 "Fatalities in Terrorist Violence in Pakistan 2003–2017."
5 "Global Terrorism Index 2014," 20.
6 "Global Terrorism Index 2015."
7 Eule, "Temporal Limits on the Legislative Mandate."
8 McGinnis and Rappaport, "Symmetric Entrenchment."
9 For the debate on the concept of legislative entrenchment see Dana and Koniak, "Bargaining in the Shadow of Democracy"; Eule, "Temporal Limits on the Legislative Mandate"; Fisk and Chemerinsky, "The Filibuster"; Posner and Vermeule, "Legislative Entrenchment"; McGinnis and Rappaport, "Symmetric Entrenchment."
10 It is worth highlighting the scope of Article 245 and the deployment of Armed Forces. The Supreme Court has explained it in the following words:

> On a plain reading of the provisions of Article 245(1) of the Constitution the functions of the Armed Forces can be bifurcated into two categories, namely, they shall (1) defend Pakistan against external aggression or threat of war, and (2) subject to law, act in aid of civil power when called upon to do so. Under clause (1) of article 243 of the Constitution the control and command of the Armed Forces is vested in the Federal Government, therefore, in the performance of both the categories of functions, the Armed Forces act under the directions of the Federal Government. [...]Thus, essentially, a proclamation requiring the aid of the Armed Forces must come from the civilian authorities and as soon as the necessity for the exercise of the military power is over, the civil administration must, of necessity, be restored, and assume its normal role.

Sindh High Court Bar Association v. Federation of Pakistan, PLD 2009 SC 879.
11 *Bazar Gul Afridi v. Federation of Pakistan*, Writ Petition No. 360/2013.
12 HRC. No. 29388-K/13, December 10, 2013.
13 See *District Bar Association Rawalpindi*, 2015 SC 401.
14 *Province of Punjab through Collector Sargodha v. Muhammad Bakhsh and another,* PLD 2012 SC 664.
15 *Muhammad Shafique Butt v. the State*, 2015 YLR 877.
16 *Sardar Ahmed Abbasi v. Muhammad Zaman Abbasi and 4 others*, 2015 CLC 1157.
17 *Mehram Ali v. Federation of Pakistan*, PLD 1998 SC 1445.
18 *Mehram Ali v. Federation of Pakistan*, 1998 MLD 1411 Lahore.
19 *Suo Motu Case No. 10 of 2011*, PLD 2011, S.C. 799.
20 Khan, "The Charge-Sheet against NAP."
21 It is worth noticing that in 1991 when Nawaz Shareef for the first time set up Special Courts for the trial of heinous offenses through the Twelfth Amendment Act and added Article 212-B they were also for a fixed time period—three years. The time period ended on July 28, 1994.
22 Hashim, "Army Courts to Try Pakistan Terror Suspects."
23 Kennedy, "The Creation and Development of Pakistan's Anti-Terrorism Regime, 1997–2002," 8.
24 Ordinance No. XIII, August 27, 1999.
25 According to Section 85 of the Army Act (1952) a general Court martial shall consist of not less than five officers each of whom has held a commission for not less than three whole years and of whom not less than four are of a rank not below that of captain. Section 87 says that a field general Court martial shall consist of not less than three officers.

26 See Section 133-B of the Pakistan Army Act, 1952.
27 Writ Petition No. 2979 of 2015, announced October 14, 2015.
28 Principle 7, Draft Principles Governing the Administration of Justice through Military Tribunals, UN Doc. E/CN. 4/2006/58.
29 "UN Human Rights Committee, 120th Session, Geneva: Submission Of The International Commission Of Jurists In Advance Of The Examination Of The Initial Report Of Pakistan Under Article 40 Of The International Covenant On Civil And Political Rights," 2.
30 "Military Injustice in Pakistan: Questions and Answers," 1.
31 "Military Injustice in Pakistan: A Briefing Paper," 3.
32 "Military Injustice in Pakistan: A Briefing Paper."
33 *Asma Jilani v. Government of the Punjab*, PLD 1972 SC 139; *Darvesh M. Arbey, Advocate v. Federation of Pakistan*, PLD 1977 Lahore 846.
34 *District Bar Association, Rawalpindi*, PLD 2015 SC 401.

5 Security and the absolute right to life

Critical reflections on the revival of capital punishment

Introduction

The December 16, 2014 terrorist attack on school children at the Army Public School in Peshawar, Pakistan, was one of the deadliest in the country's history. In this attack, 132 students and nine teachers were killed, including one female teacher who was burnt alive.[1] The attack, carried out by the Tehreek-e-Taliban Pakistan (TTP), left the entire nation reeling in shock.

The attack led to increased political pressure on the government to exercise its punitive authority, as well as to upgrade its criminal justice system. It specifically renewed the debate on whether death sentence executions should be restored in the country. Moreover, it was debated whether the proposal to lift the moratorium on death sentence executions would be an effective deterrent against senseless attacks of terrorists—particularly those in the same vein as the Peshawar school attack.

One particular question that interests me in this chapter, raised in the context of the debate on the resumption of the death sentence, is why the hands of the state were tied while killings were taking place in the country. Families of the victims of the Peshawar school killings bemoaned the need to exact justice on the perpetrators on behalf of their loved ones, and some demanded it to come in the form of public hangings. Supporters of the death sentence argued that it was the only effective way to deal with the scourge of terrorism. Some even questioned whether convicts and terrorists have the right to life. In one form or the other, these questions and demands came to centre on the legitimacy, and indeed the efficacy, of lifting an existing moratorium on death sentence executions that had been put in place for six years. Pakistani civil society and human rights groups, on the other hand, questioned whether the resumption of death sentence executions in Pakistan would serve as an effective deterrent against terrorists and to win the fight against terrorism.

In a significant political development, a day after the school attack, Prime Minister Nawaz Sharif decided to lift the moratorium on death sentence executions of persons involved in terrorism.[2] This decision was crucial, as there had been no civilian hangings in Pakistan for six years.[3] The Pakistan

People's Party had declared a *de facto* moratorium on death sentence executions in 2008 to achieve economic gains from the European Union.[4] In January 2015, the government decided to lift the moratorium on other capital cases as well. The Pakistani interior ministry directed provincial governments to proceed with hangings of convicts who had exhausted all avenues of appeal and clemency. Finally, in March 2015, the government completely lifted the moratorium and effectively restored death sentence executions across the country.[5] From the resumption of executions in 2014 until the end of April 2015, more than one hundred convicts have been hanged.[6] Presently, there are more than 8,000 prisoners on death row in the country.[7]

Historically speaking, the call for a moratorium on the death sentence originated in the West and it is relatively new. Its academic origin lies in critical legal scholarship and its popular origin in human rights activism, both in the post-WWII period (after 1945).[8] The context for the moratorium on the use of death penalty, especially in the West, was introduced with the view to protect "the right to life" of the perpetrators of homicide (and earlier, treason and rebellion).

With the War on Terror, there has grown a need to distinguish between terrorism and organised killings from other crimes. This calls into question the need to redefine the legal equation between the "absolute" right to life and "heinous" crimes, wherein the crime is deemed so abject that apparently the death sentence is absolutely justified. However, whether this equation can be legitimately defined, discussed and fixed in a secular representative assembly, in the context of Pakistan's parliament, remains to be seen.

The pathos of Pakistan's politics

On Pakistan's political stage, the decision to lift the moratorium was difficult. Six years earlier, when the moratorium was imposed, arriving at the decision was not as difficult. This was despite the fact that it contravened one school of thought in Islamic jurisprudence (specifically, the "blood for blood" principle). Even Pakistan's major Islamic parties did not protest the imposition of the moratorium.

In fact, both decisions—the imposition in 2008, as well as the lifting in 2015—did not generate any meaningful debate in the parliament, the courts, or within the public domain. The pathos of national politics is that decisions to enhance the sovereign power of the state are taken despite a lack of debate. This lack of debate also reflects a remarkable political failing in acknowledging the relationship of the death sentence to the state of democracy and criminal justice system in the country. Also, interestingly, those who showed their concern, especially human rights advocates and the Pakistani Taliban, opposed the government's decision to lift the moratorium, although for divergent reasons and interests.

The major political parties, on their part, assumed ambivalence towards the lifting of the moratorium. The religious political parties—for instance,

Jamiat Ulema-e Islam (Fazl ur Rehman) (JUI(F)) and Jamaat-e-Islami (JI)—were torn between their ideological commitment to "punishment by death" and their sympathy for those engaged in the so-called armed jihad. In regards to the two liberal-secular parties, namely the Pakistan People's Party (PPP) and Pakistan Tehreek-e-Insaf (PTI) ("Movement for Justice"), although they agreed on principle with the lifting of the moratorium, they remained reluctant to identify themselves with the decision or to lend their representative support to the government.

The ruling political party, the Pakistan Muslim League-Nawaz (PML-N), a moderate Islamic party headed by Pakistan's current Prime Minister, Nawaz Sharif, found itself locked in a political conundrum dealing with the issue. On the one hand, the Taliban threatened to initiate more attacks and jailbreaks if the moratorium was lifted.[9] On the other hand, the major political parties dragged their feet in reaching a consensus. Moreover, the government faced the question of whether death sentence executions would be effective in deterring would-be terrorists, as on the surface, it would appear that those who had taken vows of martyrdom would not be afraid of death sentence executions. However, supporters of the death sentence argued that the psychological and emotional readiness that accompanies such vows is often only temporary, pointing to instances where convicts had suffered from cardiac arrest and depression before their hangings.[10] They also pointed to the fact that death sentence executions should be seen as a matter of principle, a rule of law. For them, a greater degree of certainty of the application of the rule of law would prove as an effective deterrent against would-be terrorists. However, human rights advocates point to inadequacies in this argument by identifying existing flaws in the trial procedures. They list, for instance, the exorbitant fees of hiring a learned lawyer, the poor investigations carried out by the police, the lack of protection given to witnesses, and the abridged trial procedures as some of these existing flaws. Further, in retributive justice, the eye-for-an-eye principle is discarded and the two-wrongs-don't-make-a-right principle is embraced, where ending a person's life (even if that person has taken another's life) is not perceived as justice or a solution to the wrong committed; in the case of a terrorist, comprehensive rehabilitation and reintegration would be in order for the transformation of that individual.

Expanding necropower

Over the past few years, despite their ostensible differences or manifest ambivalence towards the decision to lift the moratorium, the major political parties and other stakeholders, especially the Pakistan Armed Forces, police and the country's bureaucratic officials, have agreed to enhance the state's sovereign power, or more precisely, "necropower," a term coined by a Cameroonian scholar to refer to the state's exercise of sovereign power in dictating who lives and who dies.[11]

For instance, in July 2014, the ruling and opposition parties agreed to codify the Protection of Pakistan Ordinance of 2013 into an act. This ordinance and act widened the scope of power accorded to security and law enforcement agencies, granting the authorities the power to shoot at sight, especially aliens, terrorists, suspected terrorists and their abettors. It needs to be noted that the category of "aliens" is wide enough to target anyone who is without legal identity documents. Essentially, the act is a document that declares that all peace-disrupting elements are deemed "enemies of the state" and that the protection of civilian life remains Pakistan's top priority.

Additionally, the government's frequent use of Article 245 of the constitution has resulted in an enhancement of the state's sovereign power. Under this article, the government can call the army and paramilitary forces to assist Pakistan's civil administration in ensuring law and order throughout the country. Furthermore, after the Peshawar school attack, the government approved both the National Action Plan (NAP) and the Pakistan Army (Amendment) Act in 2015 to empower the Pakistani Army. The act has also been extended to the Afghanistan-Pakistan borderland, where the Pakistan Army is presently engaged in counterterrorism operations. As part of the act, military courts for "speedy trials" of suspected terrorists would also be set up in the country. The bills were presented to the parliament after political parties and the army agreed, in a marathon meeting, on the mode of setting up the military courts. As of February 2015, the army had set up nine military courts—three each in Khyber-Pakhtunkhwa and Punjab, two in Sindh and one in Balochistan. In order to further strengthen these courts, an ordinance was issued to grant judges the power to exclude the public from hearings.[12] With these laws in place, it seems that the lifting of the moratorium is a continuation of the recent juridical developments to enhance the state's sovereign power. These judicial developments (vis-à-vis its anti-terrorism laws) were intended to collectively grant the state greater teeth in enforcing law and order but have ostensibly resulted in the enhancement of the state's necropower.

The ethos of Islamic Jurisprudence

In an Islamic state like Pakistan (second only to Indonesia in terms of the size of its Muslim population), there is hardly any escape from reconciling with, or at least explaining, a law in the ethos of Islamic jurisprudence, i.e., the broader spirit of Sharia (Islamic Law). The use of the death penalty also concerns its accordance to a moral right. In other words, the victim is not only entitled to a legal, justifiable right through the state's judicial system but also a moral right acceptable in the eyes of society. In Islamic tradition, the legal right is in fact, the realisation or manifestation of a codified moral right. When it comes to seeking mercy or clemency, the killer has to seek it from the victim's family. This is the view predominantly held by religious parties in Pakistan. For instance, JUI(F)'s Secretary, General Maulana Abdul Ghafoor Haidri, in response to a question on the lifting of the moratorium on the death penalty, remarked: "Only a victim's kin has the right to pardon the killer, whether in deciding to take or not take compensation. This is an Islamic way of justice, and being an ideological state, Pakistan should have Islamic laws."[13] In the judicial process that ensues, the role of the state is, therefore, primarily procedural. The moratorium on the death sentence in a way complicates and contravenes the Islamic legal right of the victim (Islamic principle of blood for blood). Hence we can make a preliminary assumption that the codification of a moral canon right into legal secular right thus defines the constitution of sovereignty in a modern Islamic state, like that of Pakistan.

The aporia of modern justice

One of the challenges involved in dispensing criminal justice, i.e., in meting out punishment on the criminal, generally speaking, is meeting the procedural requirements of due process of law and granting the victim equal protection. From the point of view of critical legal thought, there exists a gap or incoherence between laws and acts of crime, especially as it comes to application of law.[14] In other words, what this means is that, oftentimes, applying a law on a criminal act carried out by an individual is not straightforward and involves the judge's careful deliberation and discretion. Therefore, when it comes to a decision on the life and death of a person, such a gap in the application of law puts into question the entire logic of the death sentence, especially given the fact that the death sentence execution is irrevocable. This irrevocability is the crucial aspect invoked by those who defend their argument against the death sentence.

In Pakistan, it was in this light—to afford due process and equal protection—that Section 10A was introduced to the Constitution in 1973. The section guarantees the right of every citizen to a fair trial, no matter how grave an act of crime he or she is involved in. The right to a fair trial technically means a full-length trial procedure. Although the right to a fair trial was guaranteed with this section, there arose problems in the wake of the 9/11 attacks on the United States and the resultant "War on Terror," which brought back the idea of "speedy justice." The idea of speedy justice, originally, was to dispense justice, along with prudence and wisdom observed in the final disposition of cases, without undue delay.

In actual fact, the idea of speedy justice in Pakistan was first introduced in 1992, although in a different context: when the government under Prime Minister Nawaz Sharif passed two important counterterrorism acts—Act X or the Terrorist Affected Areas (Special Courts) Act, and Act IX or the Special Courts for Speedy Trials Act. The aim of the acts, as declared in the preamble of Act X, was "to provide for the suppression of acts of terrorism, subversion and other heinous offences in the terrorist affected areas." Later, these acts provided the basis for an expanded Anti-Terrorism Act (ATA) of 1997. The 1997 act was further amended and expanded on August 14, 2001, about a month before the 9/11 attacks. In practice, in Pakistan, the idea of speedy justice came to stand for a speedy procedure of trial, or more precisely, an abridged procedure of trial. It was interpreted in such a way as to shorten the overall process of the trial duration. Anti-terrorism courts with speedy trial procedures have remained active since the 1992 acts were put into place. The government again amended the Military Act of 1952 in 2015 to provide military courts with a further abridged procedure of speedy justice.

Conclusion

At present, when life and the political sensibility necessary to a meaningful life are extremely vulnerable in Pakistan, the nation is confronted with the profound question of death sentence executions. There is a need for a public debate, including an academic one, to explore how the death sentence is intimately related to the transitional character of Pakistan's liberal criminal justice system and to the very potential of a democratic character to take shape within Pakistani society.

The legitimacy of death sentence executions remains contested and controversial. This is due to (a) the lack of a political debate in Parliament, (b) ambivalence of major parties to death sentence executions, and (c) inadequacies in the criminal trial procedure. On the other hand, the sovereign power (or the necropower) of the state has increased over the past few years with the passage of several security laws, and especially with the resumption of death sentence executions. The school attack only added new laws to increase the state's necropower. These laws are adversely affecting the state of liberal democracy in the country. Moreover, the state's liberal posture has further suffered as the "blood for blood" principle in Islamic jurisprudence has effectively trumped the egalitarian and humanitarian spirit of Islam.

Notes

1 Yusufzai and Spencer, "Taliban Burned Teachers Alive in Pakistan School Attack."
2 Haider, "Nawaz Removes Moratorium on Death Penalty."
3 "Pakistan to Continue Moratorium on Capital Punishment."
4 Abbasi, "Why Hanging Was Banned."
5 khan, "Bar on Death Penalty Lifted in Toto."
6 "Pakistan Hangs 100th Convict, Amnesty Slams 'Shameful Milestone.'"
7 "Death Penalty Moratorium Lifted Completely in Pakistan."
8 See Sarat, *The Killing State*.
9 Sherazi, "Jailbreak Threat Looms for KP Prisons as Execution Moratorium Lifted."

10 Riaz, "Death Row Convict Dies of Brain Hemorrhage in Lahore Hospital"; "Death-Row Prisoner Dies of Heart Attack."
11 See Mbembe, "Necropolitics."
12 "Protection for Military Courts."
13 Haider, "Nawaz Removes Moratorium on Death Penalty."
14 See Agamben, *State of Exception*.

6 Aliens, identity and legal regime of security on the border

Introduction

A few years ago, in an essay engaging critical geography, I explored the tendency or preoccupation among the geopoliticians and military geostrategists of the War on Terror with "unveiling" the supposedly obscure battleground of the northwestern borderland of Pakistan.[1] I pointed out how the preoccupation with unveiling the borderland led to the deployment of new military technology, cartographic practices, and cultural quantitative analysis on the basis of visual data, which, while giving a strategic advantage over the adversary, took the obscurity of the borderland to another level—the digital–technological level. More importantly, I argued that geopoliticians and military geostrategists were indirectly engaged in building an imaginative geopolitical representation of the borderland. In order to critically analyse their endeavours, I engaged Michael J. Shapiro's concept of a violent cartography. The concept explains how geopolitical and geostrategic representations of a given space were/are basically "historically developed, socially embedded interpretations of identity and space," and hence are "based on models of identity-difference."[2] In light of this concept, I highlighted the implications of employing geopolitical cartographic practices based on an identity-difference framing. Here, in the present essay, I want to further extend my analysis to security practices that involve the use of lethal force sanctioned by law, which create a legal regime of security derogatory to human rights on the borderland. In other words, I pursue the concept of violent cartography, along with certain other concepts—especially structural violence and necrobiography—to present a critical analysis of the *legally embedded* interpretations of identity and place on the border.

Two recent incidents of cold-blooded killings at the hands of the law enforcement agencies (LEAs) of Pakistan present the context for this essay. These incidents took place in the summer of 2011—the first incident involved a killing of a group of aliens/foreigners who were travelling across the border from Afghanistan into Pakistan, and the second involved the killing of a young man (a Pakistani citizen) who happened to be in an area under curfew and who was suspected of theft in a local park in the metropolitan city of Karachi. Although these incidents took place one after the other, within a period of less than a month, the attention and responses they received from the government, and especially the superior judiciary, were quite different. While the latter incident (Karachi killing of a citizen) moved the Supreme Court to take a *Suo Moto* action and to replace the heads of LEAs in charge, the former incident (Kharotabad killings of foreigners) went almost overlooked, subsequently passing into oblivion. The judicial ambivalence towards the Kharotabad incident raises the question as to what was so different in the two incidents, especially from the point of view of the law or (formal) justice, that gave them such different responses.

However, before we begin to seek an answer to that question, I deem it useful to narrate the details of the two incidents. This narration is crucial for the second half of the essay, in which I engage in a critical analysis of these events of violence. On May 17, 2011, a group of five foreign travellers set out on the journey, in a hired cab, across the Pakistan-Afghanistan border and headed towards the city of Quetta in the province of Baluchistan. They crossed a couple of checkpoints from the border to the outskirts of the city. Here, outside the city, when they reached a checkpoint in Kharotabad, a small town, and disembarked from their cab for a routine check, the Frontier Corps (FC) personnel opened fire on them. Three of them died on the spot, while two women fell on ground, injured. They lay there for more than half an hour while the officers in command deliberated on their fate. Meanwhile, a few media men arrived at the spot. The FC personnel sent an armoured vehicle down to the injured women to see if they were armed with suicide jackets. The vehicle returned without finding anything conclusive. After their brief deliberation, the FC personnel decided to kill the wounded women. A second fusillade was discharged and the wounded women were killed despite their calls for mercy. Interestingly, a local media man recorded this second half of the incident, including the fusillade of fire on video camera. The recording soon hit local news networks and social media and generated a public outcry for an inquiry. It also turned out, soon after the post-mortem, that the victims were neither Chechens nor armed, as initially claimed by the LEAs. As the public pressure for accountability increased, the government promised to carry out an inquiry. After many delays, the Pakistani Government put together an "internal inquiry committee" under the Anti-Terrorism Act (ATA), 1997, to investigate the killings. However, at the end of the investigation, the report of the committee was not made public in its full original version, nor was a trial registered.

In less than a month, on June 8, 2011, a young man was shot dead by the Rangers, a paramilitary force deployed to aid the police in the metropolitan city of Karachi. A private TV channel crew that coincidentally happened to be nearby recorded this incident on camera. The video recording was shown on local news channels, and it went viral on social media. In the video recording, the victim is shown being roughly handled by a group of five Rangers, and then one of the personnel shoots the victim twice in the leg. The victim falls to the ground, crying in pain and begging to be taken to a hospital. However, the Rangers disregard his imploring and let him bleed to death. The erstwhile Chief Justice of the Pakistani Supreme Court, Iftikhar Chaudary, took a *Suo Moto* action ordering the registration of a case of murder against the Rangers personnel involved. He also advised the government to remove the incumbent Director General of Rangers and the Inspector General of Police to ensure that a fair investigation in the case could take place. The case proceeded in an anti-terrorism court (ATC), which ensured speedy criminal procedure and decided within a couple of months to award heavy punishments to the personnel involved.

The point that I want to emphasise in these incidents is that they received diametrically different responses from the Supreme Court. Although both incidents involved cold-blooded violence and were equally reproachable, what differentiated them in the eyes of the criminal justice system was the difference of personal legal identity. It should be noticed that in the Kharotabad incident, foreigners or non-citizens were involved, while in the Karachi incident, a citizen was involved. In the former incident, the court didn't intervene to order the registration of a case, while in the latter, not only did the court order to register a case under the anti-terrorism law against the Rangers personnel, but it also ensured speedy procedure in the trial. In this chapter, I emphasise these different responses to highlight the tendency towards discrimination in the criminal justice system of Pakistan, inasmuch as its operation rests on the political condition of personal identity rather than the ethical and empathic conditions of human rights law. In other words, the system makes distinctions in personal legal identity of individuals in matters as basic as the right to life. Furthermore, I argue that the practice of making these identity-difference distinctions in the personal legal status of individuals does not just victimise aliens/non-citizens but also, at times, victimises citizens. In the course of my analysis, I highlight that the practice of making identity-difference distinction is associated with the border, both historically and conceptually: the border is its potent source of initiation and enforcement. The practice of making identity-difference distinction is normally condoned through a persistent security discourse and gradually begins to take root in law. The border creates an ontological crisis of identity in everyday encounters of individuals with LEAs. In this line of argument, I question the relationship of the border with the violence of law enforcement. My exploration in the essay is divided into two parts. The first part traces the practice of making identity-difference distinction in security administration and law to highlight the legal structures of violence; the second part explores the applied side of this practice—that is, the events of violence.

Legal sovereignty on border

Legally embedded identity-difference model

When viewed from the perspective of an "empathic vision," to borrow Jill Bennett's phrase,[3] the two incidents of violence occasion the need for critical self-reflection, especially on the part of lawmakers, to assess the growing powers of LEAs vis-à-vis the state of human rights—specifically the right to life. However, the local political stage, remarkably charged with a pervasive security discourse that is predicated on the ostensible existence of an existential threat to state security, spares no room for a debate that takes as its object ethical human rights deliberations. Thus, in the years that followed the incidents, the government went on to introduce more security laws and greater powers for LEAs. The government thought it had strong reasons for doing so: first, the Haqqani network of the Taliban, based along the border in North Waziristan, had increased its suicide bombing campaign inside the country; second, the Army, engaged in operations along the border and elsewhere in the country, had been levelling complaints against the criminal justice procedure, which often let apprehended terrorists go for want of substantive evidence or other procedural requirements; and third, as a consequence of their frustration with the criminal justice procedure, the Army, through its intelligence agencies, resorted to extrajudicial detentions of suspected terrorists and carried out secret investigations. The extrajudicial detentions, however, led to the much-vexed issue of "missing persons," which, towards the end of 2012, generated serious tension between the judiciary and the intelligence agencies. It is in this fraught political environment and with a self-conscious effort to address extrajudicial practices that the newly elected government of Nawaz Sharif (May 2013) decided to amend the ATA, 1997 (Act XX of 2013) and to issue an ordinance called the Protection of Pakistan Ordinance (PPO), 2013.[4] Later, in June 2014, after the Haqqani Taliban attacked the Karachi Airport, and after the Army's subsequent operation against them, the government passed the PPO into an act—the Protection of Pakistan Act (PPA), 2014. It is interesting to note that the government hoped to address the problem of the extrajudicial practices of LEAs by only giving more powers to them. Thus the government indirectly empowered them to engage in almost the same extrajudicial practices, but now by legal means.

Before I shed light on these security laws, I want to spend a few lines on the methodological purpose and approach in the essay. My approach is informed by Michel Foucault's insight that the law is a complex site of enunciation of specific governmental programmes. It is through the law that these programmes are couched in normative and positive codes of conduct and avoid practical and political difficulties in their implementation. When these laws come into force, Foucault writes, "They crystallize into institutions, they inform individual behavior, and they act as grids for perception and evaluation of things."[5] It is this grid of perception and evaluation of *things*—in our case, identity—that interests me, especially because it opens the way to understanding and conceptualising the applied side (i.e., the possibility of violence) of security laws. Since as Julia Kristeva writes, "it is precisely with respect to laws that a foreigner exists,"[6] we need to focus on security laws and the grid of perception and evaluation that they create.

The latest security laws, as mentioned previously, contain provisions that inscribe and embed the identity-difference distinction making and the use of lethal force. For instance, the primary subject in the PPA, 2014, is the category of the enemy alien. This category was defined for the first time in the PPO, 2013, even though it was present in Article 10(9) of the current Constitution. The definition of the category of enemy alien in PPO, 2013, was worded in simple terms: an enemy alien is a person (a) who failed to establish his/her Pakistani citizenship and (b) he/she is found engaged in any of the offences of waging war, insurrection, and/or depredation. This definition of enemy alien is, however, redefined and made complex in the PPA, 2014, as it is indirectly defined through another category—that of the militant.

In the Protection of Pakistan (Amendment) Ordinance (PPAO) 2014, introduced six months before the PPA, 2014, the government also introduced a new category of the "combatant enemy." Although the government did not give reasons for introducing this new category, it can be surmised that the scope of the earlier category of the enemy alien was perhaps not broad enough to serve the security purposes of the state. The definition of the category of the combatant enemy in PPAO, 2014, comprises at least two main dimensions—identity of the individual and involvement in offences. First, a combatant enemy could be just "any person," unlike the enemy alien who had to be an alien. Second, such person should be involved in (a) raising of arms or waging war, or in aiding and abetting of the same; (b) threatening of the security and integrity of the state; (c) committing or threatening to commit a scheduled offence; and/or (d) involved in depredation. The category of combatant enemy is substituted with the category of militant in the PPA 2014, while the definition of the former category is retained from the PPAO 2014 to define the latter category in the PPA 2014. The definition is however broken down into five clauses and some new phrases are added to it. For instance, in clause (c) of Section 2(f) two new phrases—"advocating" and "encouraging"—are added to define the act of engagement in an offence. Apart from that, a new offence of "violent struggle" is introduced. These new phrases and the offence of violent struggle have neither been defined in the act or any previous security laws, nor debated in the case law. Hence, it remains to be seen how the superior courts define and fix the meaning of these new additions. With these additions, nevertheless, the scope of the law to deal with security threats from both aliens and citizens has already widened even beyond the scope of the ATA, 1997.

In PPA 2014, with the introduction of the category of the militant, the category of the enemy alien is also redefined. Now, an enemy alien is not simply an alien person, but a militant, who happens to be an alien. In other words, he/she is a militant "whose identity is not ascertainable as a Pakistani" or who has been deprived of his/her naturalised citizenship. Obviously, this is a nuanced change in the definition from the active tense (in PPO 2013, where it was said that an enemy alien is "a person who fails to establish his citizenship") to the passive tense (in the PPA). However, this change does not suggest that the burden of proof has been brought back on the shoulders of the state. Rather, it points to an enhanced power of the state over the individual by giving the state the power to determine the individual's identity, to pronounce him/her an alien and potentially a militant. Theoretically this power is akin to the sovereign power to determine, in a state of exception case, whether an exception exists and to make a decision on it.[7] It should also be noted that the category of the militant stands at a point midway between the categories of citizen and alien. In fact, it transforms both: if a citizen commits a scheduled offence, he/she becomes a militant, and if an alien commits a scheduled offence, he/she becomes a militant of an enemy alien type. This legal strategic category of the militant challenges another theoretical insight in critical legal studies that separates a political decision (to exclude an alien) from a sovereign decision (to exclude a citizen).[8] Inasmuch as the sovereign can create middle categories like the militant, as in the case of the PPA 2014, we notice that the political and the sovereign decision collapse into a legal black hole.

It is worth pointing that the Protection of Pakistan laws provide for a double burden of proof—one relating to proving (national) identity and the other to proving non-involvement in a scheduled offence. The first type of burden of proof requires an individual to prove his/her identity as a citizen of Pakistan or of another country, or to prove that he or she has a different international legal status. The second type of burden of proof requires the individual to produce evidence to dispel the criminal charge made against him/her by a law enforcement agency. Another controversial aspect of the Protection of Pakistan laws relates to the use of lethal force sanctioned within them. The LEAs, under Section 3 of the PPA (2014) and PPO (2013), can open fire to kill an individual suspected of being an enemy alien or militant. This power to fire to kill was earlier provided under the ATA 1997, although later, some restrictions were placed on it by the superior courts. In a number of cases, the courts ruled that if law enforcement personnel are not fired upon or if they overpower a terrorist, the use of lethal force against him/her is illegal.[9] On the other hand, it is interesting to note that the power to use lethal force is not provided in the Foreigners Act, 1946, which has been a law dealing with aliens for a long time. I shall return to this act in a moment.

Furthermore, the Protection of Pakistan laws, like the earlier ATA 1997, afford unfettered search and arrest powers to LEAs. In Section 3 of the PPA 2014, the section that provides for the use of force, it is provided that LEAs can arrest a suspect and search any building or premises without warrant. Such arrests and searches can be made if there is reasonable suspicion or credible information that a person has committed or is about to commit a scheduled offence. It should be noted that the phrase "about to commit" is coterminous with the scope of another phrase: "preparation to commit." These phrases are quite broad in their legal scope/construction, and as I have elsewhere shown, they were first developed against rebellion and treason cases as long ago as the mid-19th century in colonial times.[10] Now they are being used in cases of the "protection" of the state.

For providing speedy justice, the Protection of Pakistan laws and the ATA 1997 provide for setting up special courts. Both PPO 2013 and PPA 2014 provide the government the discretion to set up "as many" special courts as it deems appropriate. Moreover, the government can set up special courts in high security prisons, which can be built under this act. In order to carry out speedy and effective prosecution, the Protection of Pakistan Laws also provide for establishing an independent Prosecuting Agency. Moreover, they provide for "joint trials" of the accused—that is, the government can transfer any case against an accused from any other court to a special court to be tried alongside the case already being heard.

Lastly, the Protection of Pakistan laws provide for a greater increased punishment than the ones provided in the Criminal Code. The PPO 2013, for instance, provided that a maximum of ten years of imprisonment, along with fines and confiscation of property, could be awarded for a scheduled offence. The PPA 2014 increased the ceiling to ten years. Moreover, both laws provide that if the punishment in the Panel Code for a scheduled offence is higher than the one given in these laws, then the court can consider the higher punishment as well. And finally, a special court can also deprive a person of his naturalised citizenship. It is interesting to notice that the punishment of confiscation of property from a citizen is symbolic of the crime of treason. Such confiscations were provided in colonial times to punish offences against the state. The provenance of this punishment of confiscation of property came from the treason laws of Britain.[11]

A historically embedded identity difference model

In order to understand what the making of the identity-difference distinction in the Protection of Pakistan laws encompasses, we need to dig deeper into the layers of history, therefore illuminating the various stages of its development and embedding. The genealogy of the identity-difference distinction, as per this study, goes as far back as the initial stages of the British state making in colonial India in the mid-19th century. As I have pointed out elsewhere, this state making began with penal laws and a penal code, rather than with constitutional law and defined rights and duties for the subjects.[12] In the wake of a burgeoning state-making project in India, the British colonial administration deemed it essential to draw defined borders and harness the endemic trans-regional mobility of the people. On the North-West frontier, apart from the reason of state making, the geostrategic imperatives of the Great Game and other British-sponsored state-making projects in Afghanistan led the administration to consider a well-defined and securitised border. Hence, the border that was drawn at the turn of the century, which is often counted as a milestone political achievement of the colonial administration, was but a result of the contemporary geopolitics of war and state making in the region.

It is important to note that the British colonial administration took its first practical step towards this geopolitical act of drawing and securitising the colonial border in the realm of penal law. The administration passed a series of laws to check the free movement of people, especially those migrant peoples who valued their territorial identity (as often indicated by their territorially based surnames) and who refused to identify themselves with any specific territorial state or government. According to some recent studies, "Mobility has been a key feature of life on the Frontier, with its inhabitants employing movement as strategy of survival and response to political pressure, as well as economic opportunism."[13] On the other hand, Chris Bayly explains how the British administration was averse to free movement in the region:

> Nomads and wanderers were seen as disorderly elements—carriers of roguery and dissidence. This stereotype was often applied to traveling groups as harmless as ironsmiths and potters who linked up areas of production and consumption. It is not difficult to see how attitudes like this derived from experience of the great increase in social control which had taken place in contemporary England.[14]

In contemporary England, the government had introduced laws restricting the free movement ("vagrancy") of disorderly elements, including poor wandering people ("paupers"), aliens with criminal records, or aliens without means of subsistence.[15] Similar laws were then introduced in colonial India in the forms of Act XXXIII of 1857, Act I of 1861, and Act III (Foreigners Act) of 1864. The legal harnessing of free trans-regional movement was the logical result of the contemporary political vision in England (and for that matter, in the West in general) in which the modern state was essentially a territorial state with a defined territory, population, and law of the land. In his seminal work, *The Status of Refugees in International Law*, Atle Grahl-Madsen, for instance, writes that it was the 19th century that witnessed the birth of nationality law in Europe. In several countries, nationality laws came with other laws relating to aliens (the Aliens Acts),[16] much as their "correlative other."[17] Both these types of laws—nationality acts and aliens acts—Nevzat Soguk further points out, carried relevance for "the crafting of the sovereign territorial state." In other words, they constituted "yet another field of statist activity clearly linked to the name of the alien."[18]

In a recent play on the negotiations of the Durand Line, Ron Hutchinson illuminates this British territorial vision for the modern state by juxtaposing it with its opposite vision entertained on the North-West Frontier of colonial India. In his play, the British representative Sir Mortimer Durand debates with King Abdur Rehman over the need for drawing a border between colonial India and Afghanistan. His primary argument underpins the contemporary British vision for a state to be territorially defined. Rehman, on the other hand, is not only hesitant to negotiate a border but also averse to the very idea of the border. Durand therefore tries to convince him by pointing to the geopolitical benefits of the border for the project of state making in Afghanistan. A part of the dialogue merits quoting here at length:

REHMAN: Is there not a case for leaving the exact borders undefined for now?

DURAND: (*Even more perplexed*) A thing has to be defined—Good God, that's what this whole century has been about. A disease, a law of science, an international border—they need defining; progress flows from the act of it.

REHMAN: But to define a country? Where there have been only tribes?

....

You want order—this is how to get its opposite.

DURAND: My head spins...

He brandishes the map, passionate—

There is no government without a map. You can put it on a wall, stick pins in it, point at it, make policy about it, if you have a go to war over it see what you've won and what you've lost. It is the abstract of decision, it is fact unvarnished. Absent it, there's nothing there, the world has no shape and that which has no shape has no meaning.

REHMAN: If it leads to greater problems than it pretends to cure?

DURAND: We'll fix those in turn.

REHMAN: If it leads to endless war?

DURAND: Then we'll fight it.[19]

Durand's adamant advocacy of a territorially defined state reflected the contemporary political vision of the colonial administration, which was centred on "fact," "order," "shape," and "progress." In geopolitical terms, the vision entailed controlling the tribes, mapping the topography, and harnessing the free movement on the frontier to give it some semblance of "order" and "shape," thereby potentially registering a modern/colonial "fact." In this way, it can be argued that the vision reflected the "birth of biopolitics" on the frontier.[20] While Rehman might have agreed to Durand's proposal for a defined border, however, the former's interest in acquiring the mountainous region conflicted with the Forward Policy of the Raj, which was designed to expand the colonial sphere of political influence and control in the mountainous region. What this policy and the territorial vision immediately afforded the colonial administration was the increased control of the state over—and vis-à-vis, the individual's long-standing practice, if not right of—free movement. While the colonial administration was negotiating the border with the Emir of Afghanistan, the control of free movement on the border was already in place in the legal realm (e.g., through The Foreigners Act, 1846). The administration had also developed politico-moral predicates of justification (which, in a way, also reflected the colonial political morality) for controlling the border. These politico-moral justifications were poverty or the lack of means of subsistence, lack of professional skills, mental soundness, criminality, and/or simply foreignness/alienage of individuals involved in trans-regional movement.

Thus, in the Foreigners Act, 1864, the colonial administration introduced a number of substantive and procedural controls on free movement. The aim, which was quite telling, was "preventing foreigners from residing, sojourning, and passing through or traveling in British India without *consent* of the Government" (emphasis added). Here it can be noticed that because both local subjects and foreigners were already subject to the Penal Code, 1860, which addressed crimes, it can be surmised that the political aim of the act was not simply to check crimes committed by itinerant groups and wanderers but also to harness free movement across the region. In this line of policy, then, the colonial administration often placed emphasis on the principle of nativity to the land and loyalty to the Crown (Indian Council Act, 1861). Although both these principles were derived from the contemporary British political vision, they lacked legitimate local political roots. Nevertheless, the administration went on to introduce them and thereby differentiated and discriminated between foreigners and natives. The act clearly stipulated that difference by providing that anyone who was not a natural born subject of Her Majesty the Queen or a native of British India would thus be considered a foreigner. Although this new definition provided for an Indian subjectivity that was quite broad, in practice it excluded those living in princely states, autonomous or tribal territories, and border territories. Moreover, the act placed the burden of proof of identity—establishing whether or not an individual was a foreigner—on the individual. This provision was directly borrowed from British laws relating to aliens in England, and it inverted the principle of presumption of innocence: innocent until proven guilty.[21] From the very early laws on the subject of aliens in England, it should be noted that the principle of presumption of innocence was never extended to aliens. This exclusion of aliens from fundamental legal principles of justice has since been at the base of the discriminatory legal regime (now globally in force), which privileges subjects/citizens over aliens/foreigners. In the wake of the War on Terror in Pakistan, the burden of proof on aliens has since doubled, as they are now not only required to prove their identities but also their non-involvement in alleged offences.

In order to check free movement after a foreigner had entered British India, the Foreigners Act provided that he/she should be placed under police surveillance as long as the requirement of peace and security demanded it. Apart from police surveillance, the act also gave powers to the government to place foreigners in "safe custody," which could extend for an indefinite time and with their release dependent on the "conditions of peace and security." Thus we see that the use of state authority over aliens was institutionalised long ago, and it kept on growing.

The critical legal significance of the Foreigners Act, 1864, it can be argued, is not limited to how the colonial administration inscribed the substance and procedure for exercising control over the free movement in the penal laws. Rather, the significance goes beyond that, inasmuch as it is related to the foundational aspect of defining personal legal identity on the basis of the fledgling Western political principle of "difference"—the difference between subjects and foreigners, nativity and foreignness, local and foreign birth, and loyalty and treason. In this way, the act gave effect to oppositional binaries, which in turn related to the border and to the characteristic of foreignness as their permanent point of reference and, therefore, that of personal legal identity as well. In other words, these oppositional binaries, as well as the personal legal identity that is based on them, surface and take their roots in the law because there existed a (geostrategic will to) border. Thus a point can be made that legal subjecthood in colonial India began with imagining and defining its outside, i.e., with imagining the border and defining border law.

Over the next half century, the colonial administration engaged in drawing a complex and legally embedded border cartography of the North-West Frontier. The geopolitical exigency of the Great Game, combined with an outward deference for the social customs of local tribal people, led the colonial administration to introduce a series of criminal regulations called the Frontier Crimes Regulations (FCRs), 1872, 1876, 1887 and 1901, and the Criminal Tribes Act, 1871, especially to border the frontier. With these regulations, the mountainous strip of the North-West Frontier was transformed into a virtually legal grey zone, with an external international border separating British India from Afghanistan and an internal border separating the mountainous tribal belt from the settled districts of British India. Inside this legal grey zone, the colonial administration inscribed two further zones: *Ilaqa ghair* (Area Foreign/Other) and *Ilaqa Sarkar* (Area Administration). In this mountainous strip, apart from controlling certain other strategically important tracts, the colonial administration took control of and securitised mountainous passes, roads, and forts—collectively, these constituted the *Ilaqa Sarkar,* and the rest, the lawless *Ilaqa ghair.* It is also worth noting that from the letter and spirit of the FCRs, the legal subjectivity of tribal people living in the mountain belt suffered immensely, as they were recognised as neither Indian subjects nor foreigners but instead as somewhere between these two categories. With the creation of this complex legal grey zone, and having two controlled borders, the free movement of the people (including the tribal peoples) eventually came under the effective surveillance, if not the full-fledged control, of the colonial administration.

Apart from the Foreigners Act, 1864, the Civil Procedure of 1908 presents another crucial marker of the identity-difference model in colonial legal history. At the beginning of the 20th century, before the outbreak of World War I, we find the terms "alien enemy" and "alien friends" provided for the first time in the Civil Procedure. In colonial India, the term "foreigner" was in legal use, rather than the term "alien," which was in common use in England and the United States. The Civil Procedure provided that even alien enemies could register and maintain civil suits in colonial courts. This provision meant that alien enemies had some legal standing and rights in the eyes of the law at the beginning of the 20th century. It is in this (still liberal) posture of law that Lord McNair, in his contemporaneous and seminal work on the legal effects of war, indicated that in the British Empire before World War I, there was not much difference between the legal status of subjects and aliens.[22] However, this observation should not be construed to mean that there was no legal distinction between subjects and aliens, or that the Empire did not want one. Rather, it is that the drastic change in the legal standing of aliens that at once came along with World War I made the previous distinction look negligible. By the time World War I ended, we notice that the category of "enemy friend" is phased out: in the United States, a century-long debate on immigration involving the concepts of enemy friend versus enemy alien comes to an end, and in colonial India, the term "alien friend" is not used again in any penal or civil law.[23] With these developments, the possibility of engaging in a liberal debate on human rights is negatively affected, as one valuable concept drops out of the formal lexicon of the debate. In England, the government introduces the Defence of the Realm Act and the Defence of the Realm Regulations, 1914 through 1919, which place strict checks on the free movement of aliens. In colonial India, the Defence of India Act, and the Defence of India Regulations, 1915 through 1919, are passed, which impose similar checks on the free movement of foreigners. The Foreigners Act, 1864, is also then strictly enforced for the registration of foreigners, their police surveillance, and safe custody. On the other hand, the British government transfers a large number of European enemy aliens to India and detains them in makeshift camps. Towards the end of the war, the Government of India Act, 1919, transfers the power to deal with foreigners and enemy aliens to the central government. To enhance this power further, the government introduces the Passport Act in 1920. With this act, the discretionary power of the government to check free movement of both subjects in and out of the country tremendously increases. The act becomes the first colonial political instrument to formally and effectively separate the legal identities of foreigners and subjects. Furthermore, at the end of World War I, three Imperial Conferences (1918, 1921, 1923) are held, which accepted the discretion of the state to allow or expel an alien from its territories. It is also worth mentioning that in January 1920, the colonial government of India decides to completely bar the entry of enemy aliens for a period of five years.

The identity-difference distinction making, especially in the form of the subject-foreigner binary, was further embedded in the next round of security laws passed in the wake of World War II. The Registration of Foreigners Act, 1939, for instance, made it mandatory for all foreigners to report both their arrivals and departures, as well as carry their legal proof of identity with them at all times. Then, under Defence of India Rules, 1939, a foreigner could be stopped from both entering and leaving the country. The government could also order foreigners to submit to procuring their photographs, thumb impressions and specimens of handwriting. Moreover, they could be kept under safe custody, or moved to any prescribed detention camp. At the end of the war, a new Foreigners Act, 1946, is passed, which incorporates a number of provisions from these regulations and the previous Foreigners Act—for instance, police surveillance, medical tests, prohibition from associating with certain groups or activities, and safe custody. One of the additions the new act makes, however, is the provision that if the identity of a foreigner could not be known or was difficult to ascertain, then the government would have the discretion to decide on his/her identity. This provision is reflective of a similar provision and discretion available to the government in the latest Protection of Pakistan laws. Here, I also want to point to the Enemy Agents Ordinance, 1943, to note that the local root of the term "enemy" in the concept of "enemy alien" goes back to this ordinance. The ordinance came with provisions for special courts and speedy criminal procedures. The present concept of enemy alien in the Protection of Pakistan laws takes the term "enemy," as well as the special courts and procedure, from this ordinance, and the term "alien" from the Foreigners Act. In its undefined form, the category of enemy alien is also later provided in Article 10 of the Constitution (1973).

In this Article 10, the Constitution guarantees safeguards against arbitrary arrest and detention, except in cases of preventive detention. While the Constitution allows for indefinite preventive detention of a citizen, if he/she is declared an enemy agent, there are some formal procedural protections afforded to him/her in the form of a Review Board consisting of judges from the superior judiciary to periodically evaluate the case. However, if an individual is an alien and is reported to be involved in an offence against the security of the state, he/she is considered an "enemy alien" and does not have any protection against arbitrary arrest and detention under the Article 10(9). It is interesting to notice that in 2014 the Supreme Court ruled in the case of "missing persons" that although Pakistan is not signatory to the International Convention for the Protection of All Persons from Enforced Disappearance (2006), the convention could still be applied "to achieve the ends of justice" for the citizens who are missing.[24] While the court addressed the question of enforced disappearance of citizens, it remains to be seen whether the court would support a similar claim for aliens.

Legal sovereignty on border

Identity-difference model and the event of violence

In the previous genealogical account, I highlighted three crucial stages in the geopolitical and legal history of the border of the North-West Frontier of colonial India/Pakistan. In the first stage, during the mid-19th century, the colonial administration harnessed free trans-regional movement, which was widespread at the time. The colonial administration did this by envisioning a territorial state model for India—a model that was and still is the leading political conception of the state. With the territorial state model, there arose the need for drawing well-defined, fixed, and protected borders for colonial India. Moreover, the model also indirectly impinged on the subject's personal identity, which began to be redefined on the basis of territorial belonging/bordering. Hence, free movement was not only harnessed, it was made to seem, as a practice, in conflict with some of the foundational principles of the modern territorial state—territorial belonging and sedentary life. In the second stage, from the middle to the end of the 19th century, before the cartographic border could be negotiated and drawn, the colonial administration erected a legal border by passing a series of laws and crime regulations. The legal border was drawn primarily on the terrain of personal legal identity: subjects were distinguished from foreigners, and their rights and duties began to have a new legal base—territorial belonging and loyalty. Third, towards the beginning of the 20th century, as the cartographic border had been drawn, together with the legal border (the FCRs), it resulted in a complex border with internal and external borderlines. Inside this complex border, the colonial administration chose to suspend the operation of law and courts (by providing FCRs). The administration ensured that all mountainous passes and strategic peaks and plains were guarded and controlled. These cartographic and legal borders subsequently outlived colonialism and exist to the present day. They have been further strengthened by the provision of more powers to LEAs under the anti-terrorism and the Protection of Pakistan laws. In 2016, the government began to fence the border along the Khyber Pass.

In this genealogical account, my essential purpose was to highlight the legal dimension of the border in order to tease out the law's relationship with violence. In ways that resonate with Shapiro's concept of violent cartography, which I engaged in the beginning of the essay, the well-known sociologist, Johan Galtung introduced the concept of structural violence. According to Galtung, there are many different forms of violence, which can nevertheless be characterised into two broad forms: direct violence and structural violence. Galtung writes,

> Whereas in the first case [direct violence] these consequences can be traced to concrete persons or actors, in the second case [structural violence] this is no longer meaningful. There may not be any person who directly harms another person in the structure. The violence is built into the structure and shows up as unequal power and consequently unequal life chances.[25]

The two events of violence—the Kharotabad and Karachi killings—with which I began the essay are examples of direct violence, while the laws that I highlighted earlier in the genealogical account are examples of structural violence. The two types of violence are related in such a way that the former is not possible without the latter—the Kharotabad and Karachi killings would not have been possible without the deeper, embedded structure of violence in laws.

The two forms of violence, structural and direct violence, even though they are distinct, are not independent of each other. In a recent take on Galtung's work, James Tyner and Joshua Inwood point out that the two forms of violence can be conceptualised as distinct from each other, but making such a distinction should not elide the responsibility for action. Hence they suggest that violence should be carefully considered in its spatial and temporal contexts, especially with the aim of showing who carries out violence, why, and how.[26] In our context, which is a reading of events of violence in securitised spaces, we also notice the transformations between direct and structural violence. We notice that structural violence not only provides structural support for direct violence (or at times translates into direct violence) but also helps the latter to elide responsibility. The support is afforded through a structure created by provisions of burden of proof, indemnity in the use of force, administrative discretion to warrant detention, the defence of necessity, general administrative rules and training manuals, and the unwritten security discourse. Borrowing Agamben's concept of the security *dispositif,* I want to name the support structure of structural violence the legal-administrative *dispositif* of violence. In the Kharotabad incident, we come to clearly see the legal-administrative *dispositif* of violence at play. For instance, once the killing took place, the LEAs tried to cover it up through different tactics. The doctor who carried out the autopsies was stopped from presenting the report he prepared. The local government resisted carrying out an "internal" investigation under the ATA, 1997, and once that was done, the findings were not published in the name of state security. Moreover, in the eyes of criminal law, the victims, because they were aliens, had no legal standing to seek trial and justice. The support for these tactics was available in security laws and administration, which create, as Judith Butler puts it, the conditions for normalisation of the state of exception through the governmentality of bureaucracy.[27]

Let us turn to the operational side of direct violence in securitised spaces and the question of responsibility: in other words, how does the event of direct violence take place, and how is it subsequently justified or covered up, as in the Kharotabad and Karachi killings? I want to argue that a crucial aspect to note in most cases of direct violence is the temporality of the *modus operandi.* Obviously the speed is meant to avoid exposure, and thereby to increase the chances of eliding responsibility and hiding behind the legal-administrative *dispositif* of violence. Accordingly, most cases of direct violence in securitised spaces (even though these spaces are often equipped with CCTV cameras) go unrecorded or else are shielded by the legal-administrative *dispositif* of structural violence. However, thanks to camera technology in mobile phones and the uploading of videos to social media, some cases of direct violence do get recorded, allowing us to see and analyse the method of violence engaged.

There is no denying the fact that oftentimes LEAs, faced with security situations, have to make quick decisions on potential cases of terrorism. It is also understandable that the power to use lethal force is sanctioned by law. Moreover, we also know that in bureaucracy and public administration, the power to make such decisions based on legal provisions is recognised as an exercise of administrative discretion. However, we need to notice, as Mark B. Salter points out, that the power to exercise administrative discretion is "a decision that is not grounded in fact, but solely in the power to decide."[28] Therefore, there is a need to generate a more nuanced understanding of how this rapid operating method in direct violence works. To explain this, I want to engage a conceptual insight from Michael J. Shapiro. Writing in the context of precipitous discharge of violence by combat drones (unmanned aerial vehicles, or UAVs) on suspected terrorists/targets, Shapiro says that the personnel in charge prepare a certain "necro-biography" of the targeted persons. A necro-biography, he says, is a "murder justifying biographical speculation, which rapidly turn[s] what is arbitrary into what is regarded as 'obvious.'"[29] From this insight, I argue that in other cases of violence in securitised spaces, where armed personnel discharge violence on targeted persons, the process involves making quick biographical speculations as well, which thereby determines whether or not targeted persons are *obvious* terrorists. For instance, in the case of the Kharotabad killings, we notice that the personnel drew quick biographical speculations about the aliens, assuming and later labelling them as Chechen terrorists. We know well that in the security discourse in Pakistan—and elsewhere in the world, for that matter—Chechens may easily pass for terrorists, especially when found in securitised spaces or troubled borders. On the other hand, in the Karachi killing, the young man had roamed around in an area under curfew, and was speculated to be a *persona non grata*. In both events, the personnel relied on quick biographical speculations and resorted to the use of lethal force rather than arresting and detaining the victims, which they could easily have done.

In this context of quick decision making, I want to point to an insight by Salter that the decision involving the determination of the identity of an individual precedes any legal claim or right. He writes, "At the actual place of the border, the determination of status precedes the grant of 'leave to enter.'" He further writes that an "administrative, discretionary decision" to that effect lies at "the exceptional threshold of law."[30] This threshold is, in fact, the thinly veiled border between law and political fact, where direct violence finds its appropriate place. In the Foreigners Act, 1946 (Article 8), we find a clear provision for the determination of nationality. The act provides that in cases of difficulty in determination due to lack of, or shortcomings in, legal identity documents or oral testimony, the government will have discretion to declare the nationality of the person to which he/she seems "most closely connected" or to which he/she has been "last so connected." The act further provides that the government's discretion cannot be challenged in a court of law. Under the act, the government can practically detain a person for an indefinite period of time until his/her identity is determined. The recent Anti-Terrorism and Protection of Pakistan laws go a step forward in adding to the criminal side of the process of determination of identity. For instance, the PPA, 2014, provides that if a person's identity is "unascertainable as Pakistani," and if he/she is found to be involved in a prescribed offence against the state, then LEAs can arrest, detain, and/or use force against him. These laws relate the determination of identity to perceived involvement in an offence and/or to even the mere physical presence in the locality of the offence, and hence make individuals vulnerable. On the other hand, these laws make the use of force contingent upon the good-faith judgment of the personnel about identity. In this way, the *obvious* identity is connected directly to judgment and execution by short-circuiting the entire criminal procedure of justice.

As law enforcement personnel engage in administrative discretion while determining the identities of individuals, there is no guarantee that they will always make a correct decision. This problematic aspect is caused by what Shapiro calls "the fogging effect."[31] In other words, due to the generalised nature of training in the art of distinguishing terrorists from the common people, and/or the lack of sufficient information and understanding of the situation, social culture, and appearances of individuals, the security eyes of LEAs might cast a blurred gaze. Shapiro engages the Lacanian concept of "the gaze" or "the cultural screen" to explain the possibility of (mis-) recognition. He writes that (mis-)recognition is created because "what is perceived is what is filtered through the gaze or 'the cultural screen' that is the condition of possibility for subjectivity."[32] I have earlier pointed to a similar concept by Foucault of the "grids of perception and evaluation." The legal dimension of this gaze/grid is what I am calling the legal-administrative *dispositif*. Engaging Kant's First Critique, Shapiro further explains that an individual's consciousness is related to objects not merely in representational fashion but also in productive fashion. Our consciousness, he writes, often produces—not just identifies or represents—security threats. On the border, which remains in a permanent encounter with its alterity (for instance, the acknowledgement in the discourse of the War on Terror that the enemy has no face or identity—a faceless war[33]) this productive relationship of consciousness in creating the enemy or (mis-)recognition in creating the enemy is clearly possible and understandable.

The conscious role of border security is to hold the threshold between law and anarchy.[34] Accordingly, the border not only represents the inside (of the state) but also its outside, its alterity.[35] In its corporeal form, the border's alterity is embodied and reflected by the ontological figure of the alien/foreigner. The alien is the embodied corporeal site of the state of exception. In descriptive terms, an alien who arrives at a border risks exposing himself/herself (because of his appearance, disposition, and culture) to the burden of that country's security laws and the executive discretion of their LEAs. In the case of the Kharotabad victims, because they represented the border's alterity, which was, in a way, further screened through their Chechen appearance/labelling (at least for those who fell in the first round of firing), they exposed themselves to the burden of Pakistan's security laws and its LEAs' discretionary powers—to the legal-administrative *dispositif* of violence.

Although Shapiro's concepts of necro-biography and the fogging effect help to conceptualise the direct violence perpetrated in the two incidents, I argue that the Kharotabad incident is more complex and, therefore, needs an exercise in further conceptualisation. In this incident, we see that violence is discharged on the victims due to quick, murder-justifying biographical speculation but also because of their ethnic profiling. The assumed Chechen ethnicity of the victims provided safe warrant to the personnel to discharge violence. This type of violence, which involves murder-justifying ethnic profiling, we may name, for lack of a better term, "necro-ethnography." A necro-ethnography is a form of racial or ethnic profiling in securitised spaces, which warrants LEAs to make sovereign decisions on the life and death of individuals (belonging to, or labelled as belonging to, certain already-maligned ethnic groups in security discourse). The concept aims to expose the structure of ethnic/racial and sectarian violence built in security discourse, which warrants taking sovereign decisions on the right to life of individuals. Generally, it tends to understand the relationship between the (perceived) ethnic/racial identity of individuals and the state's legal-administrative *dispositif* of violence.

An alternative way of conceptualising and making sense of the Kharotabad killings is possible through N. A. Wonders' concept of the choreography of the border on bodies. Writing in the light of the idea of the performativity of identity, which was articulated in detail by Judith Butler, Wonders conceptualises the violent border–body relationship as an "elaborate dance" between state agents and mobile individuals.[36] Wonders argues that

> although states attempt to choreograph national borders, often in response to global pressures, these state policies have little meaning until they are 'performed' by state agents or by border crossers ... Border agents and state bureaucrats play a critical role in determining where, how, and on whose body a border will be performed.[37]

What we see in the Kharotabad incident is, in fact, the performance of the border on the bodies of these aliens. In this line of thought, when we take into account human losses at and due to the borders in today's securitised world, then I argue the geographic border is but a mere backdrop to a more performative stage of corporeal bodies of rights-denied, mobile individuals on which the choreography of violence is played.

Conclusion

To question the relationship between the border and law enforcement violence is to highlight what is at stake in the growing legal regime of security, both theoretically and practically. Part of this legal regime rests on a security discourse that conceives the figure of the alien/foreigner as an agent of uncertainty and danger who, hence, is subject to state intervention. The alien embodies otherness, alterity, and the border, but, at the same time, the alien is the correlative of order, citizenship, and the centre. The figure of the alien is located and recognised through the "grids of perception and evaluation" and is sacrificed at the altar of peace and order.

The relationship between the border and law enforcement violence originates in and/or is prompted by the state's security discourse. The border is a cartographic extension of the logic of law enforcement—to mark and maintain the threshold between inside and outside, identity and difference, and order and anarchy. Just as violence (or direct violence) is discharged to maintain the border, this logic of law enforcement is choreographed on bodies. On the other hand, the responsibility for (direct) violence is eluded with the shield of structural violence—the administrative legal provisions that warrant the good faith acts of LEAs. Moreover, as we see in the case of the Kharotabad killings, the structural violence is so effectively rationalised and deeply regimented that the courts find it beyond the point to intervene and make amends. What is at stake here, in the relationship between the border and law enforcement violence, then, is the basic right to life of every individual.

Juxtaposing the two incidents of violence in this essay is not meant to merely critique the legal regime of security and conceptualise the operation of violence. Rather, the purpose has been to expose the structure of violence both in the law and law enforcement. For this purpose, I have shed light on the latest security laws, the Protection of Pakistan laws, and how they create the possibility of enacting violence against non-citizens. Moreover, the purpose has been to remind the superior courts in Pakistan that their silence on the rights of alien/non-citizens results in the increase of the powers of LEAs, on the one hand, and on the other, it leaves the public debate (and case law) on human rights (understood as different from fundamental rights of citizens) uninformed of legal opinion and vision of the judiciary. I have tried to make the point that reforming the legal regime of security in the country is not possible without exposing and attending to those provisions in the security and panel laws that derogate against basic human rights.

Notes

1 Raza, "The North West Frontier of Pakistan: Preoccupation with 'Unveiling' the Battlefield and the Continuing Violent Cartographies."
2 Shapiro, *Violent Cartographies*, 18.
3 Bennett, *Empathic Vision.*
4 For more on the Anti-Terrorism laws of Pakistan: Kennedy, "The Creation and Development of Pakistan's Anti-Terrorism Regime, 1997–2002"; Raza, "Anti-Terrorism Legal Regime of Pakistan and the Global Paradigm of Security: A Genealogical and Comparative Analysis."
5 Michel, "Why the Prison," 79.
6 Kristeva, *Strangers to Ourselves*, 96.
7 Schmitt, *Political Theology.*
8 Salter, "When the Exception Becomes the Rule: Borders, Sovereignty, and Citizenship," 372.
9 *Mehram Ali v. Federation of Pakistan*, PLD SC 111 (2000); *Suo Motu Case No. 10 of 2011*, PLD SC 997 (2011).
10 In the 1837 draft of the Penal Code the law commissioners argued: "As the penal law is impotent against a successful rebel, it is consequently necessary that it should be made strong and sharp against the first beginnings of rebellion, against treasonable designs which have been carried no further than plots and preparations." Around the same time in the United States, however, a more

restrictive legal construction was advised by Chief Justice John Marshall. Raza, "Anti-Terrorism Legal Regime of Pakistan and the Global Paradigm of Security: A Genealogical and Comparative Analysis."

11 Raza, "Anti-Terrorism Legal Regime of Pakistan and the Global Paradigm of Security: A Genealogical and Comparative Analysis."

12 Ibid.

13 Marsden and Hopkins, *Fragments of the Afghan Frontier*, 2; Nichols, *A History of Pashtun Migration 1775–2006*.

14 Bayly, *Rulers, Townsmen and Bazaars: North Indian Society in the Age of British Expansion, 1770–1870*.

15 The first office to deal with aliens in England was created in 1793 under the Regulations of Aliens Act. It was known as the Aliens Office, and it had a Superintendent of Aliens. In 1816, another Regulations of Aliens Act was passed, which introduced an initial system of central registration of aliens. In 1826 the parliament passed the Registration of Aliens Act, which introduced registration with the local police and a declaration before leaving the country. Ten years later, a new act, the Registration of Aliens Act, 1836, is passed. With this act the small Aliens Office is merged into the Home Department.

16 Grahl-Madsen, *The Status of Refugees in International Law*, 11, 95, 319–320.

17 The expression "correlative other" belongs to Brubaker. Brubaker, *Citizenship and Nationhood in France and Germany*, 37.

18 Soguk, *States and Strangers*, 97–98.

19 Hutchinson, "Durand's Line," 45–46.

20 I borrow this phrase and the idea behind it from Michel Foucault. See Foucault, *Security, Territory, Population*; Foucault, *The Birth of Biopolitics*.

21 The requirement of burden of proof on the individual in the criminal procedure was and is the first step of (determining) culpability.

22 Lord McNair and Watts, *The Legal Effects of War*.

23 Raza, "A Preliminary Note on the Genealogy of the Concept of Enemy Alien in Pakistan."

24 *Human Rights Case No. 29388-K of 2013*, PLD SC 305 (2014).

25 Galtung, "Violence, Peace, and Peace Research," 170–171.

26 Tyner and Inwood, "Violence as Fetish: Geography, Marxism, and Dialectics."

27 Butler, *Precarious Life: The Power of Mourning and Violence*.

28 Salter, "When the Exception Becomes the Rule: Borders, Sovereignty, and Citizenship," 370.

29 Shapiro, *Politics and Time*, 123.

30 Salter, "When the Exception Becomes the Rule: Borders, Sovereignty, and Citizenship," 368.

31 Shapiro, *Cinematic Geopolitics*, 64.

32 Ibid., 65.

33 Raza, "Critical Reflections on the Reality of Drone Warfare: Thinking with Jean Baudrillard."

34 M. B. Salter drawing on R. B. J. Walker, for instance, writes, "The only 'ethic' of which governs the border is the Machiavellian 'virtue' of society." Salter, "When the Exception Becomes the Rule: Borders, Sovereignty, and Citizenship," 372.

35 Nail, *Theory of the Border*.

36 Wonders, "Global Flows, Semi-Permeable Borders, and New Channels of Inequality: Border Crossers and Border Performativity," 64.

37 Ibid., 66.

7 Epilogue

Kharotabad killings: security and political responsibility

Introduction

On May 17, 2011, breaking news regarding a potential suicide bombing attack began to flash on local TV channels in Pakistan. The law enforcement agencies claimed that a group of five (possibly Chechen) suicide bombers, including three women, were travelling towards the city of Quetta, Baluchistan. The agencies further claimed that the group was stopped at a Frontier Corps (FC) checkpoint in the town of Kharotabad, on the outskirts of the city Quetta. The agencies projected that the group, seeing they could not make it into the city, planned to attack the checkpoint instead. However, the agencies went on to say that the checkpoint had already received a radio warning from another checkpoint about this group of alleged suicide bombers. Just as the group disembarked from their cab and tried to rush towards the checkpoint, law enforcement officers gunned them down.[1]

Suicide bombings are not infrequent or unusual in Pakistan. Therefore, many such prevention operations by LEAs are viewed as a relief. However, this time something was different: the appearance of a photograph of the last alleged female suicide bomber taken just before she was ultimately killed. In the photograph, which would soon become iconic, the woman can be seen lying on the ground near a sandbag-covered picket of the checkpoint, stretching her arm upwards and apparently pointing to the sky. The photograph presented such a powerful gesture of the injured woman that it called into doubt the official claims that the operation was, in fact, a successful prevention of a suicide bombing. The photograph disrupted the security narrative before it could be consistently constructed and sold to the public. Over the next few days, the operation remained one of the top stories of the local media, and demand for more information about the concrete circumstances of the incident increased. Soon, more photographs, short video clips, and interviews of witnesses began to surface. These supplemental accounts proved convincingly that the alleged suicide bombers were not Chechens—four of them belonged to Dagestan and Russia, and one to Tajikistan—and that they had earlier travelled to Iran, from where they made their way into Pakistan. Moreover, they were all unarmed, and, shockingly, the last alleged suicide bomber to die—the woman in the photograph—was eight months pregnant.

For their part, the police and the FC personnel did whatever they could to stop the gathering of further information about the operation. The police doctor who performed the autopsy on the dead bodies was first threatened, then physically assaulted, and eventually killed by unknown men. The photojournalist who took the photo that would become iconic, as well as other photos and clips of the operation, was run out of Quetta and forced to seek refuge in the capital city of Islamabad. Despite the arbitrary and violent efforts to cover up the operation, the police and the FC personnel could not ease the popular pressure on the government to carry out an inquiry. For its part, the government, which had initially lauded the operation, felt embarrassed by what soon turned out to become a security scandal and as a result announced plans to set up a judicial inquiry commission, while parliament formed a fact-finding committee to investigate the event.

How to read the gesture in the photograph?

What do we make of the photograph in question, and what does it make of us? To put the question in other words, how does the photograph affect our political responsiveness? Our first impression of it might be quite simple: it captures a helpless, injured woman's call for mercy. However, this impression is entangled in a passive or negative frame of meaning making. Interpreting it as a call for mercy only reduces the larger political problem of violence to a singular, and hence fixed, event, and threatens to rob the photographed woman of her agency in the face of the spectacle of state violence. Put another way, our first impression is doomed to accept her as a bare sacrificial life—a *homo sacer*—unless (the state) decides otherwise.[2]

However, the *affective field of vision* created by the photograph, to borrow Judith Butler's words,[3] especially as the injured (but not necessarily helpless) woman stretches and waves her arm in the fusillade of firing AK-47s, impels us to move beyond our first impression—the call for mercy. We begin to discern the figure of violence in the photograph and experience the affective shock that at once makes us aware of a wave of revulsion, protest and resistance generating within us. Our first impression, the mercy–sympathy–singularity equation, is displaced. We are impelled to ask ourselves: is she calling for mercy or for justice, possibly even divine justice? I suggest that it is surely a call for justice or, at least, the effects this photograph generates reveal the possibility for us to treat it as a call for justice. We only need to see how she struggles to gain and assert agency in the face of violence and extreme vulnerability. The photograph captures this final moment in the act of killing: the moment when the victim registers her last expression of agency with an ambiguous and polysemic yet simple and powerful gesture. Hence, just before her death, which she sensed was coming (perhaps because she was already fatally injured), she transcends her state of helplessness to the state of sovereign subject's agency—and becomes a form of resistant life aimed at challenging state power by exposing the anarchy and anomy resident in it.

It is equally possible that some of us (the viewers) are not touched by this affective field of vision, and hence are unable to move beyond our first impression or discern the figure of agency-resistance and the call for justice. However, even if we fail to see her as a form of resistant life, we cannot fail to notice that in her iconic gesture, as she stretches her arm and points to the sky, the victim invokes a referent of justice—of God and His divine justice. This invocation of the divine referent places her gesture in at least two related, but mutually exclusive, fields of meanings: (a) have mercy in the name of God, or (b) fear His wrath and justice. In other words, her gesture is an imploration, a warning not to underestimate the sovereign subject's agency, and simultaneously begs the question of how an invocation of the divine referent relates to, and enables, the sovereign subject's agency in our profane world.

In order to give a plausible explanation of the relationship between the invocation of the Divine referent and the profane agency, as well as to move to our more central concern regarding political responsiveness, I wish to engage Walter Benjamin's concept of divine violence.[4] Benjamin introduced this concept as the nemesis of state violence, which he also sometimes refers to as the "mythic violence," and argued state violence includes two kinds of violence:

a violence used for making or constituting law, hence called "law-making violence" or "constituent violence" and
b violence used for preserving the (constituted) law, hence called "law-preserving violence" or "constituting violence."

Divine violence, on the other hand, is the violence that destroys law (and the forces on which it depends as they depend on it), and along with it, its capacity to reconstitute itself. Although Benjamin's concept of divine violence has not yet submitted itself to a complete understanding, there are important insights that his interlocutors and interpreters have made that I intend to engage, (a) to extrapolate the gesture in our iconic photograph and (b) to illustrate the concept itself through such extrapolation, especially with the purpose of putting it in operation against the mythic law of security.

Any initial extrapolation of the photograph, just as that of Benjamin's concept, essentially begins in eschatology/theology, even as the task of the photograph and concept is to prevent either from falling into that domain. From a purely eschatological perspective, I think, like numerous members of the Pakistani public who called for an investigation and justice, the gesture in the photograph is an imploration to God to witness her forced abjection and killing and to avenge her on the Day of Judgment. Hence, as she implores, the symbolic force of her gesture is directed at her perpetrators.

However, in alignment with the theological dimension of Benjamin's concept, an alternative reading sees the victim imploring God to send His wrath (violence–justice) on her perpetrators here in this profane world. Both these readings come to face the dilemma of (an indefinite) wait in the dispensation of justice. Despite a Muslim believer's faith in the Day of Judgment and in the divine miracles of wrath, we also know that divine justice either remains infinitely suspended or its moment of arrival is objectively unknowable. From the theological dimension, then, divine justice is, to use Derrida's phrase, a "justice-to-come."[5]

However, some recent interpreters of Benjamin inform us that, unlike Derrida's justice-to-come, Benjamin's divine violence/justice does arrive. It is, rather, in the state of being here already. It strikes out of nowhere, and it is pure means (without ends).[6] This interpretation might sound absurd, but as Slavoj Žižek explains and illustrates, Benjamin's concept makes more sense today than ever before. Benjamin borrows the theological and linguistic structure of the purely eschatological notion of divine violence (especially the one in the second extrapolation I gave previously) and replaces the divine referent, the big Other, with a profane referent—the people. In other words, he replaces transcendence with immanence, while the concomitant theological symbolism is not completely given up, just as the name is also not given up. Perhaps Benjamin knew, as Žižek conjectures, the value of "theological dimension without which…revolution cannot win."[7]

Just as in Benjaminian justice, the divine justice that the victim in the photograph calls for is in the state of being already here, primarily because her ultimate referent is also the people. Let us once again focus on the structure of the field of vision of the photograph. When we replace the divine referent with the people, then she appears to be pointing to the sky, but even in this pure visual dimension, we notice that the sky does exactly what the divine would do: it sends down the image (in this case, the atrocious image) to affect our responsiveness, or as Benjamin would say, to affect us in our solitudes, such that we would wrestle with it and take upon ourselves the responsibility of the event. Now, should we borrow Lacan's notion of "mirror stage," as Žižek does while explaining Benjamin's concept,[8] then the sky would appear to act as a grand mirror stage, where events are staged and sent down in the form of their mirror images. The victim points to this mirror stage, from where the divine violence will (*have*) descend(ed) in the form of atrocious mirror images. These images are, in a sense, created outside our world—somewhere on the transcendent stage—and, visually, outside the frame in which victims, perpetrators, and witnesses encounter each other. The images enable them to step outside the frame and see their mirror image speak to them. Put differently, the focus on visual dimension teases out the dimension of immanence in the victim's call for justice, just as it puts to test our own political responsiveness.

In extrapolating the victim's gesture in the photograph, and in engaging the concept of Divine violence, I do not intend to limit our task to mere conceptualisation and theory. Rather, I take the task further to praxis and identify, or perhaps project, a course of action for our political responsiveness. To be sure, I want to identify a site in the *dispositif* of state/mythic violence, which I think needs the attention of our political responsiveness, and/or where the divine violence *will have* struck. The hint to this site is given in one of the passages of Benjamin on divine violence:

> ...on the breaking of this cycle that plays out in the sphere of the mythical form of law, on the destitution (*Entsetzung*) of law with all the powers on which it depends (as they depend on it), ultimately therefore on the destitution of state violence, a new historical epoch founds itself.[9]

The site in the *dispositif* of state violence is this relationship between law and law-preserving forces. The former, as Agamben informs us, captures the anomy, and the latter, the anarchy, which together form state power/violence. Benjamin tells us that should we want to herald a new historical epoch, then we need to reckon with the possibility of destitution of law, especially the destitution of the relationship between law and law-preserving forces. And Benjamin further assures us: "If the rule of myth is broken occasionally in the present age, the coming age is not so unimaginably remote that an attack on law is altogether futile."[10]

Almost a century on from Benjamin's time, we need to ask: do we live in that unimaginably remote age in which an attack on law, to be sure, security law, is altogether futile? Given the War on Terror, has the rule of myth not expanded, strengthened, and become pervasive, such that we now live under what Agamben terms a global paradigm of security? Is this the paradigm that Benjamin had warned us against? Answering these questions depends on our ability to pose another question: is an attack on the law still possible? This is the question of the immanence of divine violence and of the right to justice.

Despite the fact that the modern security paradigm, which began during Benjamin's lifetime and has now reached its high point of penetration, we can still identify ways to depose the security law/paradigm. In this paper, I suggest that in order to depose the paradigm, we need to identify and depose its key linchpins: (a) alienage or the juridical category of aliens and (b) indemnity or the provisions of indemnity for the law enforcing agencies. My assumption is that alienage and indemnity provisions enter into a vicious relationship with the notion of security and create the *dispositif*/apparatus of security in which justice is excluded/externalised. Accordingly, the law-preserving violence of law enforcement agencies remains beyond the purview of the state justice system.

My assumption here prompts the question why I think alienage and indemnity provisions are at the heart of the security paradigm. Here are some of the reasons: (a) aliens are the individuals who are juridically most vulnerable, and they have no immunity from the right of the state to juridical derogations, (b) they cannot register claims against a state or its law enforcement agencies and are thus left to the mercy of international human rights, which are dispensable and non-justiciable, (c) anyone can become alien depending on his/her territorial location, (d) alienage is only increasing in a globalising world, partly due to increased unrest in many countries, and (e) law enforcement agencies (including military and paramilitary) are often shielded by indemnity provisions against any claims of aliens.

The Kharotabad incident is exemplary for its spectacular display of force on the one hand and the vulnerability–agency of the victim on the other. We notice in a video recording of the event, as well as from the statement of a journalist who saw the incident, that the victims could have been apprehended, but the operation commander instead ordered his soldiers to finish them off. The commander's order is clearly extrajudicial, a decision on the life and death of aliens. The concern in the wake of this incident centres around how law enforcement agencies have come to exercise this power over life and death and how they have come to usurp this power from the judiciary. What emerges is a vicious relationship between identity (here, alienage) and indemnity.

It is this aspect of the identity–indemnity relationship that is at the heart of the exercise of power over life and death. The operation officer knew well that he was dealing with aliens (who have hardly any justiciable rights). The operation officer also knew that indemnity provisions would shield his actions, and that his colleagues and higher-ups would stand by him (the *esprit de corps* will prevail over justice). This makes justice external to the security *dispositif*/apparatus. Justice is not allowed to penetrate the law-enforcing organisation. Instead, it is thought as a divisive force, causing mistrust and eventually weakening organisational coherence and functioning. Now justice lives in the interstices between different organisations and institutions, between law enforcement, prosecution, the executive, the legislature, and the judiciary itself.

Notes

1 For details, see Zahra-Malik, "Kharotabad Killings and the Cover Up."
2 See Agamben, *Homo Sacer.*
3 Butler, *Frames of War.*
4 Benjamin, "Critique of Violence."
5 Martel, "Waiting for Justice."
6 Žižek, Violence: Six Sideways Reflections.
7 Ibid., 168.
8 Ibid., 176.
9 Agamben, "What Is a Destituent Power," 70.
10 Benjamin, "Critique of Violence," 284.

Cases cited

Cases are listed alphabetically by first name of plaintiff, following the conventions of Pakistani and Indian case reporters. Abbreviations for case reporters are the following:

AIR	(All India Reporter)
FCR	(Federal Court Reporter)
MLD	(Monthly Law Reports)
PLD	(The All Pakistan Legal Decisions)
P. Cr. L. J.	(Pakistan Criminal Law Journal)
PLJ	(Pakistan Law Journal)
SCMR	(Supreme Court Monthly Review)
YLR	(Yearly Law Reporter)

Colonial India cases

Emperor v. Benoari Lall Sharma, (1943) FCR 96.
Keshav Talpade v. King Emperor, 30 AIR 1943 Federal Court 1.
Niharendu Dutt Mazumdar v. King Emperor, AIR 1942 Federal Court 22.
Piare Dusadh and others v. The King Emperor, (1944) FCR 61.

Pakistan cases

Abdullah Malik v. Crown, PLD 1949 Lahore 212.
Abdur Rahman Malik v. The Crown, PLD 1950 Lahore 234.
Abdur Rauf v. Chief Commissioner, PLD 2006 Lahore 111.
Ali Muhammad Khadian v. The Crown, PLD 1952 Lahore 573.
Ali Muhammad v. State, 2011 YLR 3055.
Ameera Khanum v. Government of Punjab, 2007 P. Cr. L. J. 527
Asadullah v. Muhammad Tariq and 2 others, PLD 2006 Lahore 651.
Asghar Ali Mubarak v. Special Judge, Anti-Terrorism Court, 2016 P. Cr. L. J. 1108
Asma Jilani v. Government of the Punjab, PLD 1972 SC 139.
Ayub Khan v. The State, 2009 MLD 793.
Azeem Khan and another v. Mujahid Khan and others, 2016 SCMR 274.
Azhar Hussain v. State, PLD 2003 Lahore 217.

Bao Saleem v. The State, 2008 MLD 647.

Basharat Ali v. Special Judge, Anti-Terrorism Court-II, Gujranwala, PLD 2004 Lahore 199.

Basharat Ali v. Special Judge, Anti-Terrorism Court, PLD 2004 Lahore 199.

Bazar Gul Afridi v. Federation of Paksitan, Writ Petition No. 360/2013.

Begum Nazir Abdul Hamid v. Pakistan (Federal Government) through Secretary Interior, PLD 1974 Lahore 7.

Chaudhary Zahur Ilahi v. Secretary to Government of Pakistan, Ministry of Home and Kashmir Affairs, PLD 1975 Lahore 499.

Darvesh M. Arbey, Advocate v. Federation of Pakistan, PLD 1977 Lahore 846.

District Bar Association, Rawalpindi, PLD 2015 SC 401.

Faisal Iqbal v. The State, PLD 1998 Lahore 371.

Federation of Pakistan v. Ch. Manzoor Elahi, PLD 1976 Supreme Court 430.

Fida Muhammad v. Province of NWFP through Home Secretary, Peshawar, PLD, 1973, Peshawar 156.

Ghulam Abbad v. Mushtaq Ahmed, 2014 YLR 201.

Ghulam Ahmed v. Govt. of Sindh, PLD 1988 Karachi 237.

Ghulam Hussain v. The State, PLD 2007 SC 71.

Government of East Pakistan v. Rowshan Bijaya Shaukat Ali, PLD 1966 SC 286

Government of West Pakistan v. Begum Agha Abdul Karim Shorish Kashmiri, PLD 1969 SC 14.

Gul Muhammad v. The State, PLD 2012 Quetta 22.

Hakim Khan and 3 others v. Government of Pakistan through Secretary Interior and Others, PLD 1992 SC 595.

Hazoor Bakhsh v. State, PLD 2008 Karachi 487.

Imran Ashraf v. The State, 2001 SCMR 424.

Jaffar Mehmood v. The State, 2016 YLR 846.

Jahangir Akbar Awan v. The State, PLD 2000 Karachi 89.

Jahangir v. State, 2011 YLR 2330 Lahore.

Jamiat-Islam Pakistan through Syed Munawar Hassan v. Federation of Pakistan, PLD 2000 SC 111.

Ketno v. Judge, Anti-Terrorism Court, 2005 MLD 353.

Khan Muhammad Yusuf Khan Khattak v. S. M. Ayub and two others, PLS 1973 Supreme Court 160.

Khawaja Mureed Hussain v. Government of the Punjab, Home Department, Lahore and 6 Others, 2013 P. Cr. L. J., 312.

Liaqat Ali v. Government of Sind through Secretary, Home Department, PLD 1973 Karachi 78.

Liaquat Hussain and others v. Federation of Pakistan, PLD 1999 SC 504.

Mahmood Khan Achakzai and others v. Federation of Pakistan and others, PLJ 1997 SC 550.

Maulana Abdus Sattar Khan Niazi v. The State, PLD 1974 Lahore 324.

Maulvi Ghulamullah Khan v. District Magistrate Campbellpur, PLD 1967 Peshawar, 195

Mehram Ali v. Federation of Pakistan, PLD 1998 Lahore 347, 1998 MLD 1411 Lahore, PLD 1998 SC 1445, 1998 SCMR 1156, PLD SC 111 (2000).

Meraj Hussain v. Anti-Terrorism Court, 2007, P. Cr. L. J., 1011.
Michroo v. State, 2015 YLR 2617 Karachi.
Mir Abdul Baqi Baloch v. Government of Pakistan, PLD 1968 SC 313.
Muhammad Amjad v. The State, PLD 2003 SC 704.
Muhammad Rasool v. The State, PLD 2012 Quetta 122.
Muhammad Shafique Butt v. The State, 2015 YLR 877.
Muhammad Shareef v. The State, 2001 YLR 900.
Muhammad Yousaf Farooqi v. Government of Punjab, 2012 P. Cr. L.J. 905;
Muhammad Yusuf v. The State, 2012 YLR 1992.
Mumtaz Ali Khan Rajban v. Federation of Pakistan, PLD 2001 S. C. 169.
Nabi Ahmad v. Home Secretary, Govt. of W. Pak., PLD 1969 SC 599.
Nadeem v. State, 2014 P. Cr. L. J. 374 FSC.
Nazeer alias Wazeer v. The State, PLD 2007 SC 202.
Nematullah v. Abdul Kahar, 2006 YLR 1036.
NLR 2005 Cr. L. J. 158.
Nooruddin v. Nazeer Ahmed, 2011 P. Cr. L. J. 1370 Karachi.
Province of Punjab through Collector Sargodha v. Muhammad Bakhsh and another, PLD 2012 SC 664.
Qamar Hussain Shah v. The State, PLD 2006 Karachi 331.
Qurban Ali and another v. The State, 2007 P. Cr. L.J. 675.
References by Judge Special Court II (Criminal References 32 and 33 of 2005), 2006 P. Cr. L. J. 921.
Roman Catholic Diocese of Islamabad/Rawalpindi through Bishop and another v. Federation through Secretary Ministry of Interior Islamabad and 6 others, PLJ 2015 Islamabad High Court, 347.
Sahibzar v. The State, 2003 P. Cr. L. J. 699.
Sakina Mai v. Government of Punjab, 2007 P. Cr. L. J. 956.
Saleem Khan and others v. The State and others, 2001 P. Cr. L. J. 503.
Sardar Ahmed Abbasi v. Muhammad Zaman Abbasi and 4 others, 2015 CLC 1157.
Sarfaraz v. Special Judge Anti-Terrorism Court Bahawalpur and 3 others, 2005 MLD 1096 Lahore.
Shaheena Nargis v. District Officer Police, 2006 P. Cr. L. J. 33.
Shahid Hussain v. the National Accountability Bureau (NAB), 2015 P. Cr. L. J. 883.
Sher Muhammad v. Crown, PLD 1949 Lahore 511.
Sindh High Court Bar Association v. Federation of Pakistan, PLD 2009 SC 879.
Sobho Gyanchandani v. The Crown, PLD 1952 FC 29.
Soorat Khan v. Anti-Terrorism Court, Sibi and 7 others, PLD 2010 Quetta 52.
State v. Dosso, PLD 1958 SC 533.
Suleman v. The State, 2012 YLR 2395.
Suo Motu Case No. 10 of 2011, PLD 2011, S.C. 799.
Suo Motu Case No. 10 of 2011, PLD SC 997 (2011).
Taj Bibi v. Government of Province of Sindh and 2 others, 2001 YLR. 1097 Karachi.

Taj Muhammad. Judge Anti-Terrorism Court and another, PLD 2003 Lahore 588.
Tariq Hakim v. The State, 2011 YLR 19 Lahore, 2011 YLR 1580.
Writ Petition No. 2979 of 2015.
YLR 2013 Lahore 92.
Zafar Iqbal v. Province of Sindh and two others, PLD 1973 Karachi 316.
Zahida Rizvi v. The State, 2011 YLR 1319.
Indian Case:
State of Tamil Nadu v. Senthil Kumar and another, AIR 1999 SC 971.

United Kingdom cases

Liversidge v. Sir John Anderson (1942) AC 206.
Rex v. Halliday (1917) AC 260.

United States cases

Ex parte Eric Bollman, 1807, 8 US 75.
Hamdan v. Rumsfeld, 2006, 548 US 557.
Hamdi v. Rumsfeld, 2004, 542 US 507.
Respublica v. Malin, 1778, 1 US 33.
United States v. Hoxie, 1808, 1 Paine US 265.
United States v. Lee, 1804.
United States v. Pryor, 1814, C.C. Penn. 349.

LEGISLATIONS *(Colonial India and Pakistan)*

1804	Regulation X, 1804.
1818	Regulation III, 1818.
1819	Bengal State Prisoners' Regulation II, 1819.
1819	Madras State Prisoners' Regulation II, 1819.
1827	Bombay State Prisoners' Regulation XXV, 1827.
1827	Sind State Prisoners Regulation, 1827.
1837	A Copy of the Penal Code 1837.
1841	Act V of 1841.
1850	An Act for the better Custody of State Prisoners, Act XXXIV of 1850.
1858	State Prisoners Act, Act III of 1858.
1860	Panel Code, Act XLV of1860.
1861	Indian Council Act of 1861, 24 & 25 Victoria, c. 67.
1872	Code of Criminal Procedure, Act X of 1872.
1872	Evidence Act, 1872, Act I of 1872.
1878	Arms Act, XI of 1878.
1885	Telegraph Act, XIII of 1885.
1890	Railway Act, IX of 1890.
1898	Code of Criminal Procedure, Act V of 1989
1908	Explosive Substances Act, VI of 1908.
1915	Defence of India (Criminal Law Amendment) Act, IV of 1915.
1919	Anarchical and Revolutionary Crimes Act, 1919.
1919	Government of India Act, 9 & 10 Geo. 5 c. 101, 1919.
1935	Government of India Act, 1935, 26 Geo. 5 & 1 Edw. 8, c. 2 (August 2, 1935)
1937	Aircraft Rules, 1937.
1939	Defence of India Act, 1939, Act XXXV of 1939.
1943	Special Courts Ordinance, No. XIX of 1943.
1944	Bahawalpur State Public Security Act, 1944.
1946	Foreigners Act, 1946, Act XXXI of 1946.
1947	Baluchistan Public Safety Regulation, No. I of 1947.
1947	Baluchistan Public Safety Regulation, 1947.
1947	Sindh Maintenance of Public Safety Ordinance, 1947.
1947	West Punjab Public Safety Act, 1947.
1947	Punjab Special Tribunals Act, XVIII of 1947.
1948	East Bengal Government Ordinance Temporary Enactment and Re-enactment Act, XII of 1948.
1948	North-West Frontier Province Public Safety Act, 1948.
1948	West Punjab Public Safety (Amendment) Ordinance, 1948.
1948	NWFP Public Safety Ordinance, 1948.
1949	Baluchistan Public Safety Regulation, I of 1949.
1949	East Bengal Preventive Detention Ordinance, VI of 1949.
1949	West Punjab Public Safety Act, XVII of 1949.
1951	East Bengal Government Temporary Re-enactment Act, 1951.
1951	East Bengal Public Safety Ordinance, 1951.
1952	Pakistan Army Act, 1952.
1952	Pakistan Public Safety Ordinance, VI of 1952.
1952	Security of Pakistan Act, 1952.
1954	Baluchistan States Union Public Safety Regulation, 1954.
1954	Khaipur Public Order and Detention Act, 1954.
1958	East Pakistan Public Safety Ordinance, 1958
1960	Press and Publication Ordinance No. XV of 1960.
1962	Preventive Detention Laws (Amendment) Act, 1962
1962	West Pakistan Maintenance of Public Order (Amendment) Ordinance, No. XXX of 1962.
1962	West Pakistan Public Order Detenu Rules, 1962. (Notification No. 8–41-H-Spl-1/57 dated: May 8, 1962.)

(Continued)

1964	West Pakistan Maintenance of Public Order (Amendment) Ordinance, No. XVII of 1964.
1964	West Pakistan Maintenance of Public Order (Amendment) Ordinance, No. Ordinance No. XVIII of 1964.
1965	Defence of Pakistan Ordinance, 1965.
1965	Defence of Pakistan Rules (Notification), 1965.
1965	West Pakistan Arms Ordinance, 1965.
1971	Defence of Pakistan Ordinance, No. XXX 1971.
1971	Defence of Pakistan Rules (Notification), 1971.
1974	Prevention of Anti-National Activities Act, No. VII of 1974.
1974	Punjab Laws (Adaptation) Order, 1974.
1974	Suppression of Terrorist activities (Special Courts) Ordinance, No. XVIII of 1974.
1975	Adaptation of Laws Order 1975.
1975	Suppression of Terrorist Activities (Special Courts) Act, No. XV of 1975.
1979	Constitution (Second Amendment) Order, 1979.
1984	Ordinance XI of 1984.
1985	Constitution (Eighth Amendment) Act, 1985.
1990	Act V of 1990.
1991	Special Courts for Speedy Trials Ordinance, No. XXXVIII, December 4, 1991.
1991	Constitution (Twelfth Amendment) Act, 1991
1992	Special Courts for Speedy Trials Ordinance, No. II of 1992.
1999	Anti-Terrorism (Second Amendment) Ordinance, 1999 (2 December 1999).
1999	Anti-Terrorism (Third Amendment) Ordinance, 1999 (December 2, 1999).
1999	Ordinance No. XIII, August 27, 1999.
2000	Ordinance No. XXIX of 2000.
2001	Ordinance No. XXXIX of 2001.
2001	Ordinance No. XXXIX of 2001.
2002	Anti-Terrorism (Amendment) Ordinance, 2002.
2009	Punjab Maintenance of Public Order (Amendment) Act 2009 (Act No. II).
2009	Punjab Maintenance of Public Order (Amendment) Act, II of 2009).
2011	Actions (in Aid of Civil Power) Regulations, 2011.
2013	The Anti-Terrorism (Amendment) Act XIII of 2013.
2014	Protection of Pakistan Act, X of 2014.
2015	Army (Amendment) Act, 2015.
2015	Constitution (21st Amendment) Act, 2015.
2015	Punjab Maintenance of Public Order (Amendment) Act, XVI of 2015.
2016	Punjab Maintenance of Public Order (Amendment) Act, XLV of 2016.
2017	Punjab Maintenance of Public Order (Amendment) Act, XX of 2017.
2017	Military (Amendment) Act, 2017
2017.	Constitution (28th Amendment) Act, 2017.

Indian Legislation

1985	Terrorist and Disruptive Activities (Prevention) Act 1985.

UK Legislation

1914	Defence of the Realm Act, 1914.
1920	Emergency Powers Act, 1920, 10 & 11 Geo, 5, c. 55.
1922	Civil Authorities (Special Powers) Act, (Northern Ireland) 1922.
1973–1996	Northern Ireland (Emergency Powers) Act, 1973, 1978, 1991, and 1996.
2000	Terrorism Act, 2000.
2001	Anti-Terrorism, Crime and Security Act, 2001.

Bibliography

A Copy of the Penal Code, 1837, Prepared by Indian Law Commissioners and Published by Command of the Governor-General of India in Council, Hertford: Stephen Austin, Fore Street, Bookseller to the East India College.

Abbasi, Ansar. "Why Hanging Was Banned." *The News International.* December 17, 2014, sec. Pakistan. www.thenews.com.pk/article-168932-Pakistan-to-end-death-penalty-moratorium-in-terror-cases.

Agamben, Giorgio. "For a Theory of Destituent Power." *Critical Legal Thinking: Law and the Political.* February 5, 2014. http://criticallegalthinking.com/2014/02/05/theory-destituent-power/.

———. *Homo Sacer: Sovereign Power and Bare Life.* California, CA: Stanford University Press, 1998.

———. *State of Exception.* Translated by Kevin Attel. Chicago: University of Chicago Press, 2005.

———. "What Is a Destituent Power." Translated by Stephanie Wakefield. *Environment and Planning D: Society and Space* 32 (2014): 65–74.

Ahmed, Ishtiaq. *Pakistan: The Garrison State.* Karachi: Oxford University Press, 2013. https://oup.com.pk/academic-generalbooks/pakistan-studies/pakistan-the-garrison-state.html.

Bayly, Chris A. *Rulers, Townsmen and Bazaars: North Indian Society in the Age of British Expansion, 1770–1870.* London: Cambridge University Press, 1983.

Benjamin, Walter. "Critique of Violence." In *On Violence: A Reader*, edited by Bruce B. Lawrence and Aisha Karim, 268–91. New York, NY: Duke University Press, 2007.

Bennett, Jill. *Empathic Vision: Affect, Trauma, and Contemporary Art.* Stanford, CA: Stanford University Press, 2005.

Blackstone, William. *Commentaries on the Laws of England: In Four Books.* 15th ed., Oxon: Professional Books Limited, 1982.

Brubaker, Rogers. *Citizenship and Nationhood in France and Germany.* Cambridge, MA: Harvard University Press, 1992.

Butler, Judith. *Frames of War: When Is Life Grievable?* London: Verso, 2009.

———. *Precarious Life: The Power of Mourning and Violence.* London: Verso, 2004.

Dana, David and Susan P. Koniak. "Bargaining in the Shadow of Democracy." *University of Pennsylvania Law Review* 148, no. 2 (1999): 473–559. doi:10.2307/3312797.

Der Derian, James. *Virtuous War: Mapping the Military-Industrial-Media-Entertainment Network.* Boulder, CO: Westview Press, 2001.

"Death Penalty Moratorium Lifted Completely in Pakistan: Officials." *Dawn*. March 10, 2015. www.dawn.com/news/1168652.
"Death-Row Prisoner Dies of Heart Attack." *Dawn*. December 21, 2014. www.dawn.com/news/1152232.
Deudney, Daniel. "Nuclear Weapons and the Waning of the Real-State." *Deadalus* 124, no. 2 (Spring 1995): 209–31.
Dinnerstein, Leonard. "The Supreme Court and the Rights of Aliens." *This Constitution* 8 (Fall 1985): 25–35.
Eule, Julian N. "Temporal Limits on the Legislative Mandate: Entrenchment and Retroactivity." *American Bar Foundation Research Journal* 12, no. 2–3 (1987): 379–459. doi:10.1111/j.1747-4469.1987.tb00542.x.
"Fatalities in Terrorist Violence in Pakistan 2003–2017." South Asia Terrorism Portal, 2017. www.satp.org/satporgtp/countries/pakistan/database/casualties.htm.
Fisk, Catherine and Erwin Chemerinsky. "The Filibuster." *Stanford Law Review* 49, no. 2 (1997): 181–254. doi:10.2307/1229297.
Fletcher, George P. "Ambivalence about Treason." *North Carolina Law Review* 82 (2003): 1611.
Foucault, Michel. *Security, Territory, Population: Lectures at the Collège de France 1977–1978*. New York, NY: St Martins Press, 2009.
———. *The Birth of Biopolitics: Lectures at the Collège de France, 1978–1979*. New York, NY: Picador, 2010.
Galtung, Johan. "Violence, Peace, and Peace Research." *Journal of Peace Research* 6 (1969): 167–91.
"Global Terrorism Index 2012: Capturing the Impact of Terrorism from 2002–2011." New York, NY: Institute for Economics and Peace, 2012. http://economicsandpeace.org/.
"Global Terrorism Index 2014: Measuring and Understanding the Impact of Terrorism." New York, NY: Institute for Economics and Peace, 2014. http://economicsandpeace.org/.
"Global Terrorism Index 2015: Measuring and Understanding the Impact of Terrorism." New York, NY: Institute for Economics and Peace, 2015. http://economicsandpeace.org/.
Grahl-Madsen, Atle. *The Status of Refugees in International Law*. Leyden: A. W. Sijthoff, 1966.
Haider, Mateen. "Nawaz Removes Moratorium on Death Penalty." *Dawn*. December 17, 2014, sec. Pakistan. www.dawn.com/news/1151408/nawaz-removes-moratorium-on-death-penalty.
Hashim, Asad. "Army Courts to Try Pakistan Terror Suspects." *AlJazeera*. January 11, 2015.
Human Rights Case No. 29388-K of 2013. PLD SC 305 (2014).
Hussain, Faqir. "Pakistan." In *Preventive Detention and Security Law: A Comparative Survey*, 173–92. Dordrecht: M. Nijhoff, 1993.
Hutchinson, Ron. "Durand's Line." In *The Great Game: Afghanistan*, edited by Nicolas Kent, 31–48. London: Oberon Books Ltd, 2010.
Jamaat-e-Islami Pakistan v. Federation of Pakistan. PLD SC 111 (2000).
Kennedy, Charles H. "The Creation and Development of Pakistan's Anti-Terrorism Regime, 1997–2002." In *Religious Radicalism and Security in South Asia*, edited by Satu P. Limaye, Mohan Malik, and Robert G. Wirsing, 387–411. Honolulu: Asia-Pacific Center for Security Studies, 2004.

Khan, Hamid. *A History of the Judiciary in Pakistan*. Karachi: Oxford University Press, 2016.

———. *Constitutional and Political History of Pakistan*. Karachi: Oxford University Press, 2005.

Khan, Iftikhar A. "Bar on Death Penalty Lifted in Toto." *Dawn*. March 11, 2015. www.dawn.com/news/1168820/bar-on-death-penalty-lifted-in-toto.

Khan, Ismail. "The Charge-Sheet against NAP." *Dawn*. August 28, 2016, Online Edition. www.dawn.com/news/1280318.

Kristeva, Julia. *Strangers to Ourselves*. New York, NY: Columbia University Press, 1991.

Lasswell, Harold D. "The Garrison State." *American Journal of Sociology* 46, no. 4 (1941): 455–68.

"LHC Told 1952 Security Act Still in Force." *Dawn*. February 15, 2003. www.dawn.com/news/82189.

Lord McNair, C.B.E., and A.D. Watts. *The Legal Effects of War*. Cambridge: Cambridge University Press, 1966.

Maddow, Rachel. "Obama Justifies FEMA Imprisonment of Civilians!" *Rachel Maddow Show*. MSNBC, May 26, 2009.

Marsden, Magnus and Benjamin D. Hopkins. *Fragments of the Afghan Frontier*. Karachi: Oxford University Press, 2013.

Martel, James. "Waiting for Justice: Benjamin and Derrida on Sovereignty and Immanence." *Republics of Letters: A Journal for the Study of Knowledge, Politics, and the Arts* 2, no. 2 (June 2011). http://arcade.stanford.edu/rofl/waiting-justice-benjamin-and-derrida-sovereignty-and-immanence.

Mbembe, Achille. "Necropolitics." *Public Culture* 15, no. 1 (2003): 11–40.

McCain, John. 2011. "Remarks by Senator John McCain in Support of the Conference Report of the National Defense Authorization Bill." *United States Senate*. http://mccain.senate.gov/public/index.cfm?FuseAction=PressOffice.FloorStatements&ContentRecord_id=42bad0e5-978f-9b8b-b74c-845aa6a7e33a.

McGinnis, John O. and Michael B. Rappaport. "Symmetric Entrenchment: A Constitutional and Normative Theory." *Virginia Law Review* 89, no. 2 (2003): 385–445. doi:10.2307/3202436.

Michel, Foucault. "Questions of Method: Why the Prison." In *The Foucault Effect: Studies in Governmentality*, edited by Graham Burchell, Colin Gordon, and Peter Miller, 73–86. London: Harvester Wheatsheaf, 1991.

"Military Injustice in Pakistan: A Briefing Paper." Geneva, Switzerland: International Commission of Jurists, June 23, 2016. www.icj.org/pakistan-military-justice-system-unjust-and-ineffective-new-icj-paper/.

"Military Injustice in Pakistan: Questions and Answers." Geneva, Switzerland: International Commission of Jurists, December 2016. www.icj.org/wp-content/uploads/2016/12/Pakistan-military-courts-QA-Advocacy-2016-ENG.pdf.

Nail, Thomas. *Theory of the Border*. New York, NY: Oxford University Press, 2016.

Neuman, Gerald L. *Strangers to the Constitution: Immigrants, Borders, and Fundamental Law*. Princeton, NJ: Princeton University Press, 2010.

Newberg, Paula R. Judging the State: Courts and Constitutional Politics in Pakistan. Cambridge South Asian Studies. Cambridge and New York, NY: Cambridge University Press, 1995.

Nichols, Robert. *A History of Pashtun Migration 1775–2006*. Karachi: Oxford University Press, 2008.

"Pakistan Hangs 100th Convict, Amnesty Slams 'Shameful Milestone.'" *Dawn*. April 28, 2015. www.dawn.com/news/1178715.

"Pakistan to Continue Moratorium on Capital Punishment." *Dawn*. October 3, 2013. www.dawn.com/news/1047193.

Posner, Eric A. and Adrian Vermeule. "Legislative Entrenchment: A Reappraisal." *The Yale Law Journal* 111, no. 7 (2002): 1665–1705. doi:10.2307/797534.

"Protection for Military Courts." *Dawn*. February 26, 2015, sec. Editorial. www.dawn.com/news/1165901.

Raskin, Marcus G. *Essays of a Citizen: From National Security State to Democracy*. Armonk, NY: Sharpe, 1991.

Raza, Syed Sami. "Anti-Terrorism Legal Regime of Pakistan and the Global Paradigm of Security: A Genealogical and Comparative Analysis." *Review of Human Rights* 2, no. 1 (Winter 2016): 4–35.

———. "A Preliminary Note on the Genealogy of the Concept of Enemy Alien in Pakistan." *Pakistan Journal of Criminology* 7, no. 2 (April 2015): 43–54.

———. "Critical Reflections on the Reality of Drone Warfare: Thinking with Jean Baudrillard." *IPRI Journal* XVI, no. 1 (Winter 2016): 1–21.

———. "Desiring Enemy: An Ontological Reading of the Military Operations and Small Wars on the North West Frontier." *Journal of Political Studies* 21, no. 2 (2014): 91–107.

———. "The North West Frontier of Pakistan: Preoccupation with 'Unveiling' the Battlefield and the Continuing Violent Cartographies." In *The New Violent Cartography: Geo-Analysis after the Aesthetic Turn*, edited by Samson Opondo and Michael J. Shapiro, 173–94. New York, NY: Routledge, 2012.

Riaz, Wasim. "Death Row Convict Dies of Brain Hemorrhage in Lahore Hospital." *Dawn*. December 31, 2014. www.dawn.com/news/1154047.

Ripsman, Norrin M. *Peacemaking by Democracies: The Effect of State Autonomy on the Post-World-War Settlement*. University Park, PA: Penn State University Press, 2002.

Ripsman, Norrin M. and T. V. Paul. *Globalization and the National Security State*. New York, NY: Oxford University Press, 2010.

Salter, Mark B. "When the Exception Becomes the Rule: Borders, Sovereignty, and Citizenship." *Citizenship Studies* 12, no. 4 (August 2008): 365–80.

Sarat, Austin, ed. *The Killing State : Capital Punishment in Law, Politics, and Culture: Capital Punishment in Law, Politics, and Culture*. Oxford: Oxford University Press, 1998.

Schmitt, Carl. *Political Theology: Four Chapters on the Concept of Sovereignty*. Translated by George Schwab. Chicago: University of Chicago Press, 2005.

Shapiro, Michael J. *Cinematic Geopolitics*. New York, NY: Routledge, 2009.

———. *Politics and Time*. Cambridge, MA: Polity Press, 2016.

———. *Reading Adam Smith: Desire, History, and Value*. Newbury Park, CA: Sage, 1993.

———. *Violent Cartographies: Mapping Cultures of War*. Minneapolis: University of Minnesota Press, 1997.

Sherazi, Zahir Shah. "Jailbreak Threat Looms for KP Prisons as Execution Moratorium Lifted." *Dawn*. December 18, 2014. www.dawn.com/news/1151610.

Siddiqa, Ayesha. *Military, Inc.: Inside Pakistan's Military Economy*. London: Pluto Press, 2007.

Singh, S. B. "Clash between Indian Judiciary and Executive during Second World War." *Proceedings of the Indian History Congress* 54 (1993): 451–57.

Soguk, Nevzat. *States and Strangers: Refugees and Displacements of Statecraft*. Minneapolis: University of Minnesota Press, 1999.

"State of Human Rights in 2016." Islamabad: Human Rights Commission of Pakistan, May 10, 2017. http://hrcp-web.org/hrcpweb/wp-content/uploads/2017/05/State-of-Human-Rights-in-2016.pdf.

Steffen, Lisa. 2001. *Defining a British State: Treason and National Identity, 1608–1820*. New York, NY: Palgrave.

Suo Motu Case No. 10 of 2011. PLD SC 997 (2011).

The Indian Penal Code (Act XLV of 1860) 1861. Compiled with Notes by Walter Morgan and A. G. Macpherson. Calcutta: G. C. Hay and Co., 56, Cossitollah. London: 2 Crescent Place, Blackfriars.

Tyner, James, and Joshua Inwood. "Violence as Fetish: Geography, Marxism, and Dialectics." *Progress in Human Geography* 38 (2014): 771–85.

"UN Human Rights Committee, 120th Session, Geneva: Submission Of The International Commission Of Jurists In Advance Of The Examination Of The Initial Report Of Pakistan Under Article 40 Of The International Covenant On Civil And Political Rights." Submission to UN Human Rights Committee. Geneva, Switzerland: The International Commission of Jurists, June 2017. http://tbinternet.ohchr.org/Treaties/CCPR/Shared%20Documents/PAK/INT_CCPR_CSS_PAK_27600_E.pdf.

Wonders, Nancy A. "Global Flows, Semi-Permeable Borders, and New Channels of Inequality: Border Crossers and Border Performativity." In *Borders, Mobility and Technologies of Control*, edited by S. Pickering and L. Weber, 63–86. Amsterdam: Springer, 2006.

Yergin, Daniel. *Shattered Peace*. Boston, MA: Houghton Mifflin, 1977.

Yong, Tan Tai. *The Garrison State: The Military, Government and Society in Colonial Punjab, 1849–1947*. New York, NY: SAGE Publications, 2005.

Yusufzai, Afshaq and Richard Spencer. "Taliban Burned Teachers Alive in Pakistan School Attack." *The Telegraph*, December 17, 2014. www.telegraph.co.uk/news/worldnews/asia/pakistan/11300078/Taliban-burned-teachers-alive-in-Pakistan-school-attack.html.

Zahra-Malik, Mehreen. "Kharotabad Killings and the Cover Up." *AlJazeera*. August 4, 2011. www.aljazeera.com/indepth/features/2011/08/ 201182103339774942.html.

Žižek, Slavoj. *Violence: Six Sideways Reflections*. London: Profile Books, 2010.

Index